# The Politics of History

Writing the History
of the
American Revolution
1783-1815

by Arthur H. Shaffer

Precedent Publishing/Chicago

Copyright © 1975
Precedent Publishing, Inc.
520 North Michigan Avenue
Chicago, Illinois 60611
All rights reserved
LC: 75-7865
ISBN: 0-913750-09-3
Manufactured in U.S.A.

To my father

Joseph Shaffer

and

to the memory of

my mother

Isabell Stept Shaffer

# The Politics of History

# Contents

# Preface

This book is an analysis of the American Revolutionary generation's attempt to create a national history that would justify the Revolution and develop a sense of nationhood. The historians are simply defined as those writers who published historical works. None among them were professional or academic scholars and only a few wrote more than one book. The study begins in 1784 when Jeremy Belknap published the first volume of his *History of New Hampshire* (1784-92), the first major work by an American historian after the Revolution. By 1815, the end of what has been called "the Second War of Independence," the creative energies of the first national generation of historians had run their course; the works written from then until George Bancroft's *History of the United States* (1834) are merely repetitious and sometimes poor copies of earlier works.

The writings here discussed are usually dismissed as inferior or biased. But, all the more for the very stridency of their bias, they offer important insights into the mind of the Revolutionary generation. The histories produced during the early national period represent the beginnings of a genre of writing new to America, one characterized by the subjugation of history to the service of nationalism. It is this element — nationalism — that gave this history its flavor, made possible its achievement, saddled it with difficulties, and, although unintentionally, produced a tone and emphasis different from that of the Enlightenment. It was not a new philosophy of history that led Americans to diverge from the general drift of Enlightenment historiography. What turned American national history into a novel kind was the impact of the Revolution as a new political and intellectual experience. Lord Acton once observed that the revolutionary upheavals at the end of the eighteenth century made the study of history "infinitely more effectual as a factor of civilization than ever before." A change took place in "the world of minds . . . deeper and more serious than the revival of ancient learning . . . those who lived through it with intelligence had a larger experience, and more intense, than other men have ever had."[1] The effect, if not the intent, was a turn away from the Enlightenment ideal of the universality of human experience to a preoccupation with a distinctly national experience.

The subject is treated not only historiographically and as a problem in the philosophy of history, but also as a reflection of the psychology of historians. To that end I have pursued a number of themes. I have attempted to establish the connection between the historians' republican ideology, political concerns, and outlook and the precise ways in which they interpreted American history. Where appropriate I have included an analysis of their background, education, profession, political persuasion, personal ambitions and circumstances, and attitudes toward the problem of union during the 1780s. In addition, I have sought to account for the fact that, although they were as multifarious as the nation itself, these men and women of strong political convictions and local loyalties produced a remarkably uniform conception of American history. Bringing to their work a sense of common enterprise, they self-consciously set out to form the entire American past into a pattern that contradicted the reality of American life. Local loyalties and internal dissensions were the persistent facts, but national unity became the interpretive credo.

That a diverse group of historians could produce, at least in its general parameters, a nearly uniform picture of the American past can best be explained as a response to political and social conditions in the early republic. Aside from personal factors that colored their writing, they did have certain common attitudes and experiences. As intellectuals in a new nation, they were anxious to define those qualities that made the nation unique, to provide an identity that would set it apart from its former metropolis. That process predisposed them to emphasize what Americans had in common at the expense of what divided them. More important, like most Americans, historians were troubled by divisive elements within society, fears that their republican ideology crystallized into a particularly menacing pattern. To them the decline of virtue and the division of society into opposing interests threatened domestic stability, with the feared ultimate consequence of civil discord and disunion. They looked back nostalgically to the harmony they believed to have existed during the Revolution, only a few years before the bitter party battles of the 1790s.[2] An article of republican political faith, widely held among Americans, was that formal political parties were incompatible with popular republican government. Republican theory, whether derived from Locke, Montesquieu, or Rousseau, declared this to be so.[3] American historians fully shared this belief, although, like so many of their countrymen, they too participated in party politics as they proclaimed the evils of faction.

The cultivated manner of the writer instructively expresses his personal past as well as the culture's ways of thinking and believing.[4] A problem arises, however, in discerning the precise relationship between political and social conditions and the motives of particular historians. These were a diverse group, and differences in background, personal circumstance, and political ambition could influence the character of an historian's work. On the other hand, the pressure for intellectual conformity affected every historian. With independence a settled issue, Americans were in no mood to tolerate views alternative to the standard Patriot interpretation of the Revolution. Moreover, since so many of the leaders of the Revolutionary movement were also leaders of the new government there was a natural reluctance to analyze critically their role in the conflict. Most historians avoided discussing personalities, and the authors of the many biographical dictionaries of the period included only the lives of the deceased persons. In like measure, there was a disinclination to discuss the politics of the 1790s. When, for example, Mercy Otis Warren, John Marshall, and Edmund Randolph wrote and published their histories they neither hoped nor expected to achieve any future political advancement — Warren as a woman, Marshall with life tenure on the Supreme Court, and Randolph in enforced retirement. They were, therefore, free to do what no other historian of the period dared: to critically evaluate the careers of living political figures and the party battles of the 1790s. By contrast, the fact that George R. Minot was ambitiously active in Massachusetts politics had an undeniable influence on his treatment of Shays' Rebellion.

The problem is compounded by the fact that among some forty-three writers the personal papers of only a handful have survived. Fortunately, they were among the most influential historians of their generation: Ramsay, Belknap, Warren, Marshall, Randolph, and Minot. When private correspondence is looked at together with their published works, with sensitivity to omissions, incidentals and implicit as well as overt structure and content, plausible inferences can be drawn. Their writings, both published and private, reveal an almost obsessive preoccupation with the problem of union. Whatever their political and individual differences, they implicitly regarded their writings as weapons in the battle against the centrifugal forces that threatened to divide society, as intellectual expressions of the political belief that the nation's success depended on a sense of personal identification with the nation-state. Because local loyalties and internal dissensions were the persistent facts of national life, their goal was to create a unified national past, define a national character, and arouse in their countrymen (and no doubt in themselves) a sense of pride in American society. While it would be an error to underestimate the impact of personal ambition and circumstance, it would also be a mistake to overlook civic pride as an important determinant of their approach to the American past. Nor did they display a lack of confidence in their audience. Whatever process of selection determined which individuals chose to write history, they seemed to agree on the subject matter and the message that would most appeal to the reading public.

Richard Hofstadter has written that history is the thread of "public identity" and "men who have achieved any civic existence at all must, to sustain it, have some kind of history though it may be history that is partly mythological or simply untrue."[5] The contribution of the Revolutionary generation of historians to the public identity represents an important aspect of the intellectual history of the early national period. They carried out an important psychological function in a new nation whose sudden and unexpected emergence left it bereft of a past. The new literature must be seen as part of a general and in part substantive change in modes of thought generated by the Revolution. With all their frequent vagueness and imprecision of formulation, almost incantatory repetitiousness, and patriotic sentimentality, the works of the first national generation of historians comprise a revealing effort to come to grips with the meaning of the Revolution and nationhood. This striving charted much of the course that American historiography was to travel thereafter.

I wish to thank several good friends for their assistance. Professor Page Smith of the University of California, Santa Cruz offered his kind support. Professor Henry Cohen of Loyola University of Chicago provided an excellent reading and a number of suggestions which I have profitably exploited. The University of Missouri — St. Louis Committee on Faculty Research furnished financial assistance. Mr. William M. E. Rachal and the Virginia Historical Society gave permission to draw from my article, "John Daly Burk's *History of Virginia* and the Development of American National History," in the *Virginia Magazine of History and Biography*, LXXVII (July, 1969), and from my introduction to Edmund Randolph's *History of Virginia* (Charlottesville: University Press of Virginia, 1970). Doreen Buerck, Janet Dunlap and Mary Supranowich typed and retyped the manuscript and saved me from many errors. Friends and colleagues offered useful advice, criticism, and encouragement: James D. Norris, Richard Mitchell, James Neal Primm, Howard Miller, Ann Lever, Charles Korr, and James Roark of the University of

Missouri — St. Louis, Esmond Wright of the Institute of United States Studies, University of London, Mary Elisabeth Lightbourn of Temple University, and James Zeidman of Los Angeles, California. Two friends deserve special mention: Lawrence Friedman of Bowling Green State University and Marian Shaffer, without whom this volume would never have reached fruition. Finally, Michelle and Elana Shaffer have given more than they can ever know.

St. Louis, Missouri, 1974

# I. Men and Motives

For a hundred and fifty years the Anglo-Saxon inhabitants of British North America thought of themselves primarily as Englishmen living abroad. Yet almost from the beginning there developed in the American colonies a sense of local identity. Over the years the diversity among the colonists in race, religion and language gradually gave way to the stronger bonds of common risks and hopes in a new world. With increasing pride in themselves as a people, colonial writers were concerned that their works should be dedicated to their New World destiny. To this developing sentiment New England gave the most persistent expression. It had a long tradition of historical writing that dated back to the generation of Bradford and Winthrop, a tradition that consistently affirmed the conviction of a special destiny. For generations ministers like William Stoughton expressed the belief that the Lord had "singled out New England . . . above any nation or people in the world."[1]

This vague sense of New World identity, found largely in the chronicles and sermons of New England during the first century of the colonial period, later began to appear with increasing frequency in other sections. Virginians in particular took almost as much pleasure as New Englanders in writing about their part of the New World, although without the same sense of a special historical destiny. Robert Beverly, for example, in his *History and Present State of Virginia* (1705) reflected American themes. He chided Virginians for excessive reliance on England, spoke in defense of local liberties, and placed the American Indian near the center of the New World stage, not as a barrier and potential enemy but as an integral part of the scene. Similarly, there are seeds of an incipient localism in William Stith's *History of Virginia* (1747). His story of the settlement of Virginia until the dissolution of the Virginia Company carried a specific complaint against royal authority in the person of King James and a more general implication of conflict between the mother country and the colony.[2]

Still, if colonial writers expressed a vague awareness of a New

World identity, it was primarily cultural and only latently political. More important, whatever sense of uniqueness they did express was limited to a particular colony or region. When writers such as William Smith, Jr. of New York or Samuel Smith of New Jersey set out to define their colony's culture they emphasized ethnic and religious diversity,[3] but they had no inclination to generalize about America as a whole. Before independence the only general theme historians found to lure them beyond local boundaries centered not in America, but on each colony's distinct relationship to Great Britain or its role in the Empire. Even the explicit New England sense of a special destiny by the mid-eighteenth century had begun to give way to a preoccupation with her place within the British Empire. Thomas Hutchinson's *History of Massachusetts Bay* (1765) was for him an account of transplanted Englishmen, an element of a larger drama.

Between the "imperial" historians of the American colonies and the Revolutionary generation there is a hiatus, chronological as well as political or ideological. Born mostly between 1743 and 1763, the American historians of the first national generation reached maturity during or soon after the attainment of independence. None had written history before the war; the Revolution and its aftermath provided the impetus for their first ventures into historical writing. During the imperial crisis few scholars could find the calm and the time for research and writing or the opportunity for the intellectual exchange essential to serious historical work. (Isaac Backus did manage to publish the first volume of his *History of New England with Special Reference to the Denomination called Baptists* (1777-96), but one suspects that, as a Baptist minister engaged in a campaign to eliminate all barriers to religious liberty, his purpose was to take advantage of the sentiment for change to influence the character of the institutions that would emerge from the Revolution.) For most historians uncertainty over the outcome of the conflict and the future shape of American society was also a serious obstacle. Indeed, few of their works were published before the Federal Constitution.

It is not surprising, then, that having reawakened in a changed world after a sleep of more than twenty years, American historical writing changed profoundly. The Revolution shattered the colonial frame of reference and created a new perspective; it transformed a colonial into a national psychology. For post-Revolutionary historians the problem of the imperial relationship had been resolved, never to be reopened, and logic demanded a national perspective. To elaborate the virtues of New Hampshire or Virginia or Pennsylvania would only serve to make the Revolution appear a mundane, fortuitous, trivial event.

American historians chose to emphasize those elements that transcended state and regional boundaries. It was the sense of patriotic duty to a national society, perhaps more than anything else, that led to the remarkable outpouring of historical works during the years from 1783 to 1815. Laboring under difficult circumstances — a small reading public, the absence of foreign copyright agreements, little or no access to archival materials, the lack of a tradition of national historical writing — some forty-three writers produced sixty books. Given a contemporary population of little more than three million, that output compares favorably with that of today's mammoth publishing industry.

It was not, of course, a completely new beginning. The style and rationale for historical writing was borrowed from the eighteenth century's outstanding British and European practitioners: Gibbon, Robertson, Hume, Voltaire, Montesquieu. From the earlier New England writers the early national historians adopted a special sense of uniqueness and destiny, the conviction that the colonies' founders were motivated by the goal of a society based on civil and religious liberty. Their conviction that the discovery and settlement of America "is the first link of a chain of causes, which bids fair to enlarge the happiness of mankind"[4] represented a revitalization and nationalization of the New England historical tradition. From colonial historians such as Thomas Prince, Stith, and Samuel Smith, and even from Loyalists such as George Chalmers and Alexander Hewatt, they culled a sparse but indispensable body of historical data.[5] What was new, however, was the manner in which they adapted and transformed the works and themes of their predecessors. Utilizing many of the old ingredients, they were manufacturers of a new past for America.

In some respects American historians did not comprise a tidy group; in background, geography, occupation and political persuasion they were as diverse as the nation itself. While a disproportionate number came from New England (fifteen of thirty-one whose birthplaces could be discovered), every area of the country was represented. The birthplaces which could be ascertained were as follows: Massachusetts, 10; Virginia, 5; Connecticut, 4; England, 3; Pennsylvania, 3; Maryland, 2; Georgia, 1; Rhode Island, 1; Ireland, 1; Scotland, 1. Moreover, historians were a more mobile group than most elements of the population. Some, like Jedidiah Morse, Hugh Williamson, Noah Webster, David Ramsay, Mason Weems, John Marshall, Hugh McCall, and Edmund Randolph, lived and traveled in various parts of the country. Politically the historian was most likely to be a Federalist, eleven of fifteen whose politics are known; but the Republican contingent, including Mercy Otis Warren, John Daly Burk, James T. Callender and James Sullivan, were prominent. Nine of the historians served in elective and appointive public office. Clergymen were the most numerous occupation, especially in New England, but members of every profession were included. The identifiable vocations of twenty-seven historians were: minister, 8; lawyer, 7; teacher, 3; writer, 3; bookseller-printer, 3; journalist, 2; physician, 2; soldier, 1; merchant, 1. (The total is more than twenty-seven because a number practiced several occupations.)

Nevertheless, the historians shared a commonality of experience and outlook that exercised a controlling influence over their work. No characteristic of historical writing in the early national period is more impressive than the general uniformity of approach and conviction among men and women of widely differing backgrounds and political persuasion. What united them was a passionate commitment to the Revolution, concern for the country's stability, and a desire to articulate a unique history that would help establish the new nation's intellectual reputation at home and abroad. An underlying similarity of attitude, then, tended to minimize differences. With their fellow scholars throughout the western world, Americans felt a sense of citizenship in the civilization of letters, in what Voltaire extolled as "a great fellowship of intellect, spread everywhere and everywhere independent."[6] In Ramsay's emulating terms, "learned men of every clime constitute but one republic."[7] Curiously, however, this intellectual cosmopolitanism had the effect of encouraging a nationalistic bias, for American men of letters were anxious to show their fellow citizens of the republic of letters that the United States, too, possessed a cultural heritage of its own.[8]

To create a sense of national identification, the first national generation felt the need to emphasize those elements that made the nation unique; the quest for a new historical identity they in turn regarded as part of a general campaign to achieve cultural as well as political independence. These sentiments were well expressed in 1787 by the Society for Political Inquiries, a group dedicated to freeing the country from the "intellectual imperialism of Europe."

> In having effected a separate government, we have as yet accomplished but a partial independence. The revolution can only be said to be compleat, when we shall have freed ourselves, no less from the influence of foreign prejudices than from the letters of foreign powers. When breaking through the bounds, in which a dependent people have been accustomed to think, and act, we shall properly comprehend the character we have

assumed and adopt those maxims of policy, which are suited to our new situation.[9]

The articulation of a national history formed an integral part of the movement to promote a national culture. Carrying on a tradition that goes back at least to the ideal of the many-sided Renaissance man, the phrase American literature generally signified not only belles-lettres, but more inclusively philosophic, historic, scientific and political writings. Sensitive to the claims of many English and European writers that the United States had not been nor was likely to be the scene of any important cultural achievements, they were anxious to expound its virtues, "to ascertain what there is peculiar and distinguishing in the state of society in the federal union." "It is now full time," wrote James Sullivan, "that we should assume a national character, and opinions of our own; and convince the world, that we have some true philosophy on this side of the globe."[10]

Many of those who wrote history also made scientific contributions. Natural history in particular attracted the interest of the historians. In a series of geographical works that earned him the reputation of the father of American geography, Jedidiah Morse sought to end native reliance on foreign accounts to learn about their own environment. Sensitive to the claims of European naturalists that the New World was harmful to animal, plant and human life, practically every historian lavished description and praise upon the American environment. Others reached out to literature. "Thy native land is big with mighty scenes," wrote Mercy Warren; some poet, she added, must "retrace, and recollect the days,/ When, by the margin of the western tide,/ Young empire sprung from oppression's side."[11] Jeremy Belknap, John Daly Burk and Warren wrote plays. Belknap defended Americanisms that had crept into the language, while Noah Webster campaigned to purify American English of aristocratic vestiges so that Americans would speak better English than the English. Webster's *Speller*, according to Hans Kohn, was "second only to the Bible in shaping the mind of the nation in its infancy."[12] The literary aim was to free the language from dependence on the mother country, win acceptance of its distinctive qualities, and fashion an American English suitable to a republic.

American historians, then, comprised an informal coalition of cultural and political nationalists. The lines of contact spread loosely throughout the nation. Jeremy Belknap, John Eliot, the members of the Massachusetts Historical Society, Hugh Williamson and Ebenezer Hazard in New York and Philadelphia, David Ramsay in Charleston, and William Gordon in England and America corresponded with each other and provided what little assistance they could to scholars lacking the resources for extensive travel and research. They lent each other research materials, read each other's manuscripts, helped find publishers for and promoted each other's books. Most important, they regarded their work as part of a common national enterprise. Unity did not always mean unanimity, for there were conflicts of political conviction and sectional jealousies; but their general harmony of outlook is all the more striking for that.

That the campaign to promote a national literature had a political as well as a literary purpose is evident in the writings of American historians. "Every engine should be employed to render the people of the country national," wrote Webster, "to call their attachment home to their country; and to inspire them with the pride of national character."[13] Their approach to history demonstrated a calculated effort to use historical writing as an instrument of public policy.[14] They self-consciously set out to establish a historical pattern that would contravene the realities of American life. Local loyalties and internal dissensions were the persistent facts, but national unity became the credo of American historians. Americans were unaccustomed to thinking in national terms, and it was no easy task to overcome deep-seated local loyalties that had had more than a century to develop, especially since even a vague sense of national identification was so recent. Historians weighted their bias in favor of the national government as the expression of American nationality. However else they were divided, they agreed that the Federal Constitution was the symbol and the reality of national life. The Anti- Federalist position was hardly represented. Even those who had been initially critical of the Constitution — Mercy Otis Warren and Edmund Randolph — had nothing but praise for it in their histories.

Even more striking is the contrast between their portrayal of a united nation and the contentious reality. The 1790s were a particularly violent period in American political life. In our history politics has not been notably calm, but the last decade of the eighteenth century was a time of peculiar emotional intensity. Physical violence, actual and threatened, occurred with disturbing regularity. There was, for example, the forceful resistance to the authority of the central government in the Whiskey Rebellion in Pennsylvania, part of the era of high emotion generated by Hamilton's financial program, the rise of party politics, and the French Revolution and the near-war with France. In 1798 and 1799 mobs roamed the streets of Philadelphia, prompting President John Adams to smuggle arms into his home through the back streets. Even more pervasive was the intensity of attitude displayed in the political rhetoric of the time. "You and I have formerly seen warm debates and high political passions," observed Thomas Jefferson to Edward Rutledge in 1797; "But gentlemen of different politics would then speak to each other. . . . It is not so now. Men who have been intimate all their lives, cross the streets to avoid meeting, and turn their heads another way, lest they should be obliged to touch their hats."[15]

Political crises have usually stimulated historical writing; warring authorities have meant warring pasts. But in the early national period the increase in historical writing did not have that effect. A number of historians were active in the bitter political quarrels of the 1790s and early 1800s and most held and expressed strong opinions. When it came to the writing of history, however, all but John Marshall and Mercy Otis Warren avoided taking sides, and even they refrained from making factional use of the years before 1789. Before the Revolution there had been few serious inter-colonial conflicts. Nationhood exacerbated sectional conflicts and transformed them into matters of serious concern, and local loyalties and partisan dissensions were now regarded not only as symptoms but sources of crisis. In this climate American historians used history to justify the whole society rather than particular groups. Of his approach to a projected history of the United States, David Ramsay wrote that he had "lightly passed over the squabbles in Congress but dwelled on the happy effects of a good government wisely administered in promoting all the important interests of our common country. I write not for a party but for posterity."[16] Such was the ideal, and for the most part they stuck to it.

Not that historical work was completely free of partisan overtones. It was too much to expect men and women with strong convictions to agree on contemporary issues. When Mercy Warren published her *History of the American Revolution* (1805) she stirred a small tempest with her characterization of Alexander Hamilton as a "foreign adventurer" with crackbrained financial schemes, and she severely strained her long-time friendship with John Adams by accusing him of "a partiality for monarchy." Adams complained to Warren that "your *History* has been written . . . to gratify the passions, prejudices, and feelings of the party who are now predominant."[17] When John Marshall announced his intention to write a life of Washington the work of so important a Federalist could not escape political notice. Republican writers had attempted to expropriate the Washington legend from Federalist possession, or at least to neutralize it. Mason Weems in his *Life of Washington* (1800) had created an image of Washington as a leader who despised faction and stood above party labels. Philip Freneau, the Republican editor and poet, similarly eulogized him:

O, Washington! thrice glorious name! What due regards can man decree— Empires are far below thy aim, And scepters have no charm for thee. Virtue alone, has your regard, And she must be your great reward.[18]

Jefferson, concerned that Marshall would undermine his party's efforts, solicited Joel Barlow to write an "impartial" history of the period as an antidote.[19]

Despite the harsh treatment of the Federalists by Warren and their equally zealous defense by Marshall, in their general approach to American history the two writers differed primarily in thematic emphasis. John Adams' objections to Warren's *History* were limited to her observations on the post-Revolutionary years. He bluntly wrote her that "after the termination of the Revolutionary War your subject was completed."[20] Jefferson's dissatisfaction with Marshall's *Washington* centered on the years after 1789; he had no great quarrel with his treatment of the colonial period or the Revolution. Moreover, both Marshall and Warren muted their partisanship by refraining from naming the parties; they preferred traditional euphemisms, like "the friends of the administration" and "the opposition."

If it appears remarkable that almost every historian avoided discussing the contemporary party battles of the early national period, the explanation may be found in traditional attitudes. While most historians were either Federalists or Republicans, they took little pride in their affiliations. A distaste for political parties, or "factions," was a universal feature of contemporary political theory. Parties were regarded as having no other objective than power and prizes. The party man ceased to be a free agent, and having conceded his freedom was deemed unfit to be trusted with the liberties of the people.[21] Even Mercy Warren and John Marshall defended particular men and policies, not parties. If historians had been inclined to favor a party system as a necessary or desirable feature of republican government, they undoubtedly would have revealed it in their writings. Instead, they ignored or minimized party conflict. In their view political parties signified disunity and instability and were incompatible with a unified United States.

---

Whether they wrote state, regional, national, or biographical history, the Revolutionary generation attempted to form the American past into a comprehensive whole that was more than a summation of its parts. The task was more difficult than it might seem. Political belief accounted less for the differences among historians than geography. The problem of American identity was multifaceted because regional and national loyalties pulled against each other. Local studies were the majority of the histories written during the period, although in part this was because of easier access to sources and the limited financial resources of non-academic scholars. In their accounts of the colonial period American historians found it difficult to break out of the straight-jacket of the state or region as the central point of reference. The most cosmopolitan writers commonly used a particular locale as the backdrop for defining the nation's character and its past. Indeed, even foreign-born historians, presumably unfettered by state and regional ties, followed the pattern of choosing state history or using a specific area as the model for a national study.

It is difficult to decide how much of this localism was the result of prevailing loyalties — after all, most states had had a century or more to develop allegiances — and how much resulted from technical difficulties like the hardships of travel and the lack of good libraries and archives. It was hard to assemble the materials to tell in depth the story of the whole people; it was relatively easy to collect state records. Much vital material was in distant English archives. So little documentation was available that many yielded to the temptation to borrow heavily from Edmund Burke and other contributors to the British *Annual Register*. Even national histories were usually organized by states and regions; the few efforts to integrate the story of the colonies into a single chronological narrative were artificial and unconvincing. When writers fastened upon a generalized concept, like the republican character of American society, they found it difficult to repel the temptation to describe a particular area as the epitome of that character. The ideal was to construct a national past that would be acceptable to all, but given the diversity of American life most historians tended to generalize from local models.

Ironically, the very impulse to surmount localism and construct a national history reinforced the tendency to generalize from local models. Consistent with the tendency of eighteenth-century historical theory to treat human nature as the same in all times and places, American historians were inclined to project the present into the past. But to superimpose the present on the past would only serve to magnify the nation's diversity, which is what nationalist historians hoped to avoid. One way out of this dilemma would have been to give unity to the American past (and present) by fitting it into the general pattern of western history. To an extent American historians did just that, proclaiming that the discovery and settlement of the American colonies and their subsequent independence had led to important advances in human knowledge and an expansion of human liberty. But they were also determined to articulate a uniquely American history. Unless one simply made a virtue of diversity, and that they were not prepared to do, to make the national past unique required a model applicable to the entire nation. The republican political system might well have provided such a model, but for the Revolutionary generation republicanism implied something far more fundamental than politics: it reflected the basic character of the society. Yet American society was diverse. Constrained by the dictates of theory and the facts of life, yet determined to provide a unified and unique national past, the only alternative was to take a segment of the society and represent it as a reflection of the whole.

Practicality confirmed what long habit and old loyalties impelled. American historians worked out a compromise. When they wrote national history they nationalized local themes; when they wrote state history they did so from a national perspective. To be sure, the writing of local history did serve to encourage local rivalries. If the Revolution stimulated an interest in discovering the nation's historical antecedents, it also created a desire to establish the role of individuals and states in its genesis. Historians reflected the dualistic character of nationality in the early Republic, the dual sovereignty and loyalty of state and nation under the Constitution.[22]

In his *Natural and Civil History of Vermont* (1794), Samuel Williams characterized his state as a microcosm and the best expression of national development. Williams explained that he limited his study to Vermont because "to represent the state of things in America in a proper light, particular accounts of each part of the federal union seem to be necessary. . . ."[23] The virtue of this approach was that one could preach loyalty to the nation without asking others to renounce their identification with Massachusetts, Virginia, or South Carolina. Provincialism and nationalism could march under the same banner. There was faith in the power of knowledge to break down local prejudices; the Union would be strengthened if only Americans knew more about each other. "I wish to see a history of every state written in the style of yours and Williams' history of Vermont," David Ramsay wrote to Jeremy Belknap. "We do not know half enough of each other. . . . Every man who is acquainted with the people of the neighboring state is I observe for the most part federal. Narrow politics are generally the offspring of insulated local views.[24]

Nowhere was the tendency to generalize from the particular to the general more pronounced than in New England. The Revolutionary generation of New England historians were the heirs of an historical tradition that dated back to the founding generation of William Bradford and John Winthrop; it was on the basis of that tradition that they built their histories of the United States. For them the national history was that of New England writ large; the characteristics and the goals of their ancestors they attributed to the American people as a whole. Even before the Revolution, Ezra Stiles, president of Yale College, began gathering material for a projected "Ecclesiastical History of New England and British America." His purpose was to articulate an historical framework that would comprehend more than New England and be distinctly American. A European, he argued, could not "do justice to the history of the American provinces."[25] Although Stiles never completed his project, he did present his vision of American history in a published sermon entitled *The United States Elevated to Glory and Honour* (1783). Stiles struck an exultant note that had been absent in New England for more than a century. He revived the old Puritan self-conception of a city upon a hill, but broadened it to include all America. For him, the creation of the United States signaled the birth of a new society which by its example would alter the world.

Among New England historians none won greater critical acclaim at home and abroad than Jeremy Belknap. Through his various activities as political activist, man of letters, naturalist, lexicographer, author of a *History of New Hampshire* (1784-92) and of a national biographical dictionary, and founder of the Massachusetts Historical Society, Belknap qualifies as a leader in the movement to create a national literature. A Harvard graduate and son of a prosperous leather dresser and furrier, he had served as a Congregational minister for twenty years at Dover, New Hampshire before moving in 1786 to Boston's Federal Street Church. Like many other New England ministers he took an active interest in public affairs. During the Revolutionary controversy he established a reputation as an ardent spokesman for the Patriot cause. It was at his meetinghouse that the Massachusetts convention met to ratify the Federal Constitution, Belknap acting as recording secretary. An early critic of slavery, he was instrumental in raising a petition which led to the passage of an act prohibiting Massachusetts citizens from engaging in the slave trade.[26]

Belknap gained his greatest reputation as an historian with the widely acclaimed *History of New Hampshire*. A work of more than twenty years labor, it was the first significant piece of historical literature to appear in post-Revolutionary America. For that reason alone it would have been influential, but it was also regarded as a work of high literary and scholarly achievement and encouraged others to join the movement to create a national historical literature. Belknap's *History* introduced the dualism of a local study that would also serve the needs of a unified national history. His major themes could easily be translated into national history. In his scenario the discovery and settlement of North America were linked to advances in human knowledge and liberty. The process of conquering a frontier led ordinary citizens to a "true use of their natural and active powers," a process of growing self-reliance that had finally brought the colonists to "that equal rank among the powers of the earth for which nature had destined, and to which the voice of reason and providence loudly called us."[27]

There was no mistaking Belknap's New England perspective. In his *American Biography* (1794-98) he drew upon the tradition of Cotton Mather and other Puritan "spiritual biographers"; in his numerous essays he theorized about American history in general and New Hampshire in particular in much the same terms; and when he described an ideal social order it was the New England town that he used as his model. Nevertheless, the themes he pursued and the attitudes he expressed — the Whig political philosophy of the Revolution, the celebration of republican morals and political institutions, the concept of America's special destiny to free mankind from the shackles of oppression — resembled the views of historians throughout the nation, and his paradigm of American development was generally accepted.

Belknap's conviction that the pattern of New England development and the character of its people represented a microcosm of the national past would be echoed by other New Englanders. They were by no means a uniform group. The providential musings of Mercy Otis Warren, Isaac Backus, and Benjamin Trumbull were balanced by the secular perspective of George R. Minot and James Sullivan. The Federalism of Minot, Jedidiah Morse, and Abiel Holmes had its Republican opposites in Warren and Sullivan. But New England historians were united by a common background and intellectual heritage that exercised a controlling influence over their work and largely submerged their differences. Descended from old Puritan stock, they had a strong sense of pride in their heritage. The only exception, Sullivan, was of Irish origins, but he was thoroughly assimilated and became President of the Massachusetts Historical Society and governor of the state. New Englanders were the heirs of an old and established tradition of historical writing through William Bradford, Cotton Mather, Thomas Prince, and Thomas Hutchinson. Unlike their colleagues in other sections of the country, they were accustomed to searching for documentary material and had no need to look elsewhere for examples and interpretations.

Whatever else divided them, New England historians were united in the conviction that their section represented what was best in

American society. If some had doubts about the future of the United States, they did not doubt that New England was the anchor of the nation's stability. What is surprising is that a number of historians from other areas concurred in that view. Found all through the first volume of Chief Justice John Marshall's *Life of George Washington*, an historical narrative under a biographical guise, is the persistent theme of New England's moral and political superiority, not seen as different from other sections but as more advanced along the same path. No doubt Marshall's judgment was colored by political bias; as a Federalist he was inclined to look with more favor upon New England than the heavily Republican South. But the pattern was not unfamiliar.

The motives of David Ramsay were more complex. Background and experience placed Ramsay in an advantageous position to discard the local attachments that characterized many of his contemporaries.[28] Born and raised in the western back country of Pennsylvania, he had been educated at the College of New Jersey and at the medical school associated with the College of Philadelphia. For several years he was a teacher in Virginia and Maryland before he settled permanently in Charleston, South Carolina to practice medicine. No doubt his varied experience helped him shed local loyalties. Moreover, Ramsay experienced the difficulties of being an outsider. In 1788 he was defeated for a seat in Congress by a man he believed to have been lukewarm to the Revolution. His opponent, William Loughton Smith, widely publicized his support for the Constitutional ban on further importations of slaves, branding him an outsider unsympathetic to local institutions and customs. Ramsay wrote that "some jealousy of offices being conferred on men who were natives has showed itself. . . . Some may and probably will object to the impolicy of trusting the legislative part of that business in the hands of a northern man by birth."[29]

Ramsay's reaction to his rejection at the polls was symptomatic of (and contributed to) a more general sense of alienation. Even after spending the major portion of his adult life in South Carolina he never felt quite at home, despite the ties of marriage and years of service in the state legislature. The longer he lived there the more critical he became, and in his *History of South Carolina* (1809) he catalogued the state's backwardness. The one area of the country which he had never visited, New England, he came to regard as the model for other sections of the country. He corresponded regularly with the New England historians, Morse, Eliot, Belknap and Hannah Adams, and became a corresponding member of the Massachusetts Historical Society. Upon completion of his *History of the American Revolution* (1789) he asked members of the New England delegation to Congress to read the manuscript. Determined to write a truly national history but uneasy with developments in regions with which he was familiar, Ramsay looked to the only section of the country that he believed could provide an historical tradition worthy of emulation.

Not every historian shared Ramsay's predilection for New England. Virginians, especially, were preoccupied with their state's place in the nation's history. In the preface to his *History of Virginia*, Edmund Randolph promised to demonstrate how she had risen "from infancy and a wilderness, through various fortunes, into a wealth, a character, and an influence which largely contributed to the establishment of American independence. . . ."[30] A member of one of the state's most prominent families, Randolph had few rivals as a student of Virginia society and history. His grandfather Sir John Randolph had spent years gathering historical materials which he passed on to William Stith, who incorporated them in his *History of the First Discovery and Settlement of Virginia* (1747). As the state's attorney-general and later governor, Randolph had access to the public records, and he also used his grandfather's papers and borrowed his cousin Thomas Jefferson's extensive collection.[31]

Steeped in the Virginia past and connected by ancestry with three generations of prominent local politicians, it is not surprising that Randolph would want to establish her place in the new national history. But the precise character of his book was determined more by personal experience than local loyalty. Randolph appeared headed for a brilliant political career, having become Virginia's wartime attorney-general at twenty-three, governor at thirty-three, Washington's first attorney-general at thirty-six, and finally, in 1794, Secretary of State at the still young age of forty-one. Yet within eighteen months he had been unjustly accused of disloyalty and corruption and forced to resign in disgrace, never to return to public life. Adhering to the tradition that a public man should stand with like-minded men on specific issues but never tie himself permanently to any faction proved extremely difficult. In the end Randolph lost the support of both Republicans and Federalists.

The ultimate blow came as a result of Randolph's opposition to the Jay Treaty. He advised Washington against approving the Treaty, while Secretary of War Timothy Pickering and Secretary of the Treasury Oliver Wolcott urged acceptance. Naturally the British were anxious to discredit Randolph, and when they intercepted a letter written by the French minister, Joseph Fauchet, to his government, the British minister, George Hammond, delivered it in July 1795 to Secretary Wolcott. The dispatch (No. 10) had been written nearly a year before (October 31, 1794) and was hardly relevant to the current dispute, but it held promise of neutralizing Randolph's inconvenient opposition to ratification. Fauchet's rambling account vaguely implied that Randolph had made improper revelations and solicited French money. When Randolph was called in and questioned by Washington and his Cabinet under humiliating circumstances, he angrily resigned. Later that year he wrote an elaborate *Vindication* that did little to clear his reputation but was notable for its intemperate attack upon Washington. Although there can be little doubt that Randolph was innocent of any wrongdoing, both the British and the partisans of Hamilton in the Cabinet were after his scalp and successfully manipulated Washington into wielding the knife. Often vacillating, Randolph obeyed his conscience and remained nonpartisan during the rancorous political struggles of the 1790s. James Madison accurately summarized Randolph's political obituary: "His greatest enemies will not easily persuade themselves that he was under a corrupt influence of France, and his best friends can't save him from the self-condemnation of his political career."[32]

Randolph's interest in writing the history of Virginia dated back to the 1780s, but not until the first decade of the nineteenth century did he begin working on it in earnest. While his *Vindication* had failed miserably to win public approval, indeed had done more harm than good, he regarded the *History of Virginia* as a more subtle way of justifying his conception of statesmanship. It occurred to Randolph that the bitter partisanship of American politics might be reduced to order if practical rules for political conduct could be established. He believed the Virginia experience could serve as a model for a virtuous republic. Randolph organized the Virginia past around a series of crises, such as the dissolution of the Virginia company, the Pistole Fee controversy, and the Revolution, that were designed to demonstrate the evolution of a political system uninfected by party spirit and dedicated to the maximum of liberty consistent with order and stability. "It is the happiness of the Virginia character," he argued, "hardly ever to push to extremity any theory which by practical relations may be accommodated." By the genius of Virginia politics he meant a system capable of producing "public agents suitable to every crisis and service," leaders who were expected to be responsive but not necessarily always responsible to the will of their constituents. In Virginia that system had demonstrated its capacity for acting responsibly and imaginatively in the face of challenges from without and stresses from within — its ability, that is, to moderate tensions.[33]

Randolph's portrayal of the Virginia political system as responsive rather than responsible and free from factionalism was self-serving. In light of his own political problems, as he perceived them, there could be no better way to justify his behavior. But he was also following an established method in defining American republicanism while insisting that Virginia was its best representative. Nationalist though he was, Randolph was also a Virginia patriot poised to defend his "native state" and its crucial role as progenitor of American republicanism. Of Pocahontas' dramatic intervention in behalf of Captain John Smith, whom he regarded as the colony's savior, Randolph wrote: "Let the Virginia patriot ascribe the preservation of Smith to that chain of grand events of which the settlement of Virginia was destined to be the foremost link, and which finally issued in the birth of our American Republic."[34]

In Belknap, Ramsay and Randolph we find, although they are separated by distance and background, a basic agreement on the need for a national history acceptable to every segment of American society. Yet each found it difficult to break the shackles of localism: Belknap, because his roots were so deeply planted in New England; Ramsay because his disillusionment with his adopted home led him to search for a vicarious alternative; Randolph, because the Virginia he knew and loved so well provided a vehicle for justifying his political career. Thus a tension was built into American historical writing: the need to articulate a national history conflicted with the continuing hold of local traditions and loyalties. No issue, not even politics, caused more dissension among historians. Yet the problem proved less troublesome than might be supposed, for the larger goal of creating a national historical literature and the desire to present a united front, especially to foreign critics, blunted what otherwise would have been a disturbingly divisive issue. The terms in which the historians discussed the basic themes of American history were similar enough to encompass their differences. If each claimed for their area a special place in the national past, those claims, as we will see, were contained within certain common philosophical and political assumptions about human nature, republicanism, national destiny, and national character.

An underlying similarity of attitude tended to assuage differences. Whatever their varying backgrounds, American historians were united by the common experience of the Revolution, for it had been the formative experience in their public lives and the impetus for their first ventures into historical writing. Psychologically and emotionally committed to the Revolution, they were anxious to represent it as a national, indeed an international, event. To treat it as a local matter born of local grievances would be to turn it into a wholly parochial affair. If the historian gave to a particular state or region a certain preeminence in the Revolutionary movement, it was offered as a model of the nation as a whole. The Revolution provided a body of common experience that was national in scope. But above all else, American historians were intent on proving that the republican system that had emerged from the Revolution had been the product of a common national experience. As a national ideology, the commitment to such ideals as representative government and the rights of man was not limited by state boundaries. Because these ideals were vague enough to exist harmoniously with state loyalties, they provided an agreeable way of emphasizing national loyalty. Moreover, by beginning with the assumption that Americans were one people even before the Revolution, it was an easy next step to treating the whole era as one in continuity with the past, despite the absence of continuity in national institutions.

There was an even more compelling reason why men and women of varying backgrounds and political loyalties were willing to minimize if not wholly submerge their differences. To yearn for harmony in the midst of contention is an understandable human trait. "In the distraction of party, or faction," observed Jared Sparks, the past "is the polestar to which all may look for safety, as presenting an object to be regarded with the same respect and confidence by all. . . ."[35] But their striving to create an illusion of harmony cannot be understood simply as a psychological response to disharmony; it was a self- conscious effort to use historical writing to achieve a set of specific objectives that could be fulfilled only by creating a sense of national unity. From the beginning of the Anglo-American conflict it was understood that some kind of national union was a necessary condition for independence. The success of the Revolution, and the republican ideology with which it had come to be identified, depended upon the success of the Union; the two were inextricably bound together. The nationalistic bias built into the works of American historians — literary, scientific and historical — formed the framework for a campaign to promote political union. "The Revolution," declared David Ramsay, "cannot be said to be completed till" the Federal constitution "or something equivalent is established." "The moral of your history," John Quincy Adams advised Senator William Plumer, should be "the indissoluble union of the North America continent," for nothing is "so likely to have a decisive influence as historical works, honestly and judiciously executed."[36]

If the Revolution was decisive in forming the attitudes of American historians towards republicanism and the need for a national literature, the 1780s were equally decisive in determining their views on the form of the nation's political institutions. During the 1780s they shared the belief that the ineffectiveness of the Confederation represented a threat to the experiment in republicanism. "We want some imminent common danger pressing hard upon us, to make us feel our need of union," wrote Jeremy Belknap. "I have always thought," he continued, "that when such a pressure was removed, internal repulsion would succeed. We must be drove to our duty, and be taught by briars and thorns." The republicanism of John Marshall, who had been an early enthusiast for "self-government," was shaken by the impotence of the Articles of Confederation and by Shays' Rebellion.

> These violent, I fear bloody, dissentions . . . cast a deep shade over that bright prospect which the revolution in America and the establishment of our free governments had opened to the votaries of liberty throughout the globe. I fear, and there is no opinion more degrading to the dignity of man, that those have truth on their side who say that man is incapable of governing himself.[37]

A devotee of orderly social and political change, David Ramsay's allegiance to republican government was severely tested in the decade of the 1780s. "This revolution has introduced so much anarchy," he complained, "that it will take half a century to eradicate the licentiousness of the people."[38] In South Carolina Ramsay observed public disorders that erupted into a wave of anti-Tory feeling: Loyalists were tarred and feathered, street riots broke out. Economic ills led to the passage of stay laws and demands for emissions of paper money to ease the financial crisis. As a member of the state legislature Ramsay was not unmindful of the heavy pressures on his fellow legislators nor unsympathetic to the plight of his fellow Carolinians. "Political necessity," he wrote to Thomas Jefferson, "has once more compelled the Legislature . . . to enact an instalment law. . . . I do not pretend to justify it. I only say that the calamities of the war and the subsequent successive failure to crops for three years in some degree palliate this interference of the legislature." But empathy did not relieve his fear that the situation might eventuate in an irreversible degeneration of public and private virtue. In despair he wrote to Benjamin Rush that "the morals of the people are so depreciated that legal honesty is all that is aimed at by most people." It is our misfortune, he continued, "that our assemblies have too much power. Most of our new governments are elective despotisms. It is the fashion to rule for the good of the people but if that fashion changes we have but feeble barriers against tyranny."[39]

Over the years Ramsay consistently backed efforts to increase the powers of the national government.[40] As the chairman of the Continental Congress he sent a letter "To the Governors of Certain

States" calling upon them "to send adequate representation" so that pressing problems could be acted upon. "The remissness of the States . . . naturally tends to annihilate our Confederation." A few weeks later he wrote gloomily of Congress's efforts "to frame a new recommendation to pass the impost" in order to pay off the country's debts. "There is a languor in the States that forbodes ruin. The present Congress for want of more states had not power to coin a copper. In 1775 there was more patriotism in a village than is now in the thirteen states."[41]

Having witnessed repeated failures to strengthen the national government, Ramsay placed his hopes on the movement to draft a new constitution. In a letter to Jefferson he predicted that unless the Philadelphia Convention devised "an efficient federal government . . . the end of the matter will be an American monarch or rather three or four confederacies."[42] In South Carolina Ramsay lobbied in behalf of the Constitution at the state convention and published a pamphlet supporting the new government.[43] Opposition to the Constitution he regarded as grounded in local fears and prejudices, and he uncharitably characterized Rawlins Lowndes, a leading local antifederalist, as a man without "one continental or federal idea in his head nor one of larger extent than that of a rice barrell."[44] It is significant that, though it was completed by late 1787, Ramsay delayed publication of his *History of the American Revolution* (1789) in order to include an account of the Constitution.

A number of historians took part in the campaign for the Constitution. Hugh Williamson and Edmund Randolph served as delegates to the Philadelphia convention. Williamson helped work out the compromise over congressional representation and played a significant part in convincing reluctant North Carolinians to ratify belatedly in 1789. Randolph headed the Virginia delegation to the Federal Convention. A member of Congress between 1779 and 1782, he served as chairman of a committee which reported on the government's inadequacies and the powers necessary for an effective national government. He had been instrumental in persuading Washington to go to Philadelphia, and as governor of the state that had taken the lead in calling the Convention he opened the proceedings by presenting the Virginia Plan.[45] Although Randolph refused to sign the Constitution he threw his considerable influence in favor of ratification, in which endeavor he was joined at the Virginia Convention by John Marshall. In Massachusetts, Isaac Backus, a Baptist minister renowned for his advocacy of religious liberty and the author of a *History of New England with Particular Reference to the Baptists,* voted for ratification, while Jeremy Belknap served as the Convention's secretary.

Concern for the future of the Union did not always imply enthusiasm for the proposed Constitution. Randolph finally decided to support ratification only after "the accession of eight states reduced our deliberations to the single question of Union or no Union." In a pamphlet listing her objections Mercy Otis Warren of Massachusetts argued that the document departed from the principles of republican government. But in their histories both Randolph and Warren were outspoken in their praise. Randolph referred to it as the "most illustrious of civil acts." Warren's objections seemed to be satisfied by the adoption of the Bill of Rights. "Perhaps genius had never devised a system . . . better adapted to the condition of man, than the American constitution," she wrote of the amended document. "Many corrections and amendments have already taken place, and it is at the present period as wise, as efficient, as respectable, as free, and we hope as permanent as any constitution existing on earth."[46]

For American historians the adoption of the Federal Constitution did not settle the central issue of whether the union of states was to become more perfect or less, or no union at all. They were not convinced that the Republic and the idea of union would endure. As late as 1807 Joel Barlow wrote, "Think not, my friends, the Patriot's task is done, or freedom safe, because the battle's won."[47] When Barlow declared his intention to write a history of the United States, he unveiled a plan for dividing the American past into three epochs: the colonial period, the Revolution, and the first twenty years of the Constitution. "I look upon the last period as the most important of the three. . . . The history of our country is the history of liberty; its two former periods may teach men how to acquire liberty, the last should teach them how to preserve it. Now in the present state of things with us it is much more important to know how to preserve than how to acquire it. For in my opinion the loss of liberty in this country is not an impossible event."[48]

Conditions within the United States — geographic, cultural and ethnic diversity, the parochialism of local loyalties, what many considered a passionate pursuit of wealth, bitter party battles — seemed to threaten the Union and the nation's experiment in republicanism. The United States suffered the trials of most newborn states, especially contests for legitimacy. To be sure, the American states had experienced neither a radical break with the past nor a drastic disruption of the structure of power. By comparison to other new nations the transfer of authority had been relatively smooth. Nevertheless, the question of legitimacy still posed perplexing problems. In 1788 Benjamin Franklin remarked that his countrymen were prone to pay too much regard to their rights and too little to their duties as citizens. By the time the

Federal Constitution went into operation in 1789, Americans had already discarded two governments in thirteen years. In his first annual address to Congress President Washington declared that the American people must learn "to distinguish between oppression and the necessary exercise of lawful authority . . . to discriminate the spirit of Liberty from that of licentiousness."[49]

The concern for governmental authority was mirrored by historians, who reflected a commonly held view of American society that transcended party and sectional disagreements. Each believed that a love of liberty was the fundamental feature of American life; but they feared that in the aftermath of their rejection British sovereignty Americans were in danger of jeopardizing the existence of their society by overemphasizing personal liberty at the expense of legitimate authority. George R. Minot observed that because the United States was a republic, the problem of legitimacy was more serious than in other countries. In a free society, he argued, factions were more likely to spring up than where freedom did not exist. While these factions might disagree among themselves, they had one thing in common: opposition to the government. Let a leader arise, such as in Shays' Rebellion, and they would unite around him in opposition. "To overset an established government," wrote David Ramsay, "unhinges many of those principles which bind individuals to each other." The United States had been born of a revolution; "the right of the people to resist their rulers, when invading their liberties, forms the cornerstone of the American republic." The problem, in Ramsay's view, was that "this principle, though just in itself, is not favourable to the tranquility of present establishments."[50]

Experience was reinforced by theory. It was an accepted dogma of eighteenth century historical and political theory that republics were frail organisms with short life expectancies. History taught that only monarchical societies had been able to establish the administrative mechanisms necessary to govern large territories, techniques that were unacceptable in a republic because they rested on force and personal loyalty to the royal person. In a republic loyalty rested on a voluntary delegation of authority. The state could not exercise authority by enlisting allegiance to an individual or a dynasty, but only by invoking a more novel loyalty. Since the coercion of monarchies was unacceptable in a republic, the United States needed something that seemed far more difficult to develop and maintain: a sense of popular identification with the new, far-flung state. In outlining a "Plan for . . . Perpetuating the Union of the American States," Noah Webster suggested manuals of history designed to convince Americans that they "ought not to consider (themselves) as inhabitants of a single state only; but as Americans; as the common subjects of a great empire."[51]

American historians worked from the assumption that the United States could only be welded into a nation by the articulation of a cohesive national heritage. We are a "young republic," observed Mercy Otis Warren in the introduction to her *History of the American Revolution*, "a confederacy which ought ever to be cemented by a union of interests and affections, under the influence of those principles which obtained their independence." The historian, wrote Benjamin Trumbull, should bring the people of the country "into a more general acquaintance with each other, awaken their mutual sympathies, promote their union and general welfare."[52] Eager to represent the American past as a collective, unifying experience, he integrated the history of the colonies into a single chronological narrative. It was this determination to use history to promote national cohesion that explains the high uniformity of the writings of American historians.

Whether they wrote national or local history (or both) American historians seldom lost sight of their primary goal: to convince their countrymen that they were united by a common heritage and that the Union represented a logical and necessary fulfillment of American history. That their purpose was didactic is evidenced by the fact that they frequently dedicated their works to young people, sometimes adopted them for use in classrooms, and used a variety of literary devices — sermons, orations, textbooks, inexpensive popular histories — to broadcast their message to the largest possible audience.[53] John W. Campbell apologized for the "extreme brevity" of his history of Virginia on the grounds that he had been motivated by a "desire to render the work accessible to those who have neither leisure nor money for voluminous publications. . . ." To furnish the public with "a cheap History of America, from its discovery, to its present state of civilization and importance," observed Richard Snowden, "is an undertaking of such general utility, that the attempt, if it ever fall short of complete execution, has a claim to a considerable share of indulgence."[54] In his *History of the American Revolution Written in the Style of the Ancients* (1795), he went to the lengths of portraying the participants in and events of the Revolution in the form of biblical characters and stories.

Whatever the technique, the purpose was always the same: to be a nation Americans must think they are a nation. The writing of American historians became the intellectual counterpart of the political concept that the nation's success depended on a sense of personal identification with the nation-state. Because local loyalties and internal dissensions was the persistent fact, their goal was to create a unified national past and arouse in their countrymen a sense of pride in

American society. We can recognize here the use of scholarship to support the social and political order. From a foundation of scholarly nationalism American historians constructed a national past. The consequences for American historiography were profound.

# II. The Development of a National History

That the works of American historians were deeply influenced by the political climate in which they were written does not mean that they can simply be dismissed as polemics. Their biases in behalf of the presumed national interest do not necessarily negate their value as history. Nevertheless, to be fully aware of the bias of their vision of the past one should remember that the use of history as a political weapon had deep roots in Anglo-American culture. Inquiring into the past had long been for Englishmen not merely an academic matter, but one of immediate and urgent importance. The peculiar precedent-minded nature of their political and legal system made this so. By the time of the American Revolution two principal interpretations of English history had developed, the Whig and the Tory. During the years of intense debate preceding the war of independence, the Patriot party converted the Whig perspective into an intellectual weapon to support its side of the imperial argument. As participants in that debate historians saw nothing unnatural or unscholarly in using their craft for political ends. With the Loyalists driven into exile or silence, the platform of the Patriot party was transformed into the ideology of a nation; party history merged into national history.

To the degree that American histories were contrived and organized to support a cause they were propaganda. Reflecting the commonplace eighteenth century assumption that their most important task is didactic, the historians wrote with a particular moral and political message in mind. "To record past events, for the instruction of the many ought to be the object of history," declared David Ramsay. "Ignorance is the enemy of liberty, the nursery of despotism." By providing the "means of education," he continued, "our yeomanry, can have nothing to fear from any man, or any association of men, however distinguished by birth, office, fortune or abilities." Therefore, if statesmen needed a knowledge of the past in order to govern wisely, in a republic it was indispensable "to the less enlightened, though not less important, citizen who supports by his labour the nation, and protects her constitution by his sword."[1]

History was to be subordinated to the moral and political instruction of the people just as, in the seventeenth century, it had been subordinated to that of princes.

At the same time, American historians were scholars schooled in and committed to the highest standards of scholarship their age could offer. Eighteenth-century historiography has been justifiably criticized for a doctrinaire didacticism that often led to unhistorical extremes and interfered with a sympathetic understanding of the past.[2] Nonetheless, the Enlightenment historians laid the modern foundations of their profession. They moved history out of the orbit of theology, went beyond mere narrative, and took the first steps in the direction of a systematic understanding of the past as a process embracing the whole of human activity. Moreover, Enlightenment skepticism encouraged a new respect for documentation and for improving standards of textual analysis, even if too often they were honored more in the breach than in the observance. "Historical truths," Voltaire wrote, "must first be proved before they can be admitted."[3] Carelessness, dilettantism, failures in use of sources were among the sins that eighteenth-century historians hoped to avoid.

What was lacking in eighteenth-century historiography was the motivation to recover source materials from earlier periods. Because the philosophes believed modern man represented the highest point yet achieved in human history, they favored the recent past over more distant epochs. But the American Revolution stimulated a new interest in documentation, not only about the event itself but about the origins and development of the people and society that had produced it. American historians believed the nation fortunate in the availability of "ample documents." "Perhaps no people on the globe," concluded John Lendrum with obvious pride, "can trace the history of their origin and progress with so much precision." That advantage, exulted Jeremy Belknap, "the historians of other countries almost universally are destitute; their first eras being either disguised by fiction and romance, or involved in impenetrable obscurity." "A new world has been discovered. . . . A new empire has arisen," observed Abiel Holmes. "That remarkable discovery, those events and actions, can now be accurately ascertained, without recourse to such legends, as have darkened and disfigured the early annals of most nations."[4]

Convinced that a unique revolution in human affairs had taken place, many Americans believed that the records of so important an event should be scrupulously preserved. Those who played important roles in the founding of the republic had a keen sense of history and were eager to see that posterity accurately portrayed the event. Jefferson meticulously copied all his letters, and Madison late in life retrieved his letters from all his correspondents so they could be collected in one complete and coherent body. A number of historians reprinted documents in appendices and in the body of their works. Along with the widespread practice of enriching historical works with primary sources there were efforts at systematic compilations of documents. Though limited to one state, William Waller Hening's edition of Virginia laws, *Statutes at Large* (1809-23), represented a landmark in American historical editing. But the first large-scale national conception for the compilation of historical documents was the brainchild of Ebenezer Hazard. A project of some twenty years labor, Hazard's *Historical Collections* (1792-94) was aimed at laying "the foundation of a good American history" and preserving those "papers" which "are intimately bound up with the liberties of the people."[5]

It is not by mere chance, then, that the United States led the world in the development of archival techniques and the establishment of repositories from the local to the national level.[6] The best known and most successful of these was the Massachusetts Historical Society. In August, 1790 Jeremy Belknap issued the "plan of an Antiquarian Society." The idea of such an organization was not new; there had been a Society of Antiquaries in London since 1572, and another was formed in Scotland in 1780. Belknap corresponded with members of the Scottish society, but their influence seems to have been limited to organizational structure. The inspiration to found a society grew out of Belknap's experience in the research and writing of his *History of New Hampshire* (1784-92). Though he had worked long and hard to gather primary materials his efforts had been hampered by inaccessibility of privately owned manuscripts and loss of materials during the revolutionary period. In particular, he lamented the partial destruction by British troops of the precious collection of Thomas Prince, author of a *Chronological History of New England in the Form of Annals* (1736) and the man who had introduced Belknap to historical studies.[6]

Aroused to action and encouraged by John Pintard, the New York merchant and later founder of the New York Historical Society, Belknap gathered together a group of like minded men who were determined "not only to collect, but to diffuse the various species of historical information, which are within their reach." True, the Massachusetts and the other societies that followed usually did most to encourage local history, but more in the desire to insure their state's place in than to fragment the nation's history. The purpose of the Society was to participate in the campaign to establish a national history; in the words of the founders, "to collect, preserve, and communicate, materials for a complete history of this country. . . ."[8]

Documentation was only the first step toward a scientific view of the past. History, the philosophers thought, could also, become a science because it was now subject to philosophy — that is, method — and because it sought the truth alone. The problem was that eighteenth-century writers seldom made clear the distinction between their doctrinal and scholarly interests. The value of a work was determined by its doctrines; for the philosophes doctrine was a weapon to further their cause. Still, to be an effective instrument it must also be truthful; without truth doctrine would be of little value. That was the theory, but in practice the issue was not so clearcut. A rift opened up, with the disciples of Montesquieu, especially his English admirers, accusing Voltaire and the Encyclopedists of abandoning the master's principles and deserting true philosophic history; that is, of becoming too polemical. Gibbon in particular attacked Voltaire as careless of accuracy and more concerned to damage his enemies than discover the truth. Yet the difference between the two groups was primarily one of degree. Gibbon's biases sometimes differed from Voltaire's, but the work of each had its own mixture of scholarship and propaganda. Each agreed that history could be made into a science. (Indeed, Voltaire cited David Hume's *History of England* as proof that the scientific ideal had been realized.) Each believed that history was philosophy teaching by example; that it should be instructive, point to a moral, enlist loyalties.[9]

American historians were sensitive to the implications of the debate over the proper uses of historical writing. They consistently, even repetitiously, affirmed their commitment to objectivity. "Sincerity and impartiality," wrote Isaac Backus, are "the most essential rules of history." Perhaps the frequency of these reminders reflected an uneasy feeling that scholarship was being compromised by polemical concerns. While defending the utility of historical studies, Backus admitted that "history has been so often written . . . either for party purposes; or mere amusement, that some serious persons have been ready to treat it as . . . of little service to mankind." "The historian," observed Hugh Williamson, no doubt with many of his contemporaries in mind, "is often biased by national prejudices, which induce him to depart from the truth. . . ."[10] The difficulty is that they wanted their histories to be both effective propaganda and objective accounts of the past. Not sur-prisingly, neither enterprise was entirely successful.

In theory they agreed that history should be both impartial and contain useful lessons. "The instruction that events afford," observed William Gordon, "is the soul of history; which doubtless ought to be a relation of real facts during the period it respects."[11] In practice those goals were frequently in conflict. There may be useful lessons to be found in the study of the past, but for Americans the writing of history served as part of a campaign to justify the Revolution and the society that had produced it. It was all too easy to let the wisdom of the past "be biased by national prejudices." When Thomas Jefferson reviewed a history of the Revolution by Carlo Botta, a member of the provisional government of Piedmont in the French Republic, he praised him for being "neutral, as an historian should be, in the relation of facts." But, Jefferson continued, "he is never neutral in his feelings, nor in a warm expression of them . . . and of honest sympathies with . . . the better cause." His work "glows with a holy enthusiasm for the liberty and independence of nations."[12] It is clear that Jefferson meant "liberty and independence" on the American model. In a like view, Isaac Backus observed that "nothing teaches like experience; and what is true history but the experience of those who have gone before us?" Having stated the ideal, Backus somewhat ingenuously gives us a glimpse at what those lessons will be. "Of the experience of those who have gone before us . . . perhaps none have been more remarkable . . . than those of this country. And as the present contests about liberty and government are very great, they call loudly for all the light . . . that can be gained from every quarter."[13]

Thus historians labored under a certain tension. They were conscious of the professional demands of critical method. Working against this was the insistence of society upon memory mixed with myth, a history that would strengthen national loyalties or confirm national pride, justify the Revolution or show that Americans possessed the traditions and character to sustain republican society and national union. It is to their credit that American historians never forgot their commitment to scholarship. Their work seldom degenerated into mere propaganda because the partisan's aim was balanced by the scholarly ideal of impartiality and accuracy. Some even took the ideal seriously enough to deal sympathetically with Great Britain during the Revolutionary crisis.[14] Although David Ramsay's *History of the American Revolution* (1789) was anything but impartial, English critics sometimes praised its generosity. One writer called it "judicious, authentic, and impartial, clearly the best extant on the subject," while another considered the work "written with knowledge, penetration, temper, and liberality."[15] Even General Sir Henry Clinton, former commander of British forces in North America, only criticized Ramsay for factual errors.[16]

Finally, practical necessity placed limits on partisanship. In the heated atmosphere of the early national period, to support a particular program was to become involved in political warfare. Therefore American historians largely avoided offering any program of their own. Since their goal was to promote a sense of national cohesion they avoided taking sides in the party battles of the 1790s and early 1800s. Even the two exceptions, John Marshall and Mercy Otis Warren, exercised restraint.[17] The historians' only particular conclusions were breathtaking in simplicity: the American past offered ample evidence that a republican society can be maintained only when men live close to nature under governments founded on popular sovereignty, religious toleration and civil liberty. Conversely, they contended that such a government would foster the virtues essential to a republic.[18] Not that they were unmindful of the complexities of government; the correspondence, political writings, and public careers of some of them indicate a sensitivity to the difficulties faced by republican societies. But their feeling that its trials could be successfully met by good government was not given substance by a program of their own. Apparently they sensed that in the heatedly partisan climate of the early national period it was more important to reinforce the social morale than to support a particular program. A preoccupation with national unity led the historians to ignore economic and political differences and over-emphasize uniformity at the expense of ethnic, cultural, and religious variety. The result was a kind of court portraiture in which the warts have been removed and the blemishes hidden. Not that the historians omitted examples of injustice, such as religious and political persecution in seventeenth-century Massachusetts, ill-treatment of the Indian, or the abuses of slavery, but they either glossed over them with facile justifications or buried them under the weight of favorable evidence.

Nevertheless, with all their distortions, occasional vagueness and imprecision of formulation, frequently repetitive, almost incantatory statements, and tendency to lapse into patriotic sentiments, the works of the Revolutionary historians were a genuine scholarly effort to come to grips with the American past. They saw new possibilities; their use of history to promote the idea of a common national past had the virtues of its vices. As pioneer national historians with no tradition of national historical writing they might have drifted aimlessly as mere chroniclers. Without some guiding cohesive principle they would have made their history incomprehensible. Their nationalism enabled them to give the United States a composite believable past. It is this element — nationalism — that gave their work its flavor, made possible its achievements, saddled it with difficulties, and, although unintentially, led to a style of history different in tone and emphasis from that of the Enlightenment.

It was not a new philosophy of history that led Americans to diverge from the general style of Enlightenment historiography. The works of the best English and European practitioners were appreciatively read and sometimes published in America.[19] Because American historians seldom used footnotes the influence of specific writers cannot be clearly determined, especially since the general tendency of eighteenth-century thought to simplification made it particularly easy to pick up ideas without going to the source. Since the substantive terminology of the Enlightenment formed the substratum of everyone's vocabulary, Americans could hardly avoid using the same words and phrases. On most counts their studies were mirror images of Voltaire, Gibbon, Hume, and Robertson, so much so that their rhetoric often seems more like random summations of established thoughts and arguments than responses to new circumstances.

The broad lines of similarity are familar: the commitment to understanding the past in human rather than theological terms, the assumption that human nature is constant and therefore human experience is universal, the conviction that beneath historical phenomena lay general laws governing the life of governments and societies. Like the Enlightenment historians, the Americans were less concerned with the facts of the past than with the lessons to be drawn from them, although as the first generation of national historians they displayed a greater concern with the details of national life. In the tradition of such philosopher-historians as Voltaire, Hume, and Robertson, they regarded their subject, in J.B. Black's terms, as "an addendum to philosophy."[20] They were anxious to disassociate their function from that of mere chroniclers. History was to be an important phase of philosophic inquiry. More specifically, they rejected, in theory if not always in practice, mere factual history as not only uninformative but dull. "Although the mass of colonial documents," wrote Edmund Randolph in his *History of Virginia* "contains some valuable information, it is crowded with matter which at this day carries with it no degree of interest. At the hazard, therefore, of the imputation that I have taken too great liberties in pruning them, I shall be chiefly attentive to such only as connect the various parts of the Virginia character and delineate the situation of Virginia at different stages most worthy of notice." By such an approach to the past Randolph believed he was emphasizing "the dignity of history."[21]

Randolph's use of the phrase "the dignity of history," which he borrowed from William Robertson, is significant. What he meant was not merely that history should be written in a dignified manner but that it should be written about dignified events and characters. This amounts to a variation of the maxims laid down by Voltaire and Hume regarding the selection of data and the subject matter appropriate to historical writing. For them it was axiomatic that many facts were altogether too trivial to be noticed by the historian, who should properly concentrate upon those transactions which commanded attention because of their inherent interest or because of the instruction to be derived from them. A history that was truly dignified would therefore be truly useful as well, because it would serve as an inspiration to dignified thought and action.[22]

American historians worked, then, from assumptions about the nature and purpose of historical inquiry that were similar to those of their European counterparts; the difference lay in their application of those principles. They turned away from the Enlightenment ideal of the universality of human experience to a preoccupation with a distinctly national experience. "It is natural," observed Jeremy Belknap, "for us to inquire into the ancient state and circumstances of the place of our own abode, and to entertain a peculiar fondness for such inquiries in preference to more foreign matters. . . ."[23]

Not that the philosophes had failed to appreciate the individuality of epochs and nations. While the idea of uniformity kept their historical vision relatively flat, it also encouraged them to make comparisons with other civilizations and periods, each with its distinctive characteristics. Even their belief in the uniformity of human nature did not rule out variety. Only the fundamental passions were uniform. Societies were susceptible to infinite variety; they were subject, observed William Robertson, to "the division of property, together with the maxims and manners to which it gave rise."[24] David Hume defined the "chief use of history" as a tool for discovering "the constant and universal principles of human nature." But he also admitted that "those who consider the periods and revolutions of human kind, as represented in history, are entertained with a spectacle full of pleasure and variety, and see, with surprise, the manners, customs, and opinions of the same species susceptible of such prodigious changes in different periods of time."[25] Hume's views were by no means unusual or idiosyncratic. Of Muslim culture, Voltaire observed that we see "customs, facts, so different from everything we are used to that they should show us how varied is the picture of the world, and how much we must be on guard against the habit of judging everything by our customs."[26]

Nevertheless, while theoretically cognizant of the individuality of epochs and civilizations, emotionally and in practice the philosophes could not accept it. Their relativism was swamped by polemical passion; as combatants in an ideological war they found it difficult to rise above the battlefield. In order to inculcate sound ideas and help bring about progress, they were bent upon exposing the deficiencies of past ages. They directed attention to the Middle Ages, for example, only to deride and dismiss them.[27] For Enlightenment writers the nature of the battle tended to reinforce uniformity, preventing them from fully exploiting their awareness of historical diversity.

The writings of American historians were also governed by polemical considerations, but for them the situation was somewhat different. True, like their European counterparts, their belief in an unchanging human nature led them to assume that they could know much about the past from a knowledge of contemporary society, a dogma that prevented them from fully comprehending the gulf between their own time and past centuries. For example, in dealing with political and religious intolerance in seventeenth century Massachusetts they could find no other explanations than the shortcomings of human nature, the imperfections of political institutions, or an incomplete under-standing of natural rights. Moreover, it was difficult for them to overcome the idea that historical events were merely repetitive variations on a theme: mankind's march toward a more rational society. Even their analysis of the causes and consequences of the Revolution contained no clear conception of historical change; it was simply the fruition of tendencies, inherent in human nature, that had existed in America from the beginning.

Yet the goals of American historians led them to exploit the relativistic strain in Enlightenment historical thought. From the notion that only the fundamental passions are uniform and universal they went on to a definition of the distinctive character of American society. Beginning with the assumption that in America human nature was fulfilling its highest potential, they explained that development in terms of the unique physical and social environment of the New World. "Nature and society," observed Samuel Williams, "have joined to produce, and to establish freedom in America."[28] Americans perceived no inconsistency in these views, for they regarded the nation's historical experience as unique only insofar as it represented the first instance in modern history of a society constructed in conformity with the laws of nature and society.

But if the presumption of universality was the point of departure for American historians, it succumbed to the need for self-justification and self-assurance. Sensitivity to criticism led to excesses of national pride. The French, Gouverneur Morris contemptuously observed, "want an American constitution without realizing they have no Americans to uphold it."[29] "All the forms of civil polity have been tried by mankind, except one," proclaimed Ezra Stiles, "and that seems to have been reserved in Providence to be realized in America."[30] Such statements could, of course, be supported on orthodox grounds. But there is a difference in tone and emphasis, a predilection for accentuating the differences between the New and Old World almost to the exclusion of what men have in common, that does set them apart from Enlightenment thought.

The contrast between American and European historians grew out of the different political and social contexts in which they worked. The philosophes were intent on exposing the follies of warriors, monarchs, and priests, who had caused untold misery and prevented progress. They saw themselves as social critics, as outsiders working to subvert and transform society. It was the depth of their disenchantment with things as they were that alienated the disciples of Montesquieu from Voltaire and the Encyclopedists. While they were reformers who believed in the possibility of progress, according to their common views a program of change depended upon the current state of society. In Protestant countries, England in particular, change could be achieved by piece-meal reform; the scholar could be content with understanding the existing forces of society and helping along their natural tendencies. But in Catholic countries such as France and Italy, the philosophes could not afford the luxury of merely understanding the world; they must change it by undermining the powers that be.[31]

Americans agreed that history is "the deposite of crimes, and the record of everything disgraceful." But, wrote Mercy Warren, it is also the record of "every thing honorary to mankind." For them the national past was primarily, if not exclusively, a record of achievements "honorary to mankind."[32] That emphasis provides a clue to what set them apart from their European counterparts. The contrasting perspectives of British and Continental reformers derived from the differences in the social and political structures of their countries and the possibilities for progressive change.[33] Similarly, the contrast between the social and political atmosphere of the United States and of Europe explains much about the differences between their writers. Disagreements between philosophes were largely a matter of intensity; but American historians were not radical social critics or reformers. They regarded themselves as an integral part of the established order and as spokesmen for a society that had already gone far toward fulfilling the dreams of reformers. Few among them were political leaders of first rank, but they identified the nation's leaders as men who, for the most part, had the same aspirations for American society as themselves.[34]

Indeed, one of the elements that gives continuing interest to their works is the relationship they established between their functions as historians and as public men. The latter were thought to be in a better position to mingle philosophy with practical experience; in the words of David Hume, "to mount up from men's actions to their motives, and to descend again from their motives to their actions." "The inferiority of modern to ancient history," observed John Marshall, exists because "the former, unlike the latter, is not written by practical statesmen." Few American historians fit Hume's definition of a man of power. But a number, including Marshall himself, were "practical statesmen," or had been close enough to the centers of authority to acquire some understanding of the problems of exercising political power. As Mercy Warren explained in the preface to her history, she was "connected by nature, friendship, and every social tie, with many of the first patriots, and most influential characters on the continent . . . and with others since elevated to the highest grades of rank and distinction. . . ."[35] Warren was a strong, sometimes bitter, critic of the Washington administration and the Federalist party; but she was not advocating that the political or social system be changed. The implicit assumption bent of her criticism was simply to vote the rascals out. Her characterizations of Washington and his supporters can hardly be compared with the philosophes' vivid descriptions of the crimes of monarchs, priests and warriors.

American historians, then, regarded themselves as insiders, spokesmen for a society to which they felt both personally and ideologically committed. The result was a kind of writing that conveys the impression that the historian is personally involved in his subject. It is this quality of involvement that makes their works valuable guides to the attitudes of their contemporaries. As active participants in and strong supporters of the Revolution they were anxious to justify the event, its ideology, and the system of government that resulted from it. That sense of personal and ideological involvement was a characteristic feature of their writings and exercised a controlling influence over them. They perceived that the success of the Revolution depended upon the success of the Union. Therefore their task was clear: the Union could not long survive, at least not as a republic, without a sense of popular identification with the nation. "Every child in America," wrote Noah Webster, "should be acquainted with his own country. . . . As soon as he opens his lips, he should rehearse the history of his country; he should lisp the praise of Liberty and of those illustrious heroes and statesmen who have wrought a revolution in his favor."[36] If few historians expressed themselves in such roseate terms, they agreed that their civic duty was to create a body of historical literature designed to convince their countrymen that they were united by a common past.

If any one work marked the beginnings of an American national history it was David Ramsay's *History of the American Revolution* (1789). Not that it compares with Parkman for beauty of style or Turner or Beard for impact upon scholarly and popular imagination; but Ramsay's study must still be regarded as the major event in the development of a distinctly national historical consciousness.[37] Read, studied and praised throughout the nation and abroad, from March, 1789 to November, 1792 it was serialized in the *Columbian* magazine, the major patriotic journal of the period, occupying far more space than any history previously published there.[38] "America has produced a Ramsay," exulted James K. Polk, who read his books while a student at the University of North Carolina, "the Tacitus of this western hemisphere to transmit to posterity in the unpolished language of truth, the spirit of liberty which actuated the first founders of our republic."[39] Among contemporaries Ramsay stands out, singular not only for his scholarly productivity but for having been the first to compose a national history specifically designed to "rub off asperities and mould us into a homogeneous people."[40]

As is often the case with basic ideas, Ramsay's version of the national past did not spring into full being out of a single mind. Less an innovator than a popularizer, his fundamental value resided in an ability to synthesize and articulate the attitudes of his contemporaries. That he viewed as his main function "to promote the union and the harmony of the different states"[41] is evidenced not only by the structure of his works but also by his efforts in behalf of scholarship. His books gave him a reputation that made him worth knowing. Ramsay kept in touch with other scholars, promoted their books, and on occasion lent materials from his unpublished manuscripts. When Hannah Adams apologized to him for having used large portions of his study of the American Revolution in her *Summary History of New England* (1799), he responded, according to Miss Adams, with "a very interesting letter, expressing . . . approbation of my work, and enclosing . . . ten dollars." Some years later Ramsay promised to delay publication of portions of his *Universal History Americanized* (1819) dealing with the history of the Jews because he did "not wish to interfere with Miss Adams." He encouraged others to write the kind of history that would break down local prejudices. "Enthusiastic as I am for the unity of our republic," he wrote to Jeremy Belknap, "I wish for every thing that tends to unite us as one people who know esteem and love each other."[42]

Like other intellectuals, Ramsay was anxious to show that the

United States possessed a distinctive cultural heritage and regarded the quest for a national historical identity as part of a general campaign to achieve cultural as well as political independence. Because "our country suffers in Europe for want of being known," he lamented to Jefferson, "Europeans affect to under value Americans."[43] He sought to devise a formula for a sense of common nationality, for the question of what was America and an American posed a perplexing problem. Unlike European countries, the United States had no long traditions as a nation; it had appeared suddenly, composed of a mixture of ethnic stocks, a variety of religions, and diverse and sometimes warring economic and geographic interests. Unifying symbols were difficult to find. The expulsion of the British monarchy displaced the arch-symbol of nationhood, and even the Constitution, subject to conflicting interpretations, had its limitations as a unifying symbol. Americans turned to classical Greece and Rome for models. Classical place names, the adaptation of Roman architectural forms in the nation's capitol, the use of the term Senate for the upper houses in most American legislatures are examples of the use of Classical lore. But such synthetic symbolism was unsatisfactory.[44]

Nineteenth-century European nationalists would proclaim national independence by referring to their old and different civilization, common religion and descent, or roots in ancestral soil. No such traditions could differentiate Americans from other peoples; they had no semi-mythical roots. The country had been too recently settled and Americans were too mobile to establish a mystical sense of attachment to an ancestral soil. Ethnic diversity, too, was conspicuous. While religion was homogeneous enough not to become a source of dangerous conflict and Protestantism imparted a certain uniformity of values, it could not be a basis for national unity. Moreover, the Revolution had weakened religious traditionalism, and the first national generation proudly adopted a policy of toleration that served to encourage diversity. Finally, if independence had discredited the old self-image by implying that Americans were not Englishmen, their English heritage continued to be the single most important ingredient. Language, law, and culture tied them to the mother country.[45]

Ramsay conceded the obvious, at least privately: "We are too widely disseminated over an extensive country and too much diversified by different customs and forms of government to feel as one people." Even so, he contended that "we really are one people" and "should consider" the inhabitants "of this country . . . as forming one whole."[46] But if "forming one whole" did not mean ethnic, cultural, or political homogeneity, what did it mean? Since the United States lacked those traits which history, tradition, ethnic and religious uniformity and a mythic past impress upon territorial societies, national identity could only be defined in abstract terms. Ramsay found the tie that made Americans "one people" unique among the peoples of the earth in the interplay of the two basic factors: the republican national character and special destiny "to enlarge the happiness of mankind, by regenerating the principles of government in every quarter of the world."[47] As he used it, the term America meant more than geography or a territorial state, more even than nationality. It meant a way of life, an ideology. The United States was not only a new nation but a new society, less bound by the customs and values of the past than the nations of Europe. Ramsay maintained that the Revolution had demonstrated the characteristic features of the nation's inhabitants and its social order, features which had marked its society from its origins. The interaction between the environment and the ideas brought to the New World by the early settlers had led to the development of "the short but Substantial political creed of an American colonist."

> He believed that God made all mankind originally equal: that he endowed them with the rights of life, property, and as much liberty as was consistent with the rights of others. That he had bestowed on his vast family of the human race, the earth for their support, and that all government was a political institution between men naturally equal, not for the aggrandizement of one, or a few, but for the general happiness of the whole community.[48]

If the nation was conspicuously lacking in cultural uniformity, Americans were still one people by virtue of their loyalty to a common set of political and social ideals and values.

Time and again Ramsay organized his presentation of the past around and to illuminate these two basic concepts, the republicanism of the national character and the nation's special destiny. For example, in his account of the decline and fall of the Carolina proprietorship he directed his heaviest criticism less at the motives of the colony's rulers than at their principles of government, which he regarded as erroneous and inconsistent with conditions in the New World. Indeed, praising the proprietors' policies of religious toleration and of encouraging immigration by people of diverse origins, he fit the story of South Carolina into the larger picture of the United States as a haven for religious liberty and the oppressed. Praiseworthy motives, however, did not prevent Carolina from quickly turning into "a scene of contention and misery." The proprietary government was, according to Ramsay, weak, unstable, and little respected. The governors were ill-qualified or shackled by unwise instructions. Money from land sales and quit-rents was insufficient for the expenses of government. The proprietors were unwilling to use their own funds for improvements or defense and they tampered with the prerogatives of the assembly, even repealing a law to insure freedom of elections.

> It may be thought somewhat astonishing, that the proprietors should have persisted in measures so disagreeable and so manifestly subversive to their authority. Many were the hardships from the climate, and the danger from the savages; with which the colonists had to struggle; yet their landlords, instead of rendering their circumstances easy and comfortable seemed rather bent on doubling their distresses. . . . It was the duty of the proprietors to listen to their complaints and redress their grievances.[49]

In the end this intolerable situation led to the Revolution of 1719.

For Ramsay the events that led to the overthrow of the Carolina proprietorship bore an unmistakable resemblance to the American Revolution. "In the course of the eighteenth century," he reminded his readers, "South Carolina underwent two revolutions; the last of which took place in 1776. Several of the actors in this are yet alive, and must be struck with the resemblance of the measures adopted by their predecessors and themselves for accomplishing these great and similar events." As in 1776, "a well-intentioned people, alarmed for their rights, were roused to extraordinary exertions for securing them." As in 1776, their inability to obtain redress of grievances through legal channels forced them to take "bolder measures." As in 1776, popular leaders came forward who "cemented their union by an association generally signed by the inhabitants" and then formed a "new government, without confusion or violence, [which] virtually superseded the existing authority." As in 1776, "all political connections" between the old government and the "people of Carolina was entirely dissolved, and a new relation formed."[50]

As elaborated by Ramsay, those events illustrated the republican character of the nation's inhabitants, with South Carolina in 1719 serving as a precursor of the nation in 1776. At the same time, he insisted that the episode demonstrated the importance of American history for all mankind: when a lack of harmony exists between government and the governed civil strife inevitably follows. The fault lay less in the follies of particular men than with the system. "Perhaps the troubles and miseries suffered by the colonists," he observed, "ought to be ascribed to their lordships' shameful inattention rather than to their tyrannical disposition."[51] Since the colony's rulers governed from a distance of 3,000 miles, they were bound to lack an adequate understanding of their subject's basic needs. The fact that the proprietors' interest in the colony lay solely in profit meant that their interests and those of the colonists were bound to conflict. Empowered to govern in an arbitrary fashion, the proprietors were free to disregard the popular will and trample on the civil and property rights of the governed.

That Ramsay focused on the republicanism of the national character and the nation's special destiny reflected a number of practical considerations. Like other nationalistic, revolutionary intellectuals, his conception of national identity was infused with ambivalence toward the former metropolis. As a nationalist he stressed those elements that made the nation unique. The awakening of a national consciousness required a point of observation and comparison from which the unity of the United States could be observed. Perhaps the people would feel more like Americans if it could be shown that they were different from other people. "That we may rightly prize our political condition let us cast our eyes over the inhabitants of the old world, and contrast their situation with our own."[52] Yet that sense of distinctiveness had to be expressed without repudiating the English heritage or the basic intellectual premises of the age, the belief in the universality of human experience and that "human nature is radically the same."[53] Ramsay never felt quite comfortable as a cultural chauvinist. "I am a citizen of the world, and therefore despise national reflections," he wrote somewhat apologetically. But, he continued, I "hope I am not inconsistent when I express my ardent wish that . . . America be . . . in all respects independent."[54] Because his intellectual roots were in the Old World he could not overcome a dependence on and preoccupation with European, particularly British, culture. While rejecting the political and class structure of the Old World as backward, he still viewed its culture as the measure of achievement.

Publicly Ramsay proclaimed that the Revolution had triggered "a vast expansion of the human mind," a flowering of literature, oratory, education, history, and the "science of government." "Our political situation, resulting from independence, tends to exalt and improve the minds of our citizens. Great occasions always produce great men."[55] Like other American men of letters, he argued that culture was moving west. "Ever since the flood," he wrote in the *United States Magazine* (1779), "true religion, literature, arts, empire, and riches, have taken a slow and gradual course from east to west, and are now about fixing their long and favorite abode in this new western world."[56] To dismiss this as naiveté or promotionalism would be to ignore the cultural determinism accepted by educated men of the era. A new land and a new society, American (and some foreign) writers affirmed repeatedly, would acquire an American muse. Such was their faith in the power of a republican transformation of society.[57]

Though in print Ramsay exuded optimism, privately he expressed disappointment. Reluctantly he conceded that America was "not the country to reward any literary publications."[58] This disparity between his public and private position was typical of the Revolutionary generation. Since they regarded historical writing as a weapon in the struggle to create a national society and culture they deliberately adopted an optimistic tone. But they were not being altogether insincere. Curiously, their doubts and fears were not set in opposition to their confidence and hopes, but reinforced them, so strong was their belief in the power of republican society to bring out the best in human nature. For Ramsay the public act of writing history provided a way of purging his private doubts: theory dictated that a republican society would free the creative energies of a free people. Still, a nagging problem remained: he could claim few genuine cultural achievements, and none that reflected a uniquely American culture. He continued to predict future achievements, while acknowledging "an inferiority" due to "the state of society."[59] In the meantime, to overcome his sense of cultural inferiority he turned to the practical alternative, discarding the premises of high culture and lauding the values of his society on other grounds. He maintained that Americans and their society represented achievements of the highest order. If the nation had yet to produce outstanding literary artists or philosophers, in the wilderness ordinary men had constructed a society that European philosophers could only dream of in their studies.[60]

By merging the concept of national character — defined as a commitment to a republican ideology — with the idea of a special destiny, Ramsay found a way to define a unique American identity without repudiating either the English heritage or the basic premises of Enlightenment thought. At the same time, only by broadening the English heritage beyond the confines of its historical-territorial limitations could the nation's distinctive cultural and political existence be established. "America's purpose," he proclaimed, "is to prove the virtues of republicanism, to assert the rights of man." In effect, he transformed an English tradition of liberty into a supranational ideology. Indeed, the idea of being an example to the world can be a parochial as well as a cosmopolitan concept. He was basing an essentially parochial ideal — nationalism — on values presumed to be universal. By focusing on the nation's destiny "to prove the virtues of republicanism," he deliberately chose the one area of national life which could be regarded as a genuine achievement, and he nationalized, even jingoized, the idea of progress. Thus did Ramsay attempt to establish the unique qualities of a national society within the accepted paradigm of eighteenth-century historical thought — that history served as a vehicle for placing "the science of politics on a footing with the other sciences, by opening it to improvements from experience, and the discoveries of future ages."[61]

Ramsay's concern was with America's uniqueness. He was interested not so much in the basic institutional arrangements of republicanism as in the formation of the particular republican, egalitarian spirit he believed prevailed in American society. Fascinated by the atmospherics of American republicanism, he failed to resolve the problems of cultural transmission and the interaction of the culture of the Old World with the environment of the New World, nor did he explain how the new fusion was transmitted as a living social force to generations of descendants and successors. But he succeeded much better in his primary goal, providing a useful paradigm to give to the national past a coherence it might otherwise have lacked.

# III. National Destiny

In their quest for a coherent national past the Revolutionary generation employed a variety of techniques, but none with more fidelity than the idea that the United States had a special mission. The belief that God or Providence or the natural order has singled out a nation for a destiny higher than its own well-being serves to give the citizen a sense of superiority and self-confidence. For Americans the sense of distinctiveness took on added importance. Lacking many of the common attributes of nationhood — ethnic and religious uniformity, long-standing national institutions such as church, army, and monarchy — they sought other sources of identification. The substance of a national tradition they found in the idea of a special American destiny. "Next to the introduction of Christianity," declared Richard Price, an English nonconformist minister whose writings were admired in the United States, "the American Revolution may prove the most important step in the progressive course of human improvement. It is an event which may produce a general diffusion of the principles of humanity and become the means of setting free mankind from the shackles of superstition and tyranny."[1]

The conviction that the American experience held universal significance grew out of the ideology of the Revolutionary movement. To justify opposition to British sovereignty the Patriot party had begun with the rights of Englishmen, but had ended by enlarging that concept to include a supranational theory of natural rights. Having proclaimed that the principles of the Revolution could be applied to all mankind, it was an easy next step to celebrating the society that had produced such an event as destined to effect a "progressive increase of human happiness." "The free system of government we have established," wrote James Madison, "is so congenial with reason, with common sense, and with a universal feeling, that it must produce approbation and desire of imitation. . . ."[2]

It was not enough to say simply that the Revolution held universal significance. To deal with it without coming to grips with the pre-revolutionary past — without making the colonial period somehow mesh with the events of 1765-1789 — would surely make the birth of the United States appear a parochial event born of chance circumstances. American historians, therefore, set out to demonstrate that from its inception the nation's history was part of a Providential plan to expand the boundaries of human knowledge and liberty. "The discovery of America," proclaimed David Ramsay, "is the first link of a chain of causes, which bids fair to enlarge the happiness of mankind by regenerating the principles of government in every quarter of the world."[3]

Preoccupied with a vision of the United States as an example to the world, the first national generation found the notion of the origins of American society as part of a grand design especially appealing. But the specific ingredients of that theme grew directly out of an historical tradition native to colonial America. For generations New Englanders had treated the ancestral migration to the New World as not merely a movement to colonize the wilderness, but a conscious act by a chosen people to found a society based on principles of civil and religious liberty. They were the heirs of a tradition that dated back to the founding generation of William Bradford and John Winthrop.[4] For seventeenth century Puritans the historian's first task was to record the workings of God. The writing of history was, however, more than a theological exercise. Placing a high premium on its social utility, they believed that the historian had a civic as well as theological responsibility. The study of the past revealed when God favored an individual, sect, or nation. "God sifted a whole nation," proclaimed William Stoughton, "that he might send Choice Grain over into this wilderness."[5] They were convinced that God had commissioned this people to fulfill the promise of the Protestant Reformation. What better proof of their righteousness than historical testimony that they had been aided by special providences? What better way to promote the cohesiveness of the community than by recounting the purposes, hardships and successes of the founders?

In time the Puritan vision of a Holy Commonwealth corroded in disappointment. Yet the use of history to promote the cohesiveness of the community by representing its founding as part of a divinely inspired mission was never abandoned. In 1672 the General Court of Massachusetts Bay Colony voted to encourage the collecting of special providences, "beyond what could in reason have binn expected," so that the inhabitants might be encouraged to serve God. This plea and the responses it elicited betray a growing fear that the enterprise was dying. New England, warned Cotton Mather in his *Magnalia Christi Americana* (1702), was in danger of forgetting its "errand into the wilderness."[6] Moreover, events in England — the defeat of the Puritans and the restoration of Anglicanism and the Stuarts — brought into question the original purpose of saving the mother country by their example.

From this crisis the cosmopolitanism of New England historical writing suffered; it became almost wholly inward looking. New Englanders were forced to examine their own peculiar experience. The sense of being part of a larger Christian past that characterized the works of Bradford and Winthrop increasingly gave way to a parochial tribalism. That tribalism led to an even greater accentuation on the founding generation and to a gradual shift in emphasis in defining what their goals had been. In particular the events of the 1680s, when the Holy Commonwealth was threatened by the Dominion of New England and then liberated by the Glorious Revolution, effected a transformation in the New England historical consciousness. The original mission of building a Holy Commonwealth was transfigured into a crusade to establish a society based on civil liberty and the right of self-government.

Political liberty and self-government were, to be sure, crucial parts of the original plan of settlement. But for the founders of New England, political liberty had a different meaning than it would in the eighteenth century. Where the first settlers had valued self-government simply as an instrument for the protection of the Holy Commonwealth, it came to be increasingly valued for itself. Before long the founders were being celebrated as the builders of a new order of human liberty.[7] As this new theme came to be used in sermons,[8] it also found its way into formal histories. In his *Chronological History of New England* (1736) the Rev. Thomas Prince asked that "the worthy Fathers of these Plantations" be remembered for their concern that "Liberty, both civil and ecclesiastical, might be continued to their successors" and for their establishment of a society "as happy as any on earth." Nearly thirty years later Thomas Hutchinson observed that "the primary views" governing their "removal" from the mother country "were the enjoyment of civil and religious liberty."[9]

If the views of the generation of Bradford and Winthrop had by the mid-eighteenth century undergone considerable revision, there remained a continuity in approach, especially in the assumption of the social utility of historical writing. A popular tradition had evolved which stated, in brief, that in driving the Puritans to come to the New World to escape persecution God had intended them to found a society based on civil and religious liberty that would serve as a model to the world.

During the Anglo-American crisis this tradition was put to new use. In the war of words that preceded independence New England Patriots exploited these arguments to convince their countrymen that the new imperial policy represented a negation of their historic rights. The major portion of Amos Adams' *Concise, Historical View of the Planting of New England* (1769) was dedicated to proving that "liberty" was "the most ardent wish" of the planters of New England. "They bore the yoke with reluctance, and never failed to improve the first opportunities to cast it off. The sacred thrust for liberty brought them hither."[10]

Perhaps the single most important application of this tradition to an ideological battle involving all of British North America was John Adams' *Dissertation on the Canon and Feudal Law* (1765). It was widely read throughout the colonies, and later historians quoted from it in their discussions of the founding of New England.[11] Here can be found the basic strategy for converting the regional tradition in to a national ideology. There was little novelty in Adams' version of the purposes of the founders. He had, after all, written the *Dissertation* primarily to encourage his countrymen to resist an assault upon their traditional liberties. Like earlier historians, he depicted New England as a society founded for religious and civil liberty; while conceding the importance of faith as a motive, he maintained that "it was not religion alone but . . . a love of universal liberty. . . ."[12]

Adams lauded the achievements of his ancestors. "After their arrival here, they began their settlement, and formed their plan, both of ecclesiastical and civil government. . . ." Although "far from being enemies to monarchy," they still established a system of government founded on the principle "that popular powers must be placed as a guard, a control, a balance, to the powers of the monarch and the priest." To render the "popular power" more effective they removed as "many of the feudal inequalities and dependencies" as possible, consistent with "the preservation of a mild limited monarchy." Though willing to "hold their lands from their king; as their sovereign lord," they refused "homage to mesne or subordinate lords." Above all, the singular achievement of the founders was to transmit "to their posterity" not only "a very general contempt and detestation of holdings by quitrents," but also a hereditary ardor for liberty. . . ."[13] While he used commonplace arguments, Adams added a new dimension by implying that the New England experience was representative of American history.

After the Revolution, New England historians continued to deal with their history in this traditional manner. In what had become familiar and stylized phrases Jedidiah Morse observed that "a rational and safe enjoyment of civil and religious privileges, was the great object of their pursuit."[14] There was, however, a serious flaw in this picture of New England's planters as champions of civil and religious liberty: the celebrated cases of political and religious persecution in seventeenth century Massachusetts. The issue was the more problematic since their countrymen sometimes ridiculed the pretensions of contemporary New Englanders by reminding them of their ancestors' intolerance. This embarrassing problem produced a variety of responses.

Benjamin Trumbull simply ignored the issue. He mentioned neither Anne Hutchinson nor the persecution of the Quakers, curious oversights for a New England historian. Although he admitted that Roger Williams "had been expelled [from] Massachusetts, on the account of his religious sentiments," a few pages later Trumbull referred to the "noble spirit and sentiments of liberty and religion" of those first settlers without bothering to reconcile the contradiction. In contrast Jeremy Belknap, a liberal Congregational minister with Unitarian leanings, believed the cause of religious toleration would best be served by exposing the bigotry of his ancestors. In a restrained but strong tone of moral revulsion, he observed that once "having the power in their hands, they effectually established their pretensions and made all dissenters and disturbers feel the weight of their indignation." Belknap did, however, redress the balance somewhat by praising the planters of Rhode Island for having executed "a plan of entire religious liberty."[15]

Mercy Warren responded directly to the needling of New Englanders for their ancestors' indiscretions. She conceded that there had been persecutions. But "the spirit of intolerance in the early stages of their settlements was not confined to the New England *Puritans,* as they have in derision been styled. In Virginia, Maryland, and some other colonies . . . dissenters of every description were persecuted, with little less vigour" than in Massachusetts. We must realize, she concluded, that "a strange propensity in human nature to reduce everything within the vortex of their own ideas, the same intolerant and persecuting spirit, from which they had so recently fled, discovered itself in those bold adventurers, who had braved the dangers of the ocean and planted themselves in a wilderness, for the enjoyment of civil and religious liberty."[16] But Warren maintained that despite predictable human failings the Puritan fathers had planted civil and religious liberty.

The approach of most historians, including Warren and Belknap, was to admit that while there had been injustices they were overshadowed by the general good that resulted from the enterprise. "What have been considered as blemishes in their character," observed Jedidiah Morse, "seemed necessary in their situation." John Adams did not particularly relish the Puritans' "religious enthusiasms," but he contended that "no great enterprise for the honor or happiness of mankind was ever achieved without a large mixture of that noble infirmity." George R. Minot argued that if "for a moment" the planters of New England had "taken a retrograde course in their progress to liberty," they "must nevertheless forever hold an envied station in the view of mankind." Even the Rev. Isaac Backus, a Congregationalist turned Baptist who campaigned to lift all religious restrictions, found much to admire in New England's early history. While critical of intolerance, especially toward his Baptist forebears, he defended the founders of Plymouth from the accusation of excessive strictness. He argued, moreover, that even in the rigid atmosphere of seventeenth century New England there emerged a tradition rich in ideological contrasts and heterodox views.[17]

If the Revolutionary generation of New Englanders, like an earlier generation, were trying to come to terms with a new self-awareness, it was not a regional but a national identity they were seeking. When they wrote state or regional history they did so with the clear implication that it was a piece of a larger national past, and when they wrote national history they generalized about the nation from the perspective of the New England past; America was New England writ large. In his history of the United States, Benjamin Trumbull employed the same language to describe the founders of all the colonies that he had used to characterize the planters of his native Connecticut. Because of the hardships endured by the first settlers, "their posterity" have inherited "an extensive country, wise institutions, and distinguished privileges, civil and religious." Trumbull pointed to particular cases which closely resembled the New England example. The "fundamental laws" of Pennsylvania, he observed, "do honor to their compilers, as statesmen, Christians, and friends to the liberties and happiness of mankind."[18]

Since a basic ingredient of the newly emerging national consciousness was the principle of religious liberty, it seemed essential to circumstantiate the founding generation's commitment to religious toleration. At the very least they must be shown to have laid the groundwork for future generations. By the same reasoning practically every American historian trod lightly on the skeletons in the New England closet. When John Marshall wrote a history of the colonies he did not ignore instances in which "the government [of Massachusetts] maintained the severity of its institutions against all those who dissented from the church; and exerted itself assidously in what was thought the holy work of punishing heretics, and introducing conformity in matters of faith." His tone was more of sorrow than outrage: "It is to be lamented that the same people possessed a degree of bigotry in religion, and a spirit of intolerance, which their enlightened posterity will view with regret." Always skeptical of man's capacity to master the instinct for self-aggrandisement, he believed that most men had been drawn to America by economic considerations. But the founders of New England, he concluded, had been guided by "a stronger motive than even interest" — a devotion to civil and religious liberty. If along the way they deviated from those principles, in the long run they left a legacy of liberty.[19]

The willingness of American historians to minimize Puritan intolerance accurately indicates an affinity for the New England approach. In his *History of Pennsylvania* (1797-98) Robert Proud proclaimed that "the restoration and enjoyment of those natural and civil rights and privileges, of which men originally, by their folly and wickedness, are often deprived, was the great end, for which the predecessors of the present inhabitants of Pennsylvania . . . peaceably withdrew into this civil government and constitution of the province" was formed to preserve these "civil rights and principles." That plan was born in the mind of William Penn, who "laid a foundation for happy consequences; as manifested in the late glorious example and prosperity of the province. . . ."[20]

Like Pennsylvania, Maryland's beginnings seemed to provide the ingredients for a history in the New England tradition. Had not the colony's founders left England to escape religious persecution? Had they not established toleration in the new colony? George Chalmers in his survey history of the colonies and James Wilson in his lectures on American law both paid tribute to Lord Baltimore as a champion of religious liberty.[21] Historians usually portrayed Maryland as a haven of toleration. But the State's first historian had doubts. Episcopalian John Leeds Bozman felt little sympathy for New Englanders or their past. A former Loyalist sympathizer, he was not inclined to interpret the American past as a groundwork for the Revolution; and he took a more critical view of the intentions of the colony's founders.[22]

In his *Introduction to the History of Maryland* (1811) Bozman agreed that the religious turmoil of seventeenth century England had led to the settlement of New England and Maryland. However, rather than accept the common view that the English government and the Church of England had treated the Puritans and Catholics unjustly, he maintained that "the established church gave many instances of her moderation, not exhibited by either of the others when in power." He defended the behavior of the Church of England, "if not entirely to excuse . . . her conduct in the causes of those first emigrations." The blame lay primarily with the Puritans and the Catholics, Bozman argued as he catalogued their intolerance.[23] Although he admired Sir George Calvert, Bozman treated his reputation as a champion of religious liberty with skepticism. He doubted that the colony's founder had been motivated primarily by a desire to establish a refuge for Catholics. He questioned whether religious toleration in Maryland resulted from a sincere conviction or "a prudent policy" based on the knowledge that "the puritans, their most inveterate enemy, were now gaining in a rapid manner the ascendancy of powers in the councils of the mother country." Still, if Bozman displayed an Anglican's suspicion for Puritans and a Protestant's distaste for Catholicism, he avoided the anti-Catholic rhetoric of many American historians. And he acknowledged, while refuting the "common remark throughout the United States, that most of these states were originally colonized by means of religious persecution," the strong appeal of that tradition in the nation's historical imagination.[24]

Unlike Bozman, most historians were anxious to claim for their state a prominent place in the national past by proving that it fulfilled the criteria of conscious purpose at its founding. John Daly Burk resented New England's widely acknowledged claim to national parenthood. He had the advantage of chronology, pointing out that Virginia was "the first permanent establishment . . . formed by the British." It was, however, difficult to make a case for Virginia's founders as conscious builders of a new political and social order, especially with the colony's reputation as a settlement established for purely commercial reasons. Burk had to concede that the real glory of the Virginia past had been crowded into the last thirty years of the eighteenth century. Nevertheless, determined to establish the Old Dominion's rightful place, he devoted a volume to the early years of settlement: "It is here we must look for those ancient documents and materials, whose discovery will throw light on the history of other states." He argued repeatedly that the first permanent settlement in Virginia was the germ of a future nation. Of Lord Delaware's squadron, which saved Jamestown from abandonment, he wrote, "This little fleet carried with it the altars and the destinies of liberty: The germ of human happiness is on board: unconscious of the invaluable treasure they possess, the wretched colonists carry with them the sacred fire, which shall bless their posterity, and animate the world."[25]

Even so, the case for conscious purpose was weak. Burk's "hardy adventurers" lacked the vision of a John Winthrop or a William Penn. If Captain John Smith was bold and brave, even Burk could not convincingly argue that Smith's mission in the New World had been to establish civil and religious liberty. He did attest, with more conviction than evidence, that the Virginia Company was "democratic" and had worked to advance that form of government. Only the Company's religious policies were illiberal, but Burk maintained that they were not enforced. If any figure emerges from his first volume with a clear idea of what Virginia should be, it is the legendary Indian chief, Powhatan, who unfortunately for Burk was not a devotee of republicanism and could hardly qualify as a national hero. Burk's settlers may have carried with them "the germ of human happiness," but he had to admit that "the vestal flame lived unnoticed amongst them, without the care of a priestess or an altar." The best he could do was to prophesy that the time would come "when their descendants, enflamed with a holy enthusiasm, shall build temples, and raise altars for its preservation."[26] Nevertheless, Burk's efforts evidence the power of this sense of special purpose.

For New Englanders it was easy to extend the tradition of their founding to the founding of all the colonies; it was a short step from interpreting their local past as part of a Divine plan to enlarging that scheme to include all of American history. As the only region with a well documented past and an established historical tradition, it is understandable that New England, which contributed a large share of the new nation's working historians, would dominate its historiography. During the colonial period other areas yielded modest crops of locally grown historians but they had only a nebulous sense of their past uniqueness and produced few genuine historical works.[27] New England suffered no such hiatus. Although uneven in quality, its distinctive style of historical interpretation pervaded the general consciousness and found its way into sermons and political tracts as well as formal histories.

With the advantage of numbers and tradition, New England historians were bound to exercise a decisive influence; yet it is difficult to say with certainty how direct that influence was. Perhaps one reason why state historians did not seek an alternative view was that so few had strong local loyalties. Of ten non-New England state histories published between 1785 and 1812, five were by men who had neither been born, raised, nor educated in the states whose history they had written: David Ramsay of South Carolina (1785 and 1809), Robert Proud of Pennsylvania (1797-98), John Daly Burk of Virginia (1804-05), and Hugh Williamson of North Carolina (1812).[28] Moreover, Ramsay and Williamson had strong New England ties: Ramsay through correspondence and as a member of the Massachusetts Historical Society, Williamson through years of residence in Boston and as a student of theology in Connecticut. Finally, a number of historians — Ramsay, John M'Culloch, John Campbell, Hugh McCall, and Williamson — came from a Scottish or Scotch-Irish Calvinist background similar to that of their New England colleagues.

The only determined efforts to provide an alternative view came from men aggressively loyal to their native states: John Bozman of Maryland and Edmund Randolph of Virginia. In Bozman's case local pride merged with a militant Anglicanism that breathed hostility to the seventeenth-century Puritans. Perhaps it is not mere coincidence that Randolph was also an Anglican, although without the overt hostility expressed by Bozman. The New England influence was so pervasive that both men felt compelled to confront it. The fact remains that most historians offered a version of the origins of American society that generally accorded with the New England view. To read John Marshall's history is to realize that he not only accepted the substance of that interpretation, but its value as the measure of what was best in colonial society. "Posterity," Ramsay remarked to Belknap, "will know much more about the early settlement of New England than they ever will of the more Southern states." He thanked John Eliot for having "rendered an essential service to the living" with his *Biographical Dictionary* (1809) "by holding up so many excellent models for their imitation from the illustrious dead. In this as well as many other particulars New England sets a good example to the other states by perpetuating the names and histories of their deceased benefactors."[29]

Except for an occasional spirit of rivalry, the New England approach was influential because it was acceptable. It fit so neatly the pattern American historians wanted to establish for the national past that it is difficult to say how much was borrowed and how much was arrived at independently. A Quaker writing about the founding of Pennsylvania did not need to be reminded that his ancestors sought to establish a society in conformity with enlightened principles of civil and religious liberty. What better way to show that the Revolution and the creation of the United States were not chance events than to portray the founders of the colonies as men who had consciously set out to establish a new social and political system?

Perhaps the New England view was acceptable to men of varying backgrounds because by the late eighteenth century it was expressed within a primarily secular framework that separated it from the specific creed of the churches. From the 1690s on New Englanders began placing more emphasis on political values. Not that they denied the importance of religion; but increasingly they separated political and religious motives, usually at the expense of religion. By the mid-eighteenth century they had laid the groundwork for a secular interpretation. For the old Puritan preoccupation with the relationship between man and God they substituted a concern for the relations between man and man. Hannah Adams and Abiel Holmes even de-emphasized religious in favor of civil liberty, despite the fact that Holmes was a minister and the devout Adams had written on religious topics. Adams maintained that the political principles of the first settlers were based on "an ardent love of liberty, an unshaken attachment to the rights of men. . . ." According to Holmes, the Pilgrim Fathers had managed "to erect themselves into a Republic, even though they had commenced their enterprise under the Sanction of a royal charter, a case, that is rare in history, and can be effected only by that perseverance, which the true spirit of liberty inspires."[30] This emphasis on political values and institutions made New England history seem less unique and more American, especially since it so readily fit a whig definition of the Revolutionary movement and the first national generation's preoccupation with political institutions.

The New England tradition provided two related themes: the American colonies were founded on principles of civil and religious liberty, and the original planters had consciously set out to achieve that purpose. An extension of these themes linked the founding of the colonies with a grand design to "liberate the slavish part of mankind." Since the secular thought of the period was already dominated by a cosmography that interpreted the world in terms of purposive qualities, it was easy to express a sense of special destiny in secular terms. Eighteenth century men had coined the word Enlightenment to distinguish theirs from earlier ages. The Revolutionary generation was especially conscious of living in a distinctive epoch and wrote history out of pride in its achievements, which it compared favorably with those of Europe. "Inferences may be fairly drawn from our present happy political situation, which lead to the extirpation of despotism from the face of the globe," proclaimed Ramsay. "Let us forward this desirable revolution, by exhibiting such an accumulation of private virtue and happiness, that other nations, struck with the fruits of our excellent constitution, may be induced, from free choice, to model their own, on similar principles."[31] In these few lines he echoed a secular version of the Puritan "city on a hill."

If eighteenth century historians effected a revolution in historical writing they did so by secularizing its subject matter, reconstructing the past in terms that explained the destiny of man by his own nature.[32] American historians operated within the conceptual framework of the Enlightenment. Yet their writings retained elements of a Christian interpretation. Virtually every American historian referred to the role of God, although with varying degrees of personal religious conviction. Few of them rejected their religious heritage or fully embraced Enlightenment skepticism. Some were or had been clergymen, while others were laymen with strong religious loyalties.[33] They ignored the intellectual problems and inconsistencies involved in the simultaneous use of both secular and Providential interpretations. Though their views varied — from Benjamin Trumbull's and Mercy Warren's genuine belief in the role of Providence to Jeremy Belknap's and John Daly Burk's occasional references to the Divine — the results were similar. Practically every historian presented a secular explanation of events, using Providence only as a vague general, not a specific, cause. They did not represent God as impelling particular events nor did they establish any casual relationship between the two.

For Trumbull the grand design to "liberate the slavish part of mankind" came directly from the mind of God. In the preface to *A History of the United States* he announced that his primary goal was "to excite gratitude and praise in the hearts of all believers in a divine providence, to confirm their trust in him . . . and to be a perpetual testimony of his goodness and wonderful works, particularly toward his American Israel."[34] It is hardly surprising that a Congregational minister would see the hand of God directing human affairs. But the God of late eighteenth century American writing was distant and depersonalized; his presence was acknowledged but seldom held responsible for specific events. American historians invariably thanked Providence for the nation's freedom and prosperity and the success of the Revolution, but such statements were preceded by a secular explanation. Not even Trumbull could recapture the seventeenth-century Puritan sense of a personal God directing the most trivial of events. To have deleted the Almighty from his *History* would have made little difference; without Jehovah his narrative lent itself to secular interpretation. Such references as he made to responsibility for the outcome of a specific event gave the appearance of being grafted on to an otherwise secular explanation.

Trumbull at least attempted to revive the providential theorizing of his Puritan ancestors, but his ministerial colleague Belknap did not even make the effort. Belknap's occasional glances toward heaven for the outcome of a particular event appear to be little more than a nod to tradition. The overriding theme of his work was mankind's "true use of their rational and active powers." In his narrative God helps those who help themselves: "It ought ever to be remembered for the honor of New England, that as their first settlement, so their preservation, increase, and defense, even in the weakest infancy were not owing to any foreign assistance, but under God, to their own magnanimity and perseverance."[35] That "under God" is weak by comparison with the formulations of his Puritan ancestors. Belknap's distaste for theological explanations and his emphasis on man's rational powers indicate the influence of the Enlightenment on his approach to history.

American historians, then, seldom attributed the outcome of specific events to Providence; even Isaac Backus, a devout Baptist minister, conceded that although "the powers that be are ordained of God, neither every use that is made of this power, nor every means for the attainment of it, are from God, though every power be of him." But if the determining role was transferred to natural laws, whereby God was thought to operate in His world, the influence of Providence was not entirely eliminated. "The wise and benevolent Author of nature," observed Samuel Williams, "has made the human race capable of continual advances towards a state of perfection and happiness."[36] This commonplace doctrine of first and second causes enabled the historian to interpret events and movements in terms of human motivations while still assigning a role to Providence. Moreover, neither sphere need necessarily impinge on the other. After accounting for the events that led to the Revolution in purely human terms, Mercy Warren asked those of a "reflective mind" to remember "that Superintending Power which governs the universe."[37] Christian historians were also coming to visualize God as acting indirectly through human agents. But invariably they portrayed the most significant human shapers of history as mere marionettes of God's will. Their interest in human causation was secondary to theological explanations. Warren came as close as any of her colleagues to a traditional Christian interpretation. Yet, in her narrative, Providence simply exists side by side with human causation as an explanation of events.

Neither Warren nor any other American historian attempted to establish a precise causal relationship between God and the actions of men. Indeed, their preference for such terms as Providence and the Author of Nature implied a distance and neutrality not associated with the God of traditional Christian historiography. For example, David Ramsay concluded that "it is probable" that during the Anglo-American conflict "neither [side], in the beginning intended to go thus far, but by the inscrutable operation of Providence, each was permitted to adopt such measures as not only rent the empire, but involved them both, with their own consent, in all the calamities of a long and bloody war."[38] The implication is that if God was not necessarily the immediate and instrumental cause, He was in a direct way an efficient and mediate cause. But such a view is more apparent than real. Isolated from the body of his narrative, Ramsay here would seem to be saying that only the "inscrutable operation of Providence" could explain the otherwise mysterious fact that both sides went further than they had "in the beginning intended to go." In his account, however, there is nothing "inscrutable" about what happened; he provided a perfectly logical, believable, and secular explanation. To delete the phrase "the inscrutable operation of Providence" would in no way alter the interpretation

Despite frequent references to Providence, American historians were not detached from the mainstream of Enlightenment thought. Not even Voltaire explicitly denied Providence, in which, as a deist, he in some sense believed. Eighteenth century historians frequently found in the idea of progress a substitute for the guiding hand of God as a unifying theme in history. Especially pleasing to Americans was the transformation of the idea of progress into a natural law by such writers as Condorcet and Joseph Priestley, because they viewed the American Revolution as a step in the emancipation of mankind. Though less optimistic about man's potential, Warren and Ramsay, for example, used Providence in much the same way as Priestley. Their conviction that in effecting a Revolution and creating a republic Americans were fulfilling God's plan for mankind seemed to echo Priestley's earlier doctrine that the "great instrument in the hand of divine providence, of this progress of the species towards perfection, is society and consequently government."[39]

More than intellectual imprecision was involved in this fusion of secular and Providential interpretations, for such a view had polemical value. What better way to give sanction to the idea that the United States had a special destiny than by arguing that the course of American history, however vaguely defined, was part of a Divine plan? Even a deist like John Daly Burk saw fit to interpret such events as the salvation of the Jamestown settlement by Lord Delaware's timely arrival as providential. "If it will be believed, that the Almighty Architect is ever under the necessity of altering or regulating the plan of his providence, here certainly is an occasion, which may justify his interference."[40]

To men and women already committed to a vision of the United States as the fulfillment of mankind's millennial future, it seemed "rational to believe that the benevolent Author of Nature designed universal happiness as the basis of his works." The concept of Providence provided an ideal way of expressing a teleology implicit in the eighteenth century idea of progress. If America was realizing the destiny God planned for mankind then Belknap need do no more than thank "that superintending influence, which brings good out of evil," nor Ramsay more than agree that "Heaven smiled on our exertions." Even

Thomas Jefferson explained the American condition by an "adoring" and "an overriding Providence, which by all its dispensations proves that it delights in the happiness of man here and his greater happiness hereafter."[41]

In theorizing about the origins of American society, historians not only revealed the influence of a secularized Christian tradition but also of a more partisan Protestant version of the past. From the former they inherited the concept of a spiritual conflict between good and evil in which good would ultimately triumph because that was God's purpose.[42] Translated into secular terms, evil became ignorance and tyranny, good became reason, knowledge, and liberty. Drawing on the analogy between ignorance and evil on the one hand and knowledge and good on the other, Belknap portrayed the discovery and settlement of America as a triumph for reason. He criticized "the Ancient philosophers" for their "erroneous" belief that the torrid zone was scorched by the vertical sun and therefore no human could pass from the northern to the southern hemisphere. On the authority of these philosophers "that imperfect system became . . . a part of the creed of the Roman church. . . . Thus ignorance and error were canonized, and the feeble dawn of science was scarcely able to penetrate the dark mist of the middle ages." But with the discovery of America "those ancient systems have gradually vanished, and mankind have founded their knowledge . . . of the terraqueous globe, in fact and experience."[43]

All this would seem to derive from Enlightenment rationalism; but Belknap betrayed the continuing influence of a Protestant bias. In a *Discourse on the Discovery of America* (1792) he took as his text a chapter from the Book of Daniel that most Protestants in the sixteenth century regarded, with the Book of Revelation, as symbolically foretelling the entire course of man's career on earth.[44] "Many shall run to and fro and knowledge shall be increased" (Chapter xiii, verse 4). He interpreted this prediction as meaning that man would find salvation through a general increase in knowledge. "As the testimony of Jesus is the spirit of prophecy, so we may very properly consider the travels of the Apostles to spread the knowledge of the gospel, as one capital influence of the fulfillment of Daniel's prophecy." From the time of the Apostles there had been few events during the intervening centuries to "advance knowledge." But beginning with the discovery and settlement of North America, Daniel's prophecy was again being fulfilled. A train of events had begun which would lead to an "increase in science." By "science" Belknap meant not only a knowledge of the natural world but, more important, civil and religious liberty.

> The discovery of America . . . has opened an important era in
> the history of man. . . . Freedom, that noble gift of heaven, has
> here fixed her standard; and invited the distressed of all
> countries to take refuge under it. Our various ancestors fled
> from the imposition and persectuions to which they were subject
> in England, and found their wilderness an asylum from that
> tyranny. . . . But we were designed by Providence for a nobler
> experiment still: not only to open a door of safety to our
> European brethren here, but to show them that they are entitled
> to the same rights in their native countries. . . .

Thus, for Belknap American history was part of a grand design. Why else
had the "discovery and settlement" of North America "by Europeans
happened at a time, when they were emerging from a long period of
ignorance and darkness?"[45]

The beginning of this "vast alteration" Belknap found in the
Protestant Reformation. The philosophes were generally hostile to
organized religion: at worst as an uncivilized activity, at best as a
guardian of morals and good order. David Hume relented when a
churchman contributed to "the cause of progress;" but, like the
philosophes in general, his condemnation of all positive expressions of
belief made it difficult for him to understand the place of Christianity
among the forces shaping civilization.[46] As for the Reformation, Hume
saw it as a battle between two false religions. American historians
suffered from no such inhibitions. Not that they were insensitive to
sectarian hatreds or unconcerned about religious enthusiasms that often
ended in violations of human rights; but they regarded these as
perversions of true religion rather than an inherent flaw.

For American historians the planting of the English colonies and
the Protestant Reformation were part of a single pattern. "Had the
settlement commenced at any period before the reformation," observed
Benjamin Trumbull, "the planters would have been Roman Catholics.
The ignorance, superstition, bigotry, and slavish principles of the Roman
Church, would have been transported into America, propagated, and
probably fixed, in the colonies."[47] Such a view did not imply
Protestantism in any doctrinal sense, but a broader secular interpretation
of the Reformation as the catalyst for a movement toward a progressive
increase in civil and religious liberty. The issue is the politics of religion.
Protestantism, Catholicism, and the Reformation were treated in political
terms; theology was related to political institutions and ideology. "The
religion of the Colonists," wrote Ramsay, "nurtured a love for liberty.
They were chiefly Protestants, and all Protestantism is founded on a

strong claim to natural liberty, and the right of private judgement." Catholicism is evil because it is used as a weapon for political oppression. When Trumbull observed that the Glorious Revolution saved America from Stuart tyranny he equated "popery" with "despotism." "Had James II succeeded . . . he would probably have established the religion of the Roman church and slavery. . . . The colonists would have been reduced to such poverty and ignorance, and their spirits . . . so enslaved and broken, that they never would have enterprised the late revolution, nor have risen to their present importance and glory."[48]

The Reformation, the settlement of North America, the American Revolution and the creation of the United States were all placed in a sequence of triumphs that defeated, at least in America and England, what John Adams referred to as the unholy alliance between religion and politics. The twin tyrannies of canon and feudal law, he maintained, had been disastrous for human freedom: "as long as this confederacy lasted, and the people were held in ignorance, liberty, and with her knowledge and virtue too, seem to have deserted the earth, and one age of darkness succeeded another. . . ." But a change had begun with the Reformation. From that time knowledge had gradually spread over Europe, especially in England, and as it increased, acceptance of ecclesiastical and civil tyranny progressively decreased. "The people grew more and more sensible of the wrong that was done them by these systems . . . till at last, under the execrable race of Stuarts" the struggle against the canon and feudal law "became formidable, violent and bloody." "It was this great struggle," concluded Adams, "that peopled America."[49]

In somewhat different terms, Belknap accentuated the bond between ignorance and "the Romish church" and the "remarkable concurrence of circumstances" which had breached it. The "invention of printing began to dissipate those errors and superstitions in which Europe had long been involved." That timely and "happy invention" gave "peculiar advantage to the bold attempt of Luther, to rouse Germany from her inglorious subjection to the Roman Pontiff, and effectuate a reformation, which soon spread into the neighboring countries." But the Reformation only triggered the process. In England "the want of a just distinction between civil and ecclesiastical power . . . kept the nation in a long ferment" and drove thousands across the sea to America. The Reformation had breached the alliance between religion and ignorance, between civil and ecclesiastical power (to Belknap they amounted to the same thing). In America that bond was gradually eroded "till the happy genius of the revolution gave birth to a free and equitable toleration, whereby every man was restored to the natural rights of judging and acting for himself in matters of religion."[50]

Here was a secularized version of the seventeenth century Puritan's "city upon a hill." In New England this took on the complexion of a return to a Puritan tradition against which earlier historians such as Thomas Hutchinson had reacted in favor of an imperial perspective. For the more or less openly disbelieving rationalism with which Hutchinson opposed the primacy of God's role in history, the Revolutionary generation proposed not a revival of Christian historiography but a vague Providential conception of history. For Hutchinson's imperial reduction of Massachusetts to the status of one colony among others, they substituted the recognition of that colony's historical importance as part of an American destiny to enlighten mankind. "I always consider the settlement of America," observed John Adams, "with reverence and wonder as the opening of a grand design in Providence for the illumination of the ignorant, and the emancipation of the slavish part of mankind all over the earth." Before the Revolution British America had been merely a European backwater; but in this context the founding of the colonies could be made to appear as a significant epoch in world history, "an event which has no parallel in the history of modern ages." Inasmuch as the American past was conceived as part of a plan to "liberate the slavish part of mankind," it could be argued that there was a fundamental unity to American history.[51]

# IV. The New World, Human Nature, and the National Character

Convinced that the nation's special destiny was to exemplify the ideals of liberty, equality, and justice, it seemed particularly important for American historians to discover how such a society had come into being. Their inquiries were designed to comprehend American history in universal terms. "Human nature is always the same," observed John Marshall, "and consequently man will in every situation furnish useful lessons." At the same time, estrangement from England led Americans to ask what made the child different from the parent, while foreign criticism of the new republic stimulated them to defend the characteristics that set the New World apart from the Old. The American states claim "the attention of the curious of all nations," for in their history can be found the causes of "their progress, from the first feeble settlements made by Europeans on a savage coast, to their present state of greatness." In their desire to establish a distinct identity and remove the stigma of cultural inferiority, they tended to emphasize the "state of greatness" at the expense of what "is always the same." "The states of America," proclaimed Samuel Williams, "now present to the world a new state of society; founded on principles, containing arrangements, and producing effects, not visible in any nation before."[1] In the tension between these seemingly contradictory goals was fashioned an understanding of America's universal relevance.

---

It seemed obvious to everyone, European as well as American, admirer and critic alike, that the character of Americans and their society was somehow related to the land. Its very extent, quality and abundance invited comment. The axiom that human nature is uniform conflicted with the observation that men and societies vary from place to place. If the nature of man is uniform why did Americans alone among the peoples of the earth achieve a republican society? If all men are fundamentally the same, then the distinctions among groups of men could only be explained by differences in their circumstances.

The preoccupation with the landscape was also a response to foreign writers who described the environment of the New World as unhealthy and degenerate.[2] Not only did such views wound national pride; they challenged the vision of a model society. The quarrel first arose over the interpretation of natural phenomena. Many European naturalists believed that nature in America was in its earliest stage of development and therefore inferior. According to Corneille DePauw, the animals of America were "often ugly and deformed," "poisonous trees grew" there, and syphillis could be contracted by breathing "the pestilential air."[3] Buffon, in his *Histoire Naturelle* (1749), theorized that since America was literally a new world — geologically more recent than the Old World — it was in a stage of growth too early for the mature development of modern animals, men and institutions. Therefore, like other new things, it was savage, unformed and undisciplined.

> In this New World, therefore, there is some combination of elements and other physical causes, something that opposes the amplification of animated Nature: there are obstacles to the development, and perhaps to the formation of large germs. Even those which, from the kindly influences of another climate, have acquired their complete form and expansion, shrink and diminish under a niggardly sky and an unprolific land, thinly peopled with wandering savages who . . . held only the first rank among animated beings, and existed as creatures of no consideration in Nature, a kind of weak automatons, incapable of improving or seconding her intentions.[4]

Buffon's approach was persuasive to Europeans because in explaining deviations from nature as they knew it as evidence of inferiority it supported their prejudices.[5] They concluded that the discovery and settlement of the New World was "the greatest of all misfortunes to befall mankind."[6] In America, observed Abbé Raynal in perhaps one of the most influential books of the eighteenth century. "everything exhibits the vestiges of a malady of which the human race still feels the effects. The ruin of that world is still imprinted on its inhabitants, they are a species of men degraded and degenerated in their natural constitution, in their stature, in their way of life, and in their understanding, which is but little advanced in all the arts of civilization."[7] In a later edition published after the French alliance and the successful conclusion of the American Revolution, Raynal offered a more favorable estimate of the English settlements; but still he insisted that the discovery and occupation of the New World was a calamity for native and European inhabitants alike.

Raynal's fame, together with his thesis, made him a particularly tempting target and probably accounts for the heat with which Thomas Paine attacked his account of the American Revolution.[8] But even he did not excite as much wrath as William Robertson's incorporation of the Raynal-Buffon thesis into his *History of America* (1777). Actually Robertson avoided many of the excesses of his Continental counterparts. Like other British writers, he tended to follow the lead of Montesquieu's *Spirit of the Laws* by describing America as an example of the influence of climate on the history of society. Robertson attempted to distinguish between tribes living in different climates, attributing their primitiveness to the backwardness of their institutions, not to their being subhuman.

It would seem, then, that there was less reason to resent Robertson than Buffon or Raynal. But despite his comparative moderation, the fact that he was a Briton, a famous Scottish historian whose books were widely read and admired in America, was bound to excite greater antagonism than the writings of any number of Frenchmen. When Robertson wrote that "the same qualities in the climate of America which stunted the growth and enfeebled the spirits of its native animals proved pernicious to such as have migrated into it voluntarily," he meant Spaniards; but he did not make that clear,[9] and the logic of his argument did not necessarily exempt British Americans. Robertson's *History of America* was especially infuriating because of its publication in the midst of the Revolutionary war and its usefulness to Englishmen urging stronger government action against the rebels in terms that seemed to have scientific validity. Benjamin Franklin reported that in Parliament there were "many base reflections on American courage, religion, understanding, etc. in which we were treated with the utmost contempt, as the lowest of mankind, and almost of different species from the English and Britain. . . ."[10]

American science and ethnography received a great impetus from the campaign against British and European critics, for to refute their views required close study of the environment. "Notwithstanding the dreams of European philosophers, or the interested views of European politicians," observed Jeremy Belknap in a typical expression of cultural patriotism, "America can best be described by those who have for a long time resided in it."[11] There were many other rejoinders by American naturalists and historians.[12] The best known was Thomas Jefferson's *Notes on the State of Virginia* (1784) which inspired many subsequent works.[13] "I am induced to suspect there has been more eloquence than sound reasoning displayed in support of this theory," wrote Jefferson of Buffon's theories; "it is one of those cases where the judgement has been seduced by a glowing pen." Americans passionately defended their environment as a positive good. An "uncleared and uncultivated soil," proclaimed Belknap, "is so far from being an object of dread, that there are no people more vigorous and robust than those who labour on new plantations. . . ."[14]

The fire of Buffon, Robertson, and company was directed at the Indian, but the unmistakable implication was that if the physical environment was corroding to the native population then it was likely the European inhabitants were also undergoing a process of moral and physical degeneration. Therefore a defense of the Indian was a defense of the European population. Jefferson, for example, praised the ability of the Indians of Virginia to form well-ordered societies without having to submit "themselves to any laws, any coercive power, any shadow of government."

> Their only controls are their manners, and that moral sense of right and wrong, which like the sense of taste and feeling in every man, makes a part of his nature. An offence against these is punished by contempt, by exclusion from society, or, where the case is serious, as that of murder, by the individuals whom it concerns. Imperfect as this species of coercion may seem, crimes are very rare among them. . . .

Jefferson used his discussion of the Indian to rebuke European critics.

> . . . insomuch that were it made a question, whether no law, as among the savage Americans, or too much law, as among the civilized Europeans, submits man to the greatest evil, one who has seen both conditions of existence would pronounce it to be the last; and that the sheep are happier of themselves, than under care of the wolves. It will be said, that great societies cannot exist without government. The savages, therefore, break them into small ones.[15]

For Jefferson favorably to compare Indian with European society also served to refute the belief that the new societies were degenerate and non-productive. If the measure of a civilization is the nature of its political institutions and the European had too much government and the Indian too little, then, he reasoned, in the United States a proper balance between too much civilization and savagery had been found. Jefferson was particularly combative when he attacked Buffon's contention that America had yet to produce "one good poet, one able mathematician, one man of genius in a single art or a single science." Again he used the Indian to make his point.

> Before we condemn the Indians of this continent as wanting genius, we must consider that letters have not yet been introduced among them. Were we to compare them in their present state with Europeans, north of the Alps, when the Roman arms and arts first crossed those mountains, the comparison would be unequal, because, at that time, those parts of Europe were swarming with numbers; because numbers produce emulation, and multiply the chances of improvement, and one improvement begets another. Yet I may safely ask, how many good poets, how many able mathematicians, how many great inventors in arts or sciences, had Europe, north of the Alps, then produced? And it was sixteen centuries after this before a Newton could be formed.[16]

Thus Jefferson attributed the Indian's backwardness to the sparseness of his numbers and lack of contact with other cultures.

Jefferson emphatically denied that America had produced no geniuses.

> In war we have produced a Washington, whose memory will be adored while liberty shall have votaries . . . and will in future ages assume its just station among the most celebrated worthies of the world, when that wretched philosophy shall be forgotten which would have arranged him among the degeneracies of nature. In physics we have produced a Franklin, than whom no one of the present age has made more important discoveries, nor has enriched philosophy with more, or more ingenious solutions of the phenomena of nature. We have supposed Mr. Rittenhouse second to no astronomer living; that in genius he must be the first, because he is self-taught.

To prove "that of the geniuses which adorn the present age, America contributes its full share," Jefferson devised a numerical theory of culture similar to the one he had used to account for the Indian's diffidence. If the United States had produced a Washington, a Franklin, and a Rittenhouse from a population of only three million, then France with twenty million should have "half a dozen in each of these lines" and Great Britain with ten million should have "half that number, equally eminent."[17] On the basis of these figures Jefferson concluded that the

United States compared favorably with Great Britain and France.

Practically every historian assumed a relationship between the environment and the character of institutions. Some of them were trained as naturalists and scientists or had a lively interest in natural history. The best known was Jedidiah Morse, who had earned an international reputation as "the father of American geography," but there were also amateur naturalists such as Jeremy Belknap and Benjamin Trumbull who published geographical accounts of their immediate locales.[18] Hugh Williamson, author of a study of American climate and a *History of North Carolina* (1812), was a member of the American Philosophical Society and had collaborated with Benjamin Franklin on his experiments with electricity. In 1769 he was appointed to the prestigious commission studying the transits of Venus and Mercury, and his observation of a comet that year was widely acclaimed on both sides of the Atlantic.[19] Samuel Williams, a liberal Congregational minister, was also a noted scientist before turning to history. His scientific writings won him honorary degrees from Yale and Edinburgh and the Hollis professorship of mathematics and natural philosophy at Harvard College (1780-88). When a financial scandal resulted in dismissal he fled to Vermont. During the next three decades he served as a minister in Rutland, edited a newspaper and a periodical, surveyed disputed boundary lines, and helped found the University of Vermont, where he lectured on astronomy and natural philosophy.[20]

In the tradition of Montesquieu, American historians considered environment to be a critical factor affecting man's intellect, health, morals, and institutions.[21] David Ramsay attributed a certain variety in the manners and habits of Americans to differences in climate and soil. Despite "a comparatively barren country" the New England provinces had "improved much faster than the others," for "it seems to be a general rule, that the more nature does for any body of men, the less they are disposed to do for themselves." He blamed the humid climate of South Carolina's summer for such social problems as dueling, drunkenness and indolence. Duels "take place oftener in Carolina than in all nine states north of Maryland" because "warm weather and its attendant increase of bile in the stomach has a physical tendency to produce an irritable temper."[22]

Such sectional differences were regarded as incidental compared to the general similarity of environmental influences. "The proper nursery of genius, learning, industry, and the liberal arts," wrote Williamson, "is a temperate climate, in a country that is diversified by hills, enjoying a clear atmosphere." In no other country, he concluded, do "these circumstances occur, in so extensive a degree, as they do in

America, at least in North America." If the climate affected man, men could also affect climate. In North America the atmosphere was becoming more moderate. That beneficial alteration was due partly to natural change and partly to the industriousness of American farmers; as others had claimed, the spread of agricultural cultivation tended to improve the atmosphere. From these observations Williamson concluded that in America man and nature worked together to provide a setting favorable to great achievements of the arts, sciences, and liberty.[23]

Williamson regarded his book on climate as an introduction to the civil history of North Carolina; with Montesquieu he believed that the physical environment operated most directly in the early stages of development. It is, therefore, not surprising that he, and other historians with expertise in natural history, wrote about areas that were emerging from frontier conditions.[24] As much to the point, in each such case they had moved from urban centers to less settled regions where that connection could still be observed. As "the youngest of the states," wrote Samuel Williams, "and now rapidly changing from a vast tract of uncultivated wilderness, to numerous extensive settlements, Vermont is now in the situation, in which a new country ought to be examined." Benjamin Rush, outlining the stages by which civilization advanced in Pennsylvania, argued the superiority of its evolution to the older European mode of military conquest.[25]

To refute the opinions "of those theorizing philosophers" who represented "America as a grave to Europeans," the naturalist-historians set out to show that there civilized men not only survived but multiplied and improved. Williams and Belknap compiled an array of statistics to prove that Americans were an unusually fecund and long-lived people. "I do not know that we can find any new country," concluded Williams, "in which, every circumstance seems more favorable to increase." In a chapter entitled the "Effect of the climate and other causes on the human Constitution," Belknap eloquently proclaimed "that there are no people more vigorous and robust than those who labor on new plantations. . . ." He argued that Americans had better appetites than Europeans, lived to a "great age" and suffered from fewer diseases, and "that many of them die of no acute disease but by the gradual decay of nature." Comparing the difficulties of the first European settlers with the easy success of the founders of Kentucky and Tennessee, Williamson observed that "after all allowance had been made for . . . the men who first came over, and the circumstances under which they settled, I think it probable, that the native white American is more ambidextrous; that he has a great versatility of genius, and can more readily turn himself to all the necessary demands of life, than the natives of the other continent."[26]

Even if there had been no such debate, Americans undoubtedly would have utilized the environment to explain the character of their society. For scholars using concepts and language commonly associated with universal history and applying them to a national history, environmentalism provided a means for attributing the community's development to factors inherent in that nation alone. The process of constructing a new and, in their view, radically different form of government carried with it the implication that men were affected — favorably in this instance — by their social, political, and physical milieu. But if environmentalism was the descriptive motif of their accounts of colonial society, one cognitive theme more than any other occupied their attention: a concern for order and stability. That they had lived through a period of political revolution and social dislocation is reason enough why the issue of social stability should have concerned them.

American historians were haunted by the picture of civilizations like individuals with a distinct life cycle ending in decay and death. "Every species of human government," warned Jeremy Belknap, "contains the seeds of dissolution, which will some time or other work its ruin."[27] The cyclical view of history postulated the rise and fall of successive political empires. History demonstrated that in the past each empire had risen to a position of supremacy, achieved maturity, and then begun a course of decline. The process was irresistible. Using biological analogies, eighteenth century historians delineated the cycle of birth, growth, maturity, old age, and death. In any given case the pace of development might be extended by prudent action or foreshortened by vice and folly, but ultimately each nation was destined to the same fate.[28]

In the United States the problem was compounded by the fear that republics were more susceptible to "a constant decay in human affairs" than other forms of government.[29] Since republics were based on the sovereignty of the people their survival depended upon the character and virtue of the citizenry. In a monarchy the vigor of unitary authority, most often with the aid of a standing army and a religious establishment, reduced the need for virtue. But in a republic coercion and fear had to be replaced by persuasion; men had to be convinced to submerge their selfish desires for the greater good of the community.[30] Given the fallibility of human nature, public virtue seemed a frail reed on which to base the life of a republic. Americans liked to think of themselves as more virtuous than other people, but many feared that the party battles of the 1790s and what they regarded as a passionate pursuit of wealth were signs of declining virtue. Comparing the Revolutionary era to the

1780s, David Ramsay complained that "the sober discretion of the present age will more readily censure than admire, but can more easily admire than imitate the fervid zeal of the patriots of 1775, who in [an] idea sacrificed property in the cause of liberty, with the ease that they now sacrifice almost every other consideration for the acquisition of property."[31]

By the late eighteenth century the cyclical view of history was giving way to a vague belief in progress. Samuel Williams, for example, based his philosophy (and theology) on the assumption that the universe was not only purposeful, systematic and comprehensible, but also beneficent. In a series of "Philosophical and Astronomical lectures" delivered at Harvard College he maintained that "the wisdom and goodness of the Creator is everywhere apparent in all the works, and laws of nature."[32] That the idea of progress implicitly contradicted the concept of an unchanging and unchangeable human nature was not yet a disturbing intellectual problem. If American historians still feared that "nothing is so established among men, but that it may change and vary," their dire predictions of death and decay were exhortations, not expressions of belief in an immutable law of history. The historians sought a way out of the dilemma posed by the cyclical interpretation. They were attempting to demonstrate that the conditions of life in America provided the basis for the virtue and social stability essential to a republic. If so, the United States might prove to be the first nation in history to break the cycle of decay and death. "We cannot fail to be convinced," observed James Sullivan, "that nothing but an unreasonable indulgence of a disposition to avarice, and ambition, groundless jealousies, a criminal supineness in public concerns, or an unpardonable inattention to the modes of education, can ever deprive us . . . of the genuine seeds of republicanism, which have produced our glorious revolution, with a rich harvest of civil liberty. . . ."[33]

Experience seemed to support the idea of progress. Surveying the American past, the historians could point to a handful of colonists building a nation out of a wilderness; in their own lifetime, the Revolution indicated how men could move toward a more perfect society. The dominant mood was unquestionably optimistic, but their optimism never obscured the political problems posed by human nature. Far from basking in cheerful certainty, they qualified their hopes with reservations. Few eighteenth century Americans were willing to place their faith entirely in the purity of human nature.[34] While praising American virtue, they recognized that Americans like others were creatures of passion, and if left uncontrolled would too often act selfishly against each other. Ramsay regarded "everything human" as "imperfect" and he feared that "corruption of human nature which wishes to exalt self at the expense and over the rights of others." "The desire of distinction is inherent in the bosom of man," wrote Mercy Warren. "Few are the numbers of elevated souls, stimulated to act on the single motive of distinterested virtue."[35]

Despite strong doubts, like most Americans, historians shared a balanced view of human nature: that it has a positive as well as a negative aspect. "The study of human character," concluded Warren, "opens at once a beautiful and a deformed picture of the soul." There is built into their histories an optimism in contradiction to the frequent reminders of the vagaries of human nature. While warning against the weaknesses inherent in mankind, almost despite themselves their goals as historians forced them to offset this attitude and they smoothed over intellectual contradictions to achieve an emotionally satisfying result. Since the success of a republic depended upon the virtue of its citizens, they had to act as though men were capable under the proper conditions of thinking and doing the right thing. Even Warren, whose traditional Calvinist conscience restrained undue optimism, referred to mankind's desire for "distinction" as that "noble principle implanted in the nature of men." Inherent in the structure of her *History* is a cautious conviction that in America, by a "coincidence of circumstances," mankind's passion for "distinction" had been "kept under the control of reason, and the influence of humanity," thereby producing "the most benevolent effects." Thus Warren somewhat inconsistently recounted a general decline in public and private virtue and then proceeded to the conclusion that the United States "may perhaps be possessed of more materials that promise success than have fallen to the lot of any other nation."[36] These attitudes were by implication akin to Madison's belief, expressed in the tenth *Federalist,* that political institutions could be constructed in such a way as to divert mankind's passion for distinction and power into socially useful channels. At the very least, they implied that in the proper setting the worst in human nature could be neutralized.

In orthodox political theory a republic prospered or decayed because of the virtue or moral debility of its citizens. Since the Revolution had led to the creation of the United States it was from that event that historians read back into the past to define the character of Americans. "The genius of the Americans, their republican habits and sentiments, naturally led them to substantiate the majesty of the people, in lieu of discarded royalty." But how did Americans acquire a "genius" for "republican habits and sentiments"? By an adept reversal, historians argued that a republican society flourished because there existed in

America the conditions essential for the maintenance of a virtuous citizenry. "The colonies from their first settlement were nurseries of freemen," proclaimed John M'Culloch, and the "inhabitants . . . grew up in an acquaintance with, and attachment to his rights." "The spirit of liberty . . . lives in the minds, principles, and sentiments of the people," wrote Samuel Williams, but it is "produced, preserved, and kept alive, by the state of society."[37] What Williams meant by "the state of society" was the total environment, physical, social, and political. The task that American historians set for their accounts of the colonial period was to show how and why such a "state of society" had come into being, to describe its basic ingredients, and to gauge its impact on the nation's inhabitants; that is, to delineate the national character.

American historians found in the ideas of Montesquieu and the Scottish Enlightenment a workable theoretical framework. The influence of particular writers cannot be precisely determined; but the works of Montesquieu and such Scottish writers as David Hume, William Robertson, Frances Hutcheson, Adam Smith, Lord Kames, Thomas Reid and Adam Ferguson were well known in the United States and reprinted in American editions. The treatises of the Scots, dealing with history, ethics, politics, economics, psychology, and jurisprudence in terms of a "system upon which natural effects are explained," had become the standard textbooks of the colleges of the late colonial period. At Princeton, William and Mary, Pennsylvania, Yale, King's, and Harvard, the men of the first national generation had been trained in the texts of Scottish social science.[38] Besides this general exposure several American historians had extensive contact with institutions and individuals strongly influenced by Scottish philosophy. David Ramsay and Hugh Williamson were alumni of New London Academy and Ebenezer Hazard had attended Nottingham Academy. Ramsay was John Witherspoon's son-in-law and a protegé of Dr. Benjamin Rush, both leading disciples of Scottish thought. Williamson, of Scottish descent, had studied medicine in Edinburgh and had been a leading student of Francis Alison, the Scottish educator who established the New London academy.[39]

Beginning with the principles of human nature as they conceived them and a view of the external conditions of human life that resembled Montesquieu's, Scottish writers attempted to reconstruct the history of human progress from its simple beginnings to more complex levels of civilization. Ferguson's *Essay on the History of Civil Society* (1767), consciously patterned after Montesquieu, insisted on the uniformity of man's nature, but he argued as emphatically for the diversity of institutions and attitudes. He contended that "the forms of government must be varied, in order to suit the extent, the way of subsistence, the character, and the manner of different nations." The growth and decline of nations, as well as the observable variations among the many forms of government, Ferguson and his American disciple Samuel Stanhope Smith attributed to three general causes: the vicissitudes of fortune, national character, and differing national goals and policies.[40]

There was much in Montesquieu that Americans found disagreeable, especially his contention that it is natural for a republic to span only a small territory, but his view of the relationship between human nature and environment, physical and social, nicely complimented their own. Turned to their purpose, they found his method useful. There are, he reasoned, certain "laws" of nature that apply to all men "because they derive their force entirely from our frame and existence."[41] His general theory stated that these laws are bent into individual shape not only by physical circumstances like climate, soil, size of the country, but also by what he referred to as "moral" causes like customs and religions. True, geography pushes them in one direction or another. But for all his inclination toward an ecological determinism Montesquieu did not believe that man is necessarily to be dominated by physical necessity alone. "Wise men or learned men are not the production of any particular soil or climate," observed Williamson, a naturalist and an admirer of Montesquieu; "they are consistently begotten and nourished by civil liberty." Samuel Williams, who came as close as anyone to an ecological determinism, argued that population depended upon "two general causes, the original laws of nature, and the state of society." The latter he defined by such factors as the difficulty of procuring property, the state of religion, destruction in war, local custom, and "the genius of the civil government." Like Montesquieu, such writers believed that men can choose the kind of political organization under which they want to live; by their choice they set in motion particular influences which permeate and shape their thoughts.[42]

But, like other eighteenth century historians, Americans had no clearly defined system of causation, no clear idea of the distinction between historical causation and historical themes. Unable to translate into narrative form the systems of either Montesquieu or Ferguson, they instead relied upon lists of related causes and circumstances with no real technique for working out precise relationships or differentiating the relative importance of each factor. In attributing the causes of the "increase of mankind" both to natural factors and the state of civil society, Williams concluded that "these causes generally combine, and operate together," but "that we cannot separate their effects; or determine how much is to be ascribed to the law of nature and climate, and what is derived from the state of society." Evident in such narratives is an awareness of Montesquieu's elusive concept of the interplay between physical and "moral" causes. Less evident are Ferguson's stages of civilization, although there is the hint of a process of maturation. Without describing the process, but enumerating the "circumstances" that ensured a spirit of independence, Ramsay proclaimed that the colonies, "though not sensible of it, were growing to a greater degree of political consequence" and "had advanced nearly to the magnitude of a nation." Like other Enlightenment historians, the closest the Americans came to a theory of causation was to relate the facts of human nature as they understood them to the circumstances of life in early America. "The mind of man naturally relishes liberty," proclaimed Ramsay, and it is in a "new and unsettled country" that the "natural desire of freedom is strengthened."[43]

If American historians had no clearly defined system of causation, they knew what themes they wanted to pursue. Drawing on the relevant writings of history and political theory — Montesquieu being but the most conspicuous among many — they regarded republicanism as more than a political system; it represented the whole character of society. They could not imagine a workable form of social and political organization, whether despotism, monarchy, or republic, without an appropriate ideology. There was, the eighteenth century believed, a reciprocal relationship between the structure of government and the spirit of its people. "The period between 1620 and 1761," wrote Ramsay, "shows to what extent a country will flourish under a good government . . . and gives an historian an opportunity to make useful reflections."[44]

These were not simply academic questions. For Americans the social meaning was the point of the Revolution. The debates over the structure of government preceding and following independence, the ideological issues that divided Republicans and Federalists, grew out of concern for the kind of people Americans were and should be. A republic, with its emphasis upon the people and its limited dependence upon authority, required that its citizens be capable of using their power wisely and be ready to sacrifice their own immediate interests when necessary for the public good. In a republic, wrote Montesquieu, there must be laws and beliefs that conform to the principle of virtue, which he defined as love for the republic, equality, and sobriety, an abhorrence of luxury, and a respect for laws and willingness to act according to them.[45] American historians attempted to prove that in the New World human nature and the environment (both physical and social) had conspired to produce not only a republican political and social organization, but also the mentality essential to its survival.

The story, with some variations among different writers, went something like the following. "From the first settlement of this country everything concurred to inspire its inhabitants with a love of liberty." In the manner of Montesquieu, historians usually opened their discussions by dealing with physical causes. "While the ministers of kings were looking into their laws and records, to decide what should be the rights of men in the colonies," observed Samuel Williams, "nature was establishing a system of freedom in America. . . . " First, there was the landscape itself. "The natural seat of freedom is among high mountains and pathless deserts such as abound in the wilds of America," wrote Ramsay, and even an accident of geography "generated ideas in the minds of the colonists favorable to liberty."

> Three thousand miles of ocean separated them from the mother country. Seas rolled, and months passed, between orders and their execution. In large governments the circulation of power is enfeebled at the extremities. This results from the nature of things, and is the external law of extensive or detached empire. Colonists, growing up to maturity, at such an immense distance from the seat of government, perceived the obligation of dependence much more feebly, than the inhabitants of the parent isle, who not only saw, but daily felt, the fangs of power.[46]

From these vague and somewhat lyrical discussions of the impact of physical environment on the minds and spirits of men, historians usually turned to a more precise analysis of the influence of the land itself. The taming of "a wilderness" made it "necessary that . . . every man who did not mean to perish was obliged to engage" in clearing the land, building homes, and securing a livelihood. Nature had blessed the New World with an abundance of land. A postulate of republican theory, derived most clearly from Harrington, declared that republican governments were only practicable in communities with a broad distribution of property. "The founders of the colonies," wrote John Lendrum, "had adopted the wisest policy in settling the vacant lands, by granting them to those only who personally cultivated their purchases." For Lendrum the more equal the distribution the more republican the attitudes of the inhabitants. Since the New England colonies had more consistently pursued a policy of "equal division of lands than in any of the other provinces . . . a spirit of liberty and independence gave vigor to industry. Few individuals were either very rich or very poor. They enjoyed the happy state of mediocrity, which is equally favorable to strength of body and vigor of mind."[47]

The circumstances of life guaranteed a style of life appropriate to a republic. American society, wrote Mercy Warren, attained "that just and happy medium between the ferocity of a state of nature and those high stages of civilization and refinement, that at once corrupt the heart and sap the foundation of happiness." A community of small farmers, argued Ramsay, "held forth few allurements" to those who "aspired to hereditary honours" and "but little scope for the intrigues of politicians or the turbulence of demagogues." Jeremy Belknap summed it all up in the closing pages of his *History of New Hampshire:*

> Were I to form a picture of a happy society, it would be a town consisting of a due mixture of hills, valleys and streams of water. . . . The inhabitants mostly husbandmen; their wives and daughters domestic manufacturers; a suitable proportion of handicraft workmen, and two or three traders; a physician and a lawyer, each of whom should have a farm for his support, a clergyman of any denomination, which should be agreeable to the majority, a man of good understanding, of a candid disposition and exemplary morals; not a metaphysical, nor a polemic, but a serious and practical preacher. A school master who should understand his business and teach his pupils to govern themselves. A social library, annually increasing, and under good improvement. A decent musical society. No intriguing politicians, horse jockey, gambler or sot; but all such characters treated with contempt. Such a situation may be considered as the most favorable to social happiness of any which this world can afford.[48]

That these comments appeared at the close of his *History* is indicative of the special emphasis Belknap, and other American historians, placed on a simple agrarian style of life. In private they bemoaned changes in American society that political theory implied were dangerous to a republican society: burgeoning population, rapid economic growth, a headlong pursuit of wealth. According to theory, youthful societies were simple in structure, egalitarian in nature. Maturing societies, however, were characterized both by greater numbers and greater wealth, and the wealth tended to become concentrated in the hands of a few. Characterized no longer by a great middle grouping of independent yeomen, but by extremes of wealth, the community lost social cohesion. By the time Belknap wrote his description of life in the republic these changes were already very much in evidence, as he was aware; but American histories ignored these circumstances.[49] Although most historians lived in the more heavily populated commercial centers or in the plantation states of the Chesapeake, their histories described a society of small towns and independent yeomen farmers that varied only in degree from area to area.

Nature and society, moreover, combined to insure the emergence of republican political institutions. As portrayed by Belknap, the governments that evolved during the colonial period had the crown as an executive and the people as a legislature, but no third branch like the House of Lords to balance king and people. The House of Lords, Belknap argued, was the product of a feudal society. "Settlement began here by an equal division of property among independent freemen. . . . The yeomanry were the proprietors of the soil; and they know no superior but the king. A council whether appointed by him or chosen by the people could not form a distinct body, because they could not be independent." The economic underpinning of an aristocracy did not exist; for an independent yeomanry cannot be controlled by an aristocracy. In short, "the colonies were communities of separate independent individuals, under no general influence, but that of their personal feelings and opinions. They were not led by powerful families, nor by great officers in church or state."[50]

In some colonies "the inhabitants chose their own governors," while in others "the Crown delegated most of its power to particular persons." Whatever the method, "the prerogatives of royalty and dependence on the mother country, were but feebly impressed on the colonial forms of government." In fact, if not in actual form, the colonists "enjoyed a government which was but little short of being independent. . . . They chose most of their magistrates, and paid them all. . . . They had in effect the sole direction of their internal government." With each colony actually if not theoretically controlling its internal affairs, Americans naturally tended toward a similar philosophy of government. "The civil government of all the provinces was so far republican, that, in every one of them, the assent of the governed was indispensably necessary to acts of legislation."[51]

One consistent theme runs through these accounts: left to their own devices in the proper setting, men will opt for a republican society.

> Americans born under no feudal tenure, nurtured in the bosom of mediocrity, educated in the schools of freedom; who have never been used to look up to any lord of the soil, as having a

right by prescription, habit, or hereditary claim, to the property
of their flocks, their herds, and their pastures, may easily have
been supposed to have grown to maturity with very different
ideas, and with a disposition to defend their allodial inheritance
to the last moment of their lives.[52]

By arguing that the environment of the New World "naturally"
strengthened "the desire of freedom," American writers implied
tendencies inherent in human nature and the natural order. The frequent,
almost repetitious, use of such words and phrases as "natural" and the
"seeds of liberty" indicate the influence of Scottish common sense
philosophy; and like all eighteenth-century scholars they assumed the
uniformity of human nature. In Scottish common sense philosophy, man
was also believed to possess "Bents or Instincts implanted in our nature."
There are, wrote Thomas Reid, certain "original judgments" which
"serve to direct us in the common affairs of life. . . . They are part of our
constitution, and all the discourses of our reason are grounded upon
them. They make up what is called the common sense of mankind. . . ."[53]

There is also in the argument of American historians a quality of
self-determinism that resembled the Law of Nature as represented by the
French philosophers Holbach and Volney. Their theory that man would
naturally gravitate toward a condition of social welfare, once freed from
the superstitions and restraints of existing society, closely resembled the
arguments to be used by American writers.[54] In the same sentence
Samuel Williams observed that the "spirit of freedom was in some
degree checked" by royal authority, but these were too "irregular and
contradictory . . . to alter the natural feelings of men, or to change the
natural course and tendency of things."[55] Finally, even though there is
implicit here the beginning of a debate over the meaning of self-evident
truth, perhaps the beginning of a revolt against the empiricism of John
Locke,[56] they also relied heavily on empirical arguments.

The goals of American historians were polemical and they used
many means to prove their thesis. Eclectic in approach, they wove the
scattered strands into an intellectual fabric of their own. It suited their
purpose to show that by any standard of judgement, empirical,
institutional, or teleological, the society of the New World was superior
to that of the Old. To overcome a sense of cultural inferiority in a nation
that lacked a culture of its own, they celebrated America itself as an
achievement. Even so staunch a pessimist as John Marshall argued that in
America men had learned more from the practical experience of
constructing a society in the wilderness than all the philosophers of
Europe could teach. Consequently, when he wrote his *Life of*

*Washington* he devoted the first volume to a history of the colonial period, a chronological narrative of the principle events of the colonial era from which he drew some broad conclusions.

Like his colleagues, Marshall was anxious to demonstrate that the achievements of the United States deserved the respect of Europeans. Although no American political philosopher could be compared favorably with a Locke or Harrington or Montesquieu, he pointed instead to how the system actually functioned. Marshall turned the nation's paucity of political philosophers to advantage by the negative argument that its experience proved the poverty of predetermined schemes of government based on logic rather than on concrete experience. In relating the story of Virginia's early settlers, he contended that the Virginia Company's policy of holding property in common had hampered the colony's development because under such a system the colonists were reluctant workers. "Industry, deprived of its due reward . . . felt no sufficient stimulus to exertion." However, when Governor Dale divided the land into private lots of three acres, even though "the colonists were still required to devote a large portion of labour to the public, a sudden change was made in their appearance and habits." Marshall also cited the history of early Plymouth to illustrate the same point, observing that the Pilgrims, misguided by their religious theories, "fell into the same error which had been committed in Virginia, and in imitation of the primitive Christians, threw all their property into a common stock." Even in a small enthusiastic sect such a scheme could only have disastrous consequences; they were often in danger of starving, and whippings administered to produce labor only aroused discontent. This "pernicious policy of a community of goods and of labor so unfavorable to population, being for some few years adhered to, they increased more slowly than any other of the colonies. . . ."[57]

Marshall reiterated time and again that abstract reasoning on questions of government and society is at best unreliable and at worst pernicious. In Virginia the problem had been the misguided plans of men stationed three thousand miles away in London with little first-hand knowledge of conditions in the New World. At Plymouth the problem rested with a social policy determined by abstract religious theories rather than in the more reliable school of practical experience. No scheme of government aroused Marshall's contempt more than John Locke's Fundamental Constitutions for Carolina. First promulgated in 1670, it provided for a social hierarchy with fanciful graduations in rank, an elaborate plan of government with provisions for sundry officials bearing elaborate titles such as Chamberlain, Lord Steward, and Chancellor, and a lower house, or commons, consisting of representatives elected by freeholders who owned at least fifty acres of land.[58] Locke's plan provided a convenient target for a group of historians determined to prove that in America practical experience had proved a more reliable guide to the achievement of a free and workable political and social system than the great minds of Europe had conceived through logic and reason. His prestige as the greatest of political philosophers made his failure, compared with the success of practical experience, all the more satisfying. "This Constitution," wrote Marshall, "soon furnished an additional evidence to many afforded by the history of the human race, of the great but neglected truth that experience is the only safe school in which the science of government is acquired, and that the theories of the closet must have the stamp of practice before they can be received with implicit confidence."[59]

If American historians believed the history of the United States provided a guide to universally valid principles of society and government, their explanation of how and why the nation had come to be what it was only served to emphasize its uniqueness. It suited their purpose to show that left to their own devices in the proper setting men would naturally opt for a republican society. Samuel Williams argued that under favorable circumstances men were capable of building a society in conformity with the laws of nature. That tendency in man and in nature would prove the universality of the American experience. "This kind of government seems to have had its form and origin, from nature," proclaimed Williams. "In America every thing tended to introduce, and to complete the system of representation. Made equal in their rights by nature, the body of the people were in a situation nearly similar with regard to their employments, pursuits, and views. . . . Nothing remained for such a people, but to follow what nature had taught; . . . they naturally adopted the system of representation." But the circumstances would attest to their uniqueness, for "it is a system that has no where been suffered to prevail but in America, and what the people were naturally led to by the situation, in which Providence had placed them."[60] The paradox is that American historians based the unity of the American past on an essentially parochial concept — of a singular national character fashioned in a unique setting — yet the ingredients of that character were based on ideals and values presumed to be universal. Preoccupied with establishing the particularity of American society, they still had not abandoned the precepts of Enlightenment thought. They often spoke of the universal applicability of the American experience. But such disclaimers paled before the weight of evidence in favor of particularity.

Within the substantive theme of uniqueness can be found an

issue of equal, perhaps greater, importance to the historians: a concern for order and stability. If they worried about American society and warned of the difficulties into which it could fall, they remained convinced that these difficulties could be overcome. The key to their optimism was an abiding faith in American virtue. Though at times disenchanted with the behavior of their countrymen, especially during the 1780s and 1790s, they remained optimistic, in public if not always in private, of the predominant virtue of the society as a whole. The significant point for them was America's uniqueness: the "differentness" of the nation's historical and physical circumstances and thus, most importantly, of her people's moral character. American historians proclaimed that their people and society, conceived in virtue and liberty by the first settlers and refined by the trials of conquering a wilderness, would prove adequate to whatever was demanded of them. They marshalled an array of historical evidence, both natural and civil, to prove that Americans possessed the qualities of character indispensable to the life of a republic, especially by recounting the ways in which they reacted to the decisions thrust upon them during the colonial and revolutionary period.

But an environmental explanation of the character of the society created a problem: it implied a rejection of its origins and heritage. If Americans had severed political ties with Great Britain, they still spoke English and lived within a framework of political and legal institutions that were English in origin. They needed a formula that would affirm the Americanness of the national character without entirely repudiating its English content.

# V. English Americans

Environmentalism provided historians with a useful tool for both universalizing the American experience and testifying to the nation's uniqueness. But it also served another purpose. For a people who no longer thought of themselves as Englishmen but could not reject their heritage, environmentalism offered a formula for explaining why they were at once English and yet distinctively American. The assumption that the colonials had been transformed by natural conditions in the New World had pronounced advantages, implying gracious acknowledgement of their heritage while emphasizing the beneficence of the environment and therefore the likelihood of further improvement. Among the reasons why historians assumed an environmentalist posture, the need both to embrace their Englishness and establish the particularity of American society was one of the most compelling.[1]

For a hundred and fifty years the inhabitants of British America had thought of themselves as Englishmen living abroad. Then, within little more than a decade, the Revolution not only severed political ties with the mother country, but also discredited the old self-image. In a nation made up of varied ethnic and religious groups, one obvious approach to the question of national identity would have been to argue that the American experience had fused them into a "new American man." "The race now called Americans have arisen," proclaimed Crevecoeur; "here individuals of all nations are melted into a new race of men."[2]

Crevecoeur's idea was consistent with the notion that since human nature is uniform, differences among men must be the result of different environments. Inviting as such an approach may have been, especially since the Revolutionary generation was so fond of portraying the United States as an asylum for the oppressed, Crevecoeur was not expressing a widely held view. While it is true that the Revolution had demonstrated a certain homogeneity of the American people — the divisions over independence bore little relationship to differences of national origin — it could hardly be argued that political unity had developed out of a common ethnic and cultural background. Even during the 1790s, when Federalists asserted the nation's Englishness, Republicans, despite their electoral strength among diverse ethnic groups, did not extol the melting-pot ideal. The idea that the American had been transformed into a "new man" by some process of ethnic amalgamation was the exceptional view of a romantic French immigrant.[3]

Historians were not hostile to the concept of an ethnically diverse society; nor did they mean to repudiate the contributions of non-English Americans. But circumstance led them to emphasize their English heritage at the expense of diversity. Regardless of American resentment of Britain, it would be many years before they could overcome their psychological dependence on and preoccupation with England and things English. They spoke English and their institutions had been built on English models. Some of the most numerous of the non-English settlers, the Scots, Irish, and Scotch-Irish, almost all spoke English. The best estimates indicate that in 1790 between 61 and 66 per cent of white Americans were of English origin and between 80 and 84 per cent of English-speaking origin. Moreover, most historians were either of English descent or acculturated Englishmen, and the most numerous group, New Englanders, were from the most homogeneously English section of the country. Other factors were also important, such as priority of arrival, imperial ties, law and governmental institutions, and the isolation of cultural deviations.[4]

Even more important than cultural preponderance, historians were determined to use their writing to promote "a more perfect union." A preoccupation with national unity tempted them to emphasize uniformity, ignore economic and political differences, and stress homogeneity at the expense of ethnic, cultural and religious variety. Since Americans, whatever else divided them, shared common political attitudes and institutions of English origin, it is not surprising that they adopted an English bias in emphasizing politics and government, especially since they used the Revolution as the focus for their discussions of national characteristics. It was natural that they would be preoccupied with the Revolution and search for its roots; it represented, after all, the genesis of American nationhood. But since it was a political movement based on English Whig ideology, by concentrating on it they further strengthened the bias of their histories.

Finally, there may have been an even more compelling although not explicitly stated reason for their English bias. By implication historians praised the emergence of a new man fashioned by the unique environment of the New World; but they were troubled by that perception, perhaps by the uneasy feeling that the character of this new man would not be capable of resisting the dangers inherent in a republican society. Consciously or not, they added a new dimension to their discussions of the national character: they removed the new American a step further from his naturalistic origins by invoking the restraints instilled by his English heritage, especially by the veneration of legal and political institutions. In their accounts of the Revolution, for example, they placed special stress on constitutional issues and the willingness to be law-abiding even when no formal government existed. If the American was the product of the New World, he was also an English-American.

Thus, for a variety of reasons historians wrote with an English bias and tended to overlook or minimize the diversity of national life. In describing the colonial period they dwelt on the early years of colonization, insisting that the first colonists had founded societies that better reflected English ideals of liberty than did the mother country. Because the early years of colonization were dominated by the English this perspective tended to identify the nation's institutions with those of England. Similarly, when they wrote about the Revolution the historians insisted that the colonists were defending English principles of constitutional liberty. In his analysis of the Revolution in Virginia, Edmund Randolph contended that the predominance of English ideas was a major cause of the separation from the mother country. "We have seen that until the era of the Stamp Act almost every political sentiment, every fashion in Virginia appeared to be imperfect unless it bore a resemblance to some precedent in England." That very bias made it inevitable that Virginians would take offense at an attack on their liberties. "The spirit . . . which she had caught from the charters, the English laws, the English constitution, English theories . . . had diminished her almost idolatrous deference to the mother country and taught her to think for herself."[5]

Even historians from states with heterogeneous populations tended to accentuate the English at the expense of other elements. Pre-revolutionary writers had emphasized the ethnic and religious variety of the middle colonies; the Revolutionary generation ignored such diversity. In part their omission was due to the fact that middle state historians largely neglected local history. There were no histories of New Jersey and New York, two of the more heterogeneous states. Ebenezer Hazard collected documents for a national history and Richard Snowden and John M'Culloch, himself a Scottish immigrant, wrote general histories in which they paid little attention to local issues. Robert Proud's *History of*

*Pennsylvania* (1797-98), the one study of a mid-Atlantic state published during the early national period, referred to the early activity of the Dutch and the Swedes on the Delaware River only by way of introduction; his was the story of settlement by people who were primarily English and Quaker. Although Proud did identify the numerous German sects that settled in Pennsylvania, he gave them no significant place in his account, and he virtually ignored the Scotch-Irish settlers of the backcountry.[6] Occasionally nativists like Jedidiah Morse and Elijah Parish wrote that New England was "almost universally of English descent" and not plagued like Pennsylvania with "the wild Irish and sour Germans."[7] But most historians were not hostile to the non-English portions of the population; they simply did not concern them. By implication Englishmen alone were regarded as having set the mold of American society. Even John Daly Burk, an Irish Revolutionary who had recently fled from British rule in his native land, cast his *History of Virginia* as the story of Englishmen building a society based on English ideals of liberty.[8]

David Ramsay alone acknowledged that a process of amalgamation was taking place. An historian of unusual breadth and sensitivity, he painted a picture different from Crevecoeur's. In describing the ethnic makeup of South Carolina, Ramsay observed that "so many and so various have been the sources from which Carolina had derived her population, that a considerable period must elapse, before the people amalgamate into a mass possessing an uniform national character. This event daily draws nearer, for each successive generation drops a part of the peculiarities of its immediate predecessors. . . . The different languages and dialects, introduced by the settlers from different countries, are gradually giving place to the English." For Ramsay amalgamation was part of a long range process of acculturation in which "similarity" had been achieved only "among the descendants of the *early emigrants* from the old world." As for more recent arrivals, he had simply projected from the situation in 1809 to some unspecified future time when ethnic homogeneity would be realized. Ramsay had been born in Pennsylvania, but his father was from Scotland and his family lived in the Scotch-Irish Pennsylvania backcountry. Yet if Ramsay was more aware of non-English ethnic groups than other historians, he gave them no more credit than his colleagues for having contributed permanently to the national character and institutions. The process he saw was the absorption of the non-English white population into the dominant group, not the emergence of a new ethnic type.[9]

The relative anonymity of the non-English also held true for non-whites. Despite their numbers and the importance of slavery,

Africans received little attention. Unlike the Indian, the African had not been native to America; there was no necessity to defend him in justification of the environment. Nor was slavery accorded more than occasional comment, except for sporadic descriptions of its adverse effects. Having affirmed a relative political and economic equality in the colonies, John M'Culloch conceded that "those provinces in which slaves were the most numerous, were far inferior to their neighbors in strength, population, and wealth." Edmund Randolph referred to slavery as an "unnatural debasement" and denounced the cultivation of the "baneful weed tobacco" for having "stained our country with all the pollutions and cruelties of slavery." But if the "cruelties of slavery" gave him, like most men of his age, some anxious moments, he felt little sympathy for the Negro. His primary concern was with the institution's effect on whites. He attributed, for example, the inability of Virginians to produce military materials during the Revolutionary War to tobacco and slavery. "As soon as that noxious weed tobacco had obtained currency of fashion in Europe and the introduction of slavery had sheltered the white population from the labor and exposure incidental to its cultivation, it was seen that the raw materials of manufacture could be invested with greater profit in purchasing what she wanted from England . . . than in the application of her manual force to the tedious progress of manufactures."[10]

The attitude of other American historians toward slavery and blacks was ambiguous. They occasionally commented on the plight of the Afro-American but were far more troubled by the effect of slavery on whites. Though occasionally deploring the existence of slavery, they offered no practical plan or prospect for its abolition. Their views reflected the ambiguities inherent in the outlook of their generation. If the Founding Fathers dreamed of universal American freedom, their ideological posture was weighed down with priorities and prejudices that made the dream unrealistic. The dominant passion of the age was not with extending liberty to blacks but with erecting a republic for whites. When the slavery issue threatened the Constitutional Convention the Deep South's ultimatums were quickly met.[11] The works of historians were strongly influenced by this pattern of valueing Union more than abolition. Since they regarded historical writing as a weapon in the battle to help cement the bonds of Union, they were reluctant to raise divisive issues. Even those historians who had publicly opposed the peculiar institution did not press the issue. Jeremy Belknap, for example, had been a leader in the successful campaign to abolish the slave trade in Massachusetts; yet neither he nor any other historian used their histories to discuss the possibility of abolishing slavery. If an occasional historian bemoaned the unfairness or inhumanity of slavery, he never protrayed slaveowners as deliberately cruel or immoral, only as victims of historical circumstance.

Political expediency dominated attitudes, but there was also the issue of race. The belief that blacks were inferior made it difficult to include them in discussions of the national character. Randolph had expressed reservations about the status of Virginia blacks, but he stated with apparent approval that the phrase "all men are by nature free and independent" contained in article one of the Virginia Bill of Rights did not apply to blacks because they are not "constituent members of our society. . . ."[12] Even Crevecoeur could praise physical amalgamation only by omitting the participation of blacks.[13] Ramsay gently chided Jefferson for having "depressed the negroes too low" in his *Notes on the State of Virginia*. "All mankind," he argued, are "originally the same and only diversified by accidental circumstances." Yet he considered those "accidental circumstances" so overwhelming that "they who have been born and grown up in slavery are incapable of the blessings of freedom. Emancipation therefore would be ruinous both to masters and slaves." All he would concede was the remote possibility "that in a few centuries the Negroes will lose their black color."[14]

Unlike the blacks and non-English whites, the native American could not be ignored; and he presented a knottier problem. The Indians represented a political and military threat; they might still align with hostile European nations, especially Britain. Artistically, the Indian was the foil for dramatizing the colonist's encounter with the wilderness. A number of histories, especially those by New Englanders, were filled with dramatic tales of war and captivity.[15] More important, since European naturalists had focused on the "American man" to prove the degeneracy of the New World environment, American writers felt compelled to defend him. Samuel Williams, who came closer than any other historian to an environmental determinism, argued that since Indians lived close to nature they possessed a native strength. Because they dwelled in harmony with nature the "state of society . . . among the Indians of America" once was " beautiful and promising." If their communities were "everywhere tending to decay and dissolution," that process began with "the first arrival of the Europeans." The European had disrupted the Indian's rapport with nature. "The vices we have taught them, the diseases we have spread among them, the intemperance they have learned from us, and the destruction of their game, are evils for which the savage is unable to find a remedy."[16]

It was Jefferson who set the tone of the debate, using the Indian as a vehicle for discussing the character of American society.

> . . . were it made a question, whether no law, as among the savage Americans, or too much law, as among the civilized Europeans, submits man to the greatest evil, one who has seen both conditions of existence would pronounce it to be the last; and that the sheep are happier of themselves, than under care of the wolves. It will be said, that great societies cannot exist without government. The savages, therefore, break them into small ones.[17]

Jefferson's favorable comparison of Indian with European society served as a way of undercutting Buffon's theory that society in America was degenerate and non-productive. If the European had too much government and the Indian too little, in the United States a proper balance between the two had been found. There were a few brief and largely misinformed attempts to understand the Indian, but as a moral and social factor he was regarded as important only as part of the external environment.[18] He was not credited with having contributed to national development, much less with being a candidate for absorption into the general population. When Edmund Randolph referred to the Chickahominy tribe "as a stout, daring, and free people . . . governed in a republican form by their elders," he was not praising the Indian so much as the beneficent effects of the environment, even on "that lazy and improvident people."[19]

While American historians argued that the New World provided an ideal environment for the nurture of a republican society, they meant that it could only be exploited by a culturally and politically advanced people. They never doubted that among the nations the English were ideally suited to profit from so promising an opportunity. For countless centuries the Indian had lived "a miserable existence" in the same environment free from outside interference. The Europeans' "arts and arms . . . soon gave them an ascendancy over such untutored savages." Moreover, like the English, the New World colonies of Spain and Portugal were also separated from their parent states by distant oceans and covered by "high mountains and pathless deserts;" yet they had travelled a different path from that of English America.

> Portugal and Spain burdened theirs with many vexatious regulations, gave encouragement only to what was for their own interest, and punished whatever had a contrary tendency. France and Holland did not adopt such oppressive maxims, but were, in fact, not much less rigorous and coercive . . . these oppressive regulations were followed with their natural consequence: the

settlements thus restricted advanced but slowly in population and and in wealth.

Unlike other imperial nations, Britain had pursued an enlightened colonial policy. Even though its continental colonies were "far inferior in natural riches to those which fell to the lot of other Europeans," the "wise policy of Great Britain" enabled "her American settlements" to increase "in number, wealth and resources, with a rapidity which surpassed all previous calculations."[20]

American historians were not arguing that their history was an extension of the English past. The Saxon myth, so prominent in Revolutionary polemics, found no expression in their writings;[21] nor did any other aspect of English history unless it was directly related to America. They regarded their history as new and unique and as a new beginning, even without rejecting their English heritage. If, as they claimed, man is molded by his environment, then the environment of North America had molded Indians, Spaniards, and Englishmen in different ways. Echoing the logic of Scottish philosophy, they began with the assumptions "that there is a great uniformity among the actions of men, in all nations and ages, and that human nature remains still the same, in its principles and operations. The same motives always produce the same actions; the same events follow the same causes. . . ."[22] But if human nature is the same in all men, how was it that the English response to the environment of the New World was different from that of Indians and Spaniards? Because they were English. America may have been a new land but Englishmen did not begin anew. What differentiated the inhabitants of the New World was the level of civilization they had previously attained. Unlike the theories advanced in the *Encyclopedie* by the French philosophes, Adam Ferguson and his American disciples rejected the diffusionist theory of civilization. If nations borrow from their neighbors, they borrow only those things which they are near to inventing for themselves. "Any singular practice of one country," he observed, is seldom transferred to another, till the way be prepared by the introduction of similar circumstances."[23] It was the level of civilization of the English settlers that enabled them to take advantage of the environment and develop a republican society.

Every American historian, then, operated on the assumption, however vaguely stated, that the American was an Englishman modified by the natural conditions and circumstances of life in the New World. Some historians tended to place greater emphasis on the English heritage than on the transforming conditions of the New World. As Nathan Hale observed:

> In the two centuries since the first landing of our forefathers in
> this country . . . the posterity of a few persecuted emigrants
> have become a rich, proud, and powerful people . . . this
> remarkable growth was due not to the accidental advantages of
> soil and situation, but to the character, habits and institutions of
> our people, as they were introduced into this country by the first
> pilgrims, and have been cultivated and improved by their
> descendants.[24]

Hale emphasized the social attributes of the nation's founders, although
his comments carried the implication that the "institutions of our
people" had found an ideal if "accidental" setting for their culitvation
and improvement. Others, while concentrating on the English experience
in the New World setting, still acknowledged the crucial importance of
their tradition. John Marshall, for instance, argued that legislative
assemblies took root in America because those promoting settlement
found Englishmen reluctant to emigrate without a guarantee of
representative government. Civil and religious rights were abridged in
seventeenth century England, wrote Ramsay, but the proprietors of the
colonies found that in order to "allure settlers" they had no choice but to
"establish free constitutions." Even "the principle of avarice," therefore,
served to plant "seeds of liberty" that "grew up" into "fruit worthy of a
nobler origin."[25]

Even those who emphasized the environment argued that its
effects were most beneficial to the English. Despite his respect for the
power of environment, Samuel Williams was not certain that human
differences could be laid entirely to climate and other "circumstances."[26]
The freedom of action afforded by geography, he conjectured, enabled
the first settlers to develop to their logical conclusion the ideals they
carried with them to North America. Williams maintained that the New
England settlers had "suffered severely under the bigotry and intolerance
of ecclesiastical power, in the days of Elizabeth, James and Charles the
first." Having learned from "their situation and sufferings . . . the rights
of men," by the time they left the Old World their experiences had
prepared them "to at once understand the voice of nature."[27]

In one phrase — "they could at once discern and understand the
voice of nature" — Williams summed up, with all its ambiguities, the
American interpretation. As Englishmen the colonists were presumed to
have emigrated in the hope of establishing societies based on civil and
religious liberty. The environment and geographic isolation of the New
World afforded an opportunity to put those principles into practice and
to refashion them to conform to the circumstances of the American

setting. That Englishmen would be inclined to establish such societies was taken for granted because British America, so the argument ran, had been settled at a time when the struggle against arbitrary power was raging at home. Most settlers. moreover, were non-conforming Protestants, and "there was a similarity between their opinions of government, and those which they held on the subject of religion. Each strengthened the other. Both were favorable to liberty, and hostile to all undue exercise of authority." It was from the interplay between the physical environment and isolation of the New World and the political and religious heritage of the colonists that there evolved what M'Culloch referred to as the American's "love of liberty, of property, and an idea of their own strength."[28]

What was meant by national character, then, was a cluster of ideas, expressed not so much in a formal system as in a vague set of informal beliefs. The interplay between environment and heritage predisposed Americans to what Jefferson referred to as "the unquestioned republicanism of the American mind." But it was the colonists' struggle to establish and defend their liberties, most notably during the Revolution but also throughout their history, that formed the national character.

This emphasis on love of liberty and traditional rights reveals the powerful influence of the English Whig tradition. The works of Whig political theorists enjoyed enormous popularity and during the Revolutionary controversy constituted the single most important source of intellectual argumentation.[29] Historians used Whig ideas as a general rather than a specific framework. In Whig style, they devoted much of their narratives to recounting the emergence of a political order based on a strong legislative authority, independent landholders, and a general diffusion of political power. In George R. Minot's *History of Massachusetts Bay* (1798-1803) can be found a basic ingredient of Whig history: the struggle between republican liberty and arbitrary authority. But at strategic points his allusions to America's special environment gave to the Whig perspective a somewhat different meaning. Like other historians, he appropriated Whiggish ideas to the effort to create a national history. For example, Minot paused at the loss of the colony's charter in 1684 to declare that "with it fell not the habits it had engendered," nor, and this is the point, "the principles which the settlement of the country had inspired." In conclusion, he declared, "every germ of despotism and royal authority" will "probably be forever buried . . . in this republican soil."[30] If "soil" had for him several connotations, its literal meaning was also intended.

No less important than the Whig motif of the conflict between republican liberty and arbitrary authority was its adaptation to the American theme of imperial versus local authority. In Whig political theory the interests of the people were regarded as irreconcilably opposed to those of the executive. Historians did not deny the validity of that principle. But they gave it an American twist by focusing on the issue of home rule, thereby turning an abstract intranational political principle into a struggle between two separate peoples. In so doing they took a step toward defining American nationality in terms of national antagonisms. Moreover, by treating imperial authority as something akin to a foreign government — without questioning its legitimacy before the 1760s — historians used the issue of home rule to build an historic basis for the foremost achievement of the Federal Constitution: the equation of ruler and ruled as identical.[31] "The far famed social compact between the people and their rulers," declared Ramsay, "did not apply to the United States." Americans of the Revolutionary era destroyed the time-worn conception of mixed government and created a system that rested on an expansion of the principle of representation. "Our form of government," wrote Jeremy Belknap, "is founded on" the principle "that the people have the sole and exclusive right of governing themselves." However else the various state constitutions might differ, observed Williams, "the principle on which all the American governments are founded, is representation."[32]

In the opinion of contemporaries the classic Whig dichotomy between the interests of rulers and ruled had been extinguished. In America, observed Ramsay, "the sovereignty was in the people," who "depicted certain individuals as their agents to serve them. . . ." "All the *power* that such governments can have," declared Williams, "is derived from the public opinion." For American historians this principle was an historic fact before it had been legally established. Since the "state of society" encouraged an equality of condition "this could produce nothing but similarity of situation, rights, priviliges, and freedom." With the commencement of the Anglo-American controversy, observed Edmund Randolph, Virginia elevated new men to leadership who were recognized by the public as having "no other stake or hope than their own country."[33] It was largely in the context of challenges from imperial authority that American historians attempted to prove the principle of representative leadership and identified it with the national character.

A number of historians used New England as a fulcrum to generalize these traits to the nation as a whole. Although a Virginian, John Marshall depicted the settlement of the New England colonies in much the same way as New Englanders. His central theme was that in the long run the Puritans' devotion to liberty outweighed their intolerance. Marshall stressed their willingness to do battle to preserve their political rights, especially the cherished principle of home rule. With shrewd foresight the founders of the Bay colony had "resolved that the patent should be transferred, and the government of the colony removed from London to Massachusetts." Operating on the assumption that their charter was an inviolate compact, they had repeatedly defended their rights against the ambitions of Crown and Parliament. In 1692, for example, the General Court seized the occasion of the implementation of a new Royal charter to proclaim the principle of no taxation without consent. Marshall also recounted at length the successful struggle during the late 1720s against imperial efforts to institute a permanent salary for the royal governor. The "circumstances" of this "stubborn contest," he concluded, "have been given more in detail than is consistent with the general plan of this work, because it is considered as exhibiting, in genuine colors, the character of the people engaged in it. It is regarded as an early and an honourable display of the same persevering temper in defence of principle, of the same unconquerable spirit of liberty, which at a later day, and on a more important question, tore the British colonies from a country to which they had been strongly attached."[34]

Marshall did not ignore the rest of New England. Even "the rigor with which conformity was exacted" by the authorities in Massachusetts had the virtue of causing "the first settlement of the other colonies of New England." Roger Williams' banishment resulted in a new colony founded on the "tenet that all were entitled to freedom of conscience in worship," while a small band led by Thomas Hooker created a new polity in which "the rights of freemen" were extended "to those who were not members of the Church." Most important, these exiles carried with them the Puritans' zeal in defending their liberties. If the citizens of Connecticut were forced to submit to the restoration of Charles II, they did so "without abandoning any opinion concerning their own rights."[35] It was this rugged tradition that was for Marshall the central feature of the national character.

Marshall did not portray other regions so glowingly. To Pennsylvania he accorded only the briefest attention. Of the Quakers' devotion to civil and religious liberty he had little to say other than that William Penn's "scheme of fundamental law contains many provisions indicating good sense and just notions of government, but was too complex for an infant settlement."[36] As for the other colonies, Marshall acknowledged that their inhabitants had also defended the rights of

Englishmen; but, unlike New Englanders, most of them had been drawn to America for economic gain alone. If they had been won to the cause of home rule and defense of their liberties, it was by their experience in the New World and by the example of New England.[37]

It is difficult to say precisely why Marshall expressed so strong a preference. The history of colonial New England did well illustrate his principle of home rule. Perhaps, too, Marshall's politics predisposed him to look more favorably on Federalist New England than the Republican South, although by the time he wrote his history the political uniformity of New England was crumbling. In general, however, there appears to be little relationship between the historians' politics and their attitude toward New England. Federalist David Ramsay wrote favorably of the region while Federalist John L. Bozman was an ardent critic, as was Republican John Daly Burk and sometimes Federalist Edmund Randolph. The differences seem to have been determined by the strength of feeling for one's native or adopted place, with a somewhat alienated Ramsay and Marshall looking to greener pastures and the militantly loyal Randolph, Bozman, and Burk defending their states' reputation.

Whatever the reasons for the historian's attitudes, Marshall's view of the national character was generally acceptable; but his bias in favor of New England did not go unchallenged. In his *History of Virginia*, Burk announced his intention of countering a "universally received opinion, arising from the want of an authentic history, that Virginia was distinguished for her invariable loyalty, and her submissive and tractable temper, during the greater part of her colonial existence." The charge was even more galling since "it has been customary to contrast her yielding policy with the sturdy patriotism of New England." Not that Burk wished to detract "from the well-earned fame of New England; their noble ardor for liberty, their steady and animated resistance against force and corruption." But he maintained that "the conduct of Virginia, from the first moments of her existence, was exactly the opposite of what it has been represented." He argued, for example, that the cautious attitude of the Council toward the Glorious Revolution and its reluctance "to appoint a day for proclaiming William and Mary" was unrepresentative of true opinion in Virginia; "whatever uneasiness and embarrassment this procedure might have caused the council, it was received by the people at large with every demonstration of unfeigned joy and exultation."[38] Although Burk offered little evidence to prove his thesis, he doggedly pursued it. Yet his analysis of the Virginia character did not differ substantially from the New England version. His aim was simply to prove that Virginians were equally entitled to a place of honor by showing that they had exhibited the same qualities.

Edmund Randolph, too, was determined to authenticate Virginia's "rightful" place in the nation's history. His *History of Virginia* testifies to a concerted effort to celebrate the genius of her political system as reflected in what he referred to as the "Virginia character." In his view the inhabitants of the Old Dominion were "a people proud of English blood" who had inherited the virtues of the "English character" but had "avoided the poison of those prejudices which still ran unmitigated in the bosom of England." Randolph selected episodes from the Virginia past that illustrated the development of a spirit of freedom and independence. Somehow the physical and social environment of America enabled Virginians to fulfill their natural predisposition as Englishmen. The absence of serious religious conflict and a government so simple in form that it offered few temptations for official corruption made it possible for them to avoid the worst aspects of English politics. Pausing at the dissolution of the Virginia Company, Randolph observed that "whatever may be the defects of the foregoing narrative, an estimate may be made of the faculties or qualities which the colony actually possessed in the year 1624." He was particularly impressed that the dissolution of the Company "caused an agitation so little serious." Despite ample ground for rebellion, he found it "a lesson not unworthy of adoption in seasons even the most enlightened to count the cost of popular tumult before it is excited and clearly to see the effect of the war before it is waged." The soil of Virginia nurtured a people who had found a happy balance between over-civilization and barbarism, a people "equally aloof from the frenzy of reform and the abjectness of vassalage."[39]

These passages tell more about the "Virginia character" in action than about how or why it developed as it did. Virginians had avoided the frenzies characteristic of English politics: "It is the happiness of the Virginia character hardly ever to push to extremity any theory which by practical relations may not be accommodated." Thus, the colony was able to survive uncontaminated by "the fanaticism and hypocrisy of Cromwell" or "the poison of the licentiousness of the second Charles." Again, in the controversy over the pistole fee (1752-1755), Virginia's leaders "were as bold as the time would permit." They wisely eschewed an appeal to arms: "Their opposition would have been folly had a resort to force constituted a part of it." For "to know when to complain with truth and how to complain with dignity was characteristic of watchful patriots and ample for the only end which could then be projected." Randolph's *History* elaborates the ideals of a society uninfected by party spirit and dedicated to the maximum of liberty consistent with order and stability. "The preceding history," he concluded, "contains repeated instances of loyalty debased by no servile compliance and a patriotic watchfulness never degenerating into the mere petulance of complaint."[40]

Randolph dealt exclusively with Virginia, but he regarded its experience as more than local in importance. Of Pocahontas's dramatic intervention in favor of Captain John Smith, a man he called the colony's savior, he wrote: "Let the Virginia patriot ascribe the preservation of Smith to that chain of grand events of which the settlement of Virginia was destined to be the foremost link, and which finally issued in the birth of our American republic."[41] Randolph considered the "Virginia character" a prototype of the national character; he was not content to create a copy of New England. Burk thought the colony's leaders were tinged with an aristocratic bias at odds with the republicanism of the people; but Randolph defended the republicanism of the ruling group and treated them as a true reflection of Virginia society. Where Burk asserted that the colony's inhabitants were more militant in defense of colonial rights than their officials, Randolph portrayed the latter as representative of the "Virginia character." For Burk the period of relative calm after 1689 was "the dark age in Virginia;"[42] for Randolph moderation and compromise represented true political wisdom.

It would be easy to overemphasize the differences between Randolph's and the New England version of the national character. True, he wrote as a Virginia patriot defending the unique qualities of his "native state." Indeed, he felt a sense of urgency because after 1789 there no longer existed an independent state history. But, like other state historians, he was determined to secure his state's place in the national past by fitting the local history into the pattern of the national. Randolph's *History of Virginia* was a variation on a theme. While he could not argue that the colony's earliest settlers had set out with the avowed purpose of establishing a society with civil and religious liberty, he did maintain that in time "a spirit of mildness" provided an "antidote to the licensed severity of laws."[43] Furthermore, just as other historians emphasized that the background of the founders of New England predisposed them in favor of civil and religious liberty, Randolph pointed out that only a few years after Virginia had been founded its governing body passed into the hands of the most politically progressive elements in English society. It was, he observed, under the leadership of the noted parliamentarian Sir Edwin Sandys that the first legislative assembly in America was established.

Randolph drew his account of the rise and fall of the Virginia company from William Stith's *History of the First Discovery and Settlement of Virginia* (1747), a work written in the Whig style. Not only did Randolph closely follow Stith's narrative of the colony's first seventeen years, but he also adopted his central theme — the struggle against the imposition of arbitrary royal authority — as the organizing principle of his entire work. Thus Randolph extended the Whig interpretation of the first seventeen years to the entire Virginia past, making it a story of liberty, of repeated efforts to defend constitutional rights against the tyrannical ambitions of crown and governor.[44] He offered a version of the past that differed from those of other American historians only in emphasis. The colonists "always had rights," proclaimed Burk,

> rights which they always exercised, which they never relinquished and the least encroachment on which, on the part of the parent state, they always resisted, always resented. . . . Various attempts had been made by Great Britain previous to the stamp act; . . . she was in every instance repelled with a spirit becoming the hardy sons of the forest. . . . If those circumstances be duly considered — the revolution in those states, will be a matter of less wonder. It will be regarded as an event necessarily growing out of the temper and habits of the people.[45]

That there were ambiguities in the concept of national character seemed to provide no unmanageable intellectual problems. Eighteenth century historians had no clearly defined theories of causation. They tended to simply list causes, with no overall explanation of change that would permit them to show how causes interacted or to establish their relative importance. American historians never attempted to show precisely how the New World environment and the English heritage combined to create the American character. But if their explanation was not particularly good history or sociology, it did serve their polemical interests. For people who could no longer think of themselves as English but could not reject their heritage, environmentalism provided a useful instrument for explaining why they were at once English and yet distinctively American. By arguing that the environment could only be exploited by a culturally and politically advanced people, they could exclude the African and the Indian, whom they suspected of being inherently inferior, from inclusion in the national community. Yet if their conception of national character provided no motive for refining eighteenth century theories of causation, such was not the case when they turned to the causes of the Revolution.

# VI. The American Revolution

Even before the Treaty of Peace accounts of the Revolution began to appear.[1] Predictably, the arguments used were indistinguishable from those employed by the Patriot party during the Anglo-American crisis. Every historian agreed that the Revolution was justified, that the conflict resulted from the actions of the British government and not from any desire for independence, that the contest revolved around constitutional issues, and that the American colonists had turned to armed rebellion only after they had exhausted all legal avenues of redress.

That a uniform view of the causes and desirability of independence could be widely accepted can best be explained by the nature of the Revolutionary settlement. For the overwhelming majority of Americans, once the war had ended and independence had been achieved the Revolution seemed a happy event. It had not been very traumatic for this kind of experience; no substantial numbers of people still living in the United States nursed grievances over it. Yet, if independence was no longer a divisive issue, it did not mean that historians were free from pressure for intellectual conformity. After nearly two decades of acrimony and war with Britain, Americans were in no mood for alternatives to the Patriot interpretation of the Revolution. So possessive were they of their past that few foreign accounts earned critical approval, while the works of Loyalists were either bitterly denounced or, more often, ignored. The only way a former Loyalist sympathizer like Robert Proud could hope to gain an audience for his *History of Pennsylvania* (1797-98) was to stick to the colonial period and avoid direct references to the Revolutionary controversy.

With dissenters in exile or reduced to silence the field was left to the friends of the Revolution, but even they were apprehensive about writing its history. William Gordon, an English dissenting minister turned Patriot, decided to return home to publish his *History* because he believed that in the United States "those individuals who now occupy eminencies will be most horribly affected by an impartial history."[2]

Gordon's fears reflected the overanxiety of a somewhat neurotic personality; but the hazards seemed real enough to convince Charles Thomson, Secretary of the Continental Congress and a man who had earned a reputation as the "Sam Adams of Philadelphia," to destroy a history he claimed to have written because it was critical of some Patriot leaders.[3] Few historians risked character sketches, and those that did were subjected to bitter criticism. The authors of the many biographical dictionaries of the period were careful to include only deceased persons.[4]

No doubt these hazards account for the fact that a gifted generation of leaders, so well versed in ancient and modern history and (particularly) Plutarch's *Lives* that they could not help but be concerned with their place in history, left few published accounts of an event that had dominated their lives. Despite the high correlation between political and intellectual leadership during the early years of the Republic, no important political leader published a history of the Revolution. Statesmen such as John Adams and Thomas Jefferson lacked neither the interest nor the ability to write history. Both feared that partisan politics prevented an accurate account from being produced and both took historical writing seriously enough to be alarmed by the influence of particular histories. Adams carried on an angry correspondence with Mercy Otis Warren over her accusation that he was a monarchist, while Jefferson tried to recruit Joel Barlow to write an answer to John Marshall's *Life of George Washington*. Jefferson once argued that the Tory bias in David Hume's *History of England* had "revolutionized the public sentiment of that country more completely than the standing armies could ever have done."[5]

Since so many of the principal leaders were also prominent in the new government it would have been a hazardous business to write a history of the Revolution. In the partisan atmosphere of the early national period few acts were more dangerous for a public man than publishing a book, as John Adams discovered with his *Defense of the American Constitutions* (1787). Of course, as has often been the case in new nations, it must have been tempting to prove one's fitness for office by carving out a place of eminence in the struggle for independence or by demonstrating that one's policies derived from the principles of the Revolution. Conversely, such a work could also be used to discredit the opposition. But the disadvantages seemed to outweigh the benefits, not the least of which was the risk of offending one's friends.

Consequently, the writing of American history was left primarily to men and women who had lived through the Revolution and had been strong supporters of the Patriot cause, but had not achieved positions of first rank. Only John Marshall and Edmund Randolph held important posts in the national government, and by the time they wrote their histories they were no longer actively seeking public office: Marshall had life tenure on the Supreme Court and Randolph was in enforced retirement. For all their differences the men and women attracted to writing the history of the Revolution were united by a common bond: a psychological and intellectual commitment to the Revolution. "I am a child of the revolution," proclaimed Randolph. "I feel the highest . . . attachment to my country; her felicity is the most fervent prayer of my heart. . . . The unwearied study of my life shall be to promote her happiness."[6] Each historian had been an enthusiastic Patriot; most had been active in the army, in public life, in the pulpit and with their pens. Jeremy Belknap, William Gordon, Benjamin Trumbull, and Samuel Williams had published Patriotic tracts, while Belknap, Gordon, and Trumbull delivered sermons to the troops in the field. David Ramsay was a surgeon in the Continental army and a South Carolina legislator. When the British captured Charleston he was among the members of the Privy Council who were left behind. Accused by the British of collaborating with the enemy, he was imprisoned at St. Augustine, Florida. John Marshall had been an officer in the army, while his fellow Virginian Edmund Randolph served briefly on General Washington's staff before becoming the state's wartime attorney general. As a woman, Mercy Otis Warren could not take an active part in the war, but her brother, James Otis, Jr., and her husband, James Warren, were both prominent Massachusetts Patriots, and she was a respected confidant of important members of the Revolutionary leadership.

Hugh Williamson's service to the cause extended to trans-Atlantic intrigue. A witness to the Boston Tea Party, he sailed on the ship that carried the first news of it to England, where he predicted before the Privy Council that the colonies would revolt if British policy were not changed. During his stay he published an anonymous letter, *The Plea of the Colonies* (1775), in which he answered charges of colonial sedition and disloyalty and appealed for British Whig support. Just before leaving England, Williamson somehow obtained and turned over to Benjamin Franklin the correspondence between Thomas Hutchinson and Andrew Oliver which eventually led to Hutchinson's removal as governor of Massachusetts. After returning home in 1776 he served as a surgeon in the North Carolina militia and the Continental Army.

As old activists, historians were sensitive to criticism of the Revolution. They wrote as if they had taken as their mandate the words of the Declaration of Independence: "a decent respect to the opinions of mankind requires that they should declare the causes which impel them to the separation." They were particularly angered by the charge that the break with the mother country occurred because the colonists had desired independence from the outset. "British emissaries," wrote Ebenezer Hazard, "have diligently propagated an idea that the colonies were disaffected to the royal government, and thirsted after independence; and I think it is a duty incumbent on every American historian to use his endeavors to wipe off so unjust an aspersion."[7]

Thomas Paine reflected this defensiveness by attacking the Abbé Raynal's *Revolution of America* (1781) in a virulent seventy-page pamphlet. Like other recent arrivals in America, Paine so closely identified himself with the Patriot cause that he was enraged at what he regarded as the Frenchman's insensitivity to the tyranny of British rule. With a fury characteristic of the convert, Paine set out to repudiate Raynal's interpretation of the causes of the Revolution. Actually the Abbé had written a sympathetic account, but Paine was incensed by his contention that "none of those energetic causes, which have produced so many revolutions upon the globe, existed in North America." According to Raynal the British had violated neither religion nor laws, nor had arbitrary power been used to imprison innocent men. He asserted that the post-1763 period had witnessed no serious alteration of colonial administration. For him "the whole question was reduced to knowing whether the mother country had or had not a right to lay, directly or indirectly, a slight tax upon the colonies." Apparently Raynal was thinking of the kind of abuses that were common in France, and the question of "a slight tax" appeared to him trifling. An irritated Paine enumerated for the Frenchman's edification the "just causes," arguing heatedly that the attempt to tax the colonies "was an usurpation of the Americans' most precious and sacred rights. . . . It placed America not only in the lowest, but the basest state of vassalage."[8]

One way to prove that the colonists had not desired independence was to demonstrate the depth of their loyalty on the eve of the conflict. Even bitter Anglophobes argued that prior to 1763 Americans had been loyal subjects. James Callender was the author of one of the few overtly anti-British histories of the period. Yet, after comparing the British and Spanish empires, he admitted that English colonial policy illustrated "the eternal difference between freedom and slavery." John Daly Burk's *History of Virginia* (1804-05) betrayed the natural anti-British bias of an emigré Irish revolutionary. Nevertheless, in assessing the effects of the French and Indian War he observed that "the attachment of the colonies to the mother country was universal" and the war strengthened those ties. Americans greatly admired Britain, he concluded, and "in contemplating more nearly their own situation, as it stood relative to the parent state, they found little to abate the ardour of their attachment."[9]

While Callender and Burk grudgingly conceded the benefits of British policy, most historians cheerfully acknowledged that the colonists' loyalty had been justified. "Neither ancient nor modern history," wrote Ramsay, "can produce an example of colonies governed with equal wisdom or flourishing with equal rapidity." "At no period of time," proclaimed Marshall, "was the attachment of the colonies to the mother country more strong, or more general, than in 1763. . . . ." According to Belknap the colonists "were proud of [their] connexion with a nation whose flag was triumphant in every quarter of the globe; and by whose assistance we had been delivered from the danger of our most formidable enemies, the French in Canada."[10] No doubt these sentiments reflected a genuine admiration for Great Britain; but they also dramatized the contrast between British imperial policy before and after 1763.

Equally important, emphasis was placed on the colonials' contribution of men and treasure in defense of the empire, sacrifices little appreciated by the mother country. Drawing on his New England ancestors' accounts of war and captivity, Benjamin Trumbull recounted their participation in the numerous wars against the French. He estimated that from 1639 to 1703 they had been at war nearly continuously without substantial assistance from Britain. During the hostilities that began in 1739 the northern colonies expended a million pounds sterling, sustained heavy losses in trade and sacrificed the lives of three or four thousand young men. Yet, while they "had exhibited the most striking evidences of their loyalty and zeal, in his majesty's service, no notice was taken of the exertions of the colonies, nor of the extraordinary measures to supply the army; measures to which, probably neither the people of England, nor even of Ireland would have submitted."[11]

Finally, of the various techniques for justifying the cause none was more rigorously applied than the Patriot legal arguments. "The specific doctrine which condemned taxation without representation," wrote Edmund Randolph, "had been quoted as a fundamental one of colonial freedom, and every generation of lawyers inbibed it in their studies." The first full scale work to receive wide notice, William Gordon's *History of the Rise, Progress, and Establishment of the Independence of the United States of America* (1788), was dedicated to proving that "the colonies were very early in declaring that they ought not to be taxed, but by their own general courts, and they considered subjection to the acts of a parliament in which they had not representatives for themselves, as a hardship. . . . ."[12]

To prove his point Gordon sketched the history of each colony from the first charter to 1760. He listed all charters, assembly resolutions, petitions, and instructions to royal governors that seemed to contradict, however vaguely, Parliament's right to tax the colonies. He cited, for example, a letter of 1679 from the Massachusetts General Court to its London agents affirming "that not being represented in Parliament, they looked upon themselves to be impeded in their trade by the acts of trade and navigation, and that these could not be observed by his majesty's subjects in Massachusetts without invading their liberties and properties, until the general court made provision therein by law, which they did in October." Gordon also sought to strengthen his case by searching out past statements which resembled the legal rhetoric of the 1760s and 70s. His best but by no means only example was a letter written by Benjamin Franklin in 1754 to Governor William Shirley of Massachusetts outlining Franklin's objections to interference in colonial affairs on the grounds that "the parliament of England is at a great distance" and that body's "united interests might probably secure them against the effect of any complaint." Franklin also argued "that it is supposed to be an undoubted right of Englishmen, not to be taxed but by their own consent given through their representatives" and "the colonies have no representatives in parliament."[13] For Gordon this letter proved that the principles vigorously defended by Americans in the 1760s and 70s had been fully developed at least a decade earlier.

At first glance these histories seem to have had no other purpose than to prove the justice of the American cause. Committed as the authors had been to independence, their efforts were an understandable psychological consequence of wartime emotions. But American historians were anxious to do more than justify the revolt of thirteen colonies. If they operated on the assumption that their cause had been just and independence a benefit, the stridency of their bias should not obscure the fact that such questions, important as they were, were not the most crucial. Their views were subject to heavy pressure for conformity, from the overt pressure of a reading public that would accept no other interpretation and from the more subtle pressure of their own desire to use historical writing to serve the cause of national unity. Yet it would be a mistake to dismiss their works as only special pleading. Once having established their credentials as defenders of the American side of the controversy, they could speculate about more fundamental questions of causation and meaning, so long as their speculations did not detract from the legitimacy of the Revolution.

If American historians tailored their histories to serve a cause, they were also scholars attempting to explain an historical event. As nationalists they shaped their accounts of the Revolution to serve the cause of national unity. One obvious way to forge an identification with a national polity was to glorify the Revolution as an heroic national struggle against British tyranny. But to focus exclusively on the rejection of British authority would have been to stress a negative definition of nationality. As scholars attuned to the cosmopolitan ideals of the Enlightenment they could not help but treat the Revolution as something more fundamental than a sequence of unique and parochial events.

Generally speaking there are two types of historical discourse: first, the straightforward narrative of a linear sequence of non-recurring events; second, an account of recurring forms of thought and action characteristic of particular times and places or particular sets of circumstances. While each of these forms is designed to achieve different goals, they are not mutually exclusive; they can merge together within the same historical work.[14] Clearly, Patriot history fit the first category; but these narratives also contained basic assumptions about the motives of the participants and the dynamics of the Revolution that fit into the second category, assumptions that were determined by the historian's philosophy of history and conception of human nature.

Every historian agreed that the immediate cause of the conflict lay in the disharmony between the program of taxation put forward by the British government in 1764-65 and the colonists' perception of their rights. "As soon as this plan" for taxing the colonies "was known in America," wrote John M'Culloch, "it spread an alarm from one end of the continent to the other." But the argument over taxation was, after all, only an argument. "The remonstrances against the Stamp Act," observed Randolph, "breathed loyalty and prays for the continuance of the relation of subjects. . . . Now indeed, on the opening of the year 1774, a deeper tone broke forth." The critical question was how a protest movement had been transformed into a revolution. Randolph described the years prior to 1774 "as resembling that season between the two old friends when the language begins to be embittered and the heart is gnawed, a rupture is dreaded but the cause is not forgiven." He was suggesting that to understand the nature of the conflict required an analysis of the impact of particular events on the psychology of the participants. "In times of general sensibility," as he put it, "almost every public event is tortured into an affinity with the predominant passions."[15]

Patriot historians located the dynamic of the conflict in a cycle of response and counterresponse that assumed a logic of its own. Step by step the colonists had been driven toward independence; step by step

Great Britain hardened its resolve. "The spirit of resistance to the encroachments of the Crown of Great Britain, on the rights of the provinces in America," wrote Hugh McCall, "was increased by every revenual act of Parliament, imposed upon the colonies." The controversy over taxation served to encourage a new spirit of speculation concerning the relationship of the colonies to the mother country that ended in "the horrors of civil war." "Where Parliamentary supremacy ended, and at what point colonial independency began was not ascertained. . . . The investigation of these subjects," observed Ramsay, "brought matters into view which the friends of union ought to have kept out of sight." Before long some bold spirits, especially among the commercial populations of the Eastern states, suggested that not only British taxation but the whole imperial system was contrary to American interests.[16]

The battle over the Stamp Act and the Townshend duties added a new dimension to the conflict that transcended constitutional and imperial questions. It was transformed into a test of will in which the determination to prevail grew as each British action produced a fresh colonial response. The cumulative effect of repeated confrontations, wrote Marshall, was that "the prejudices in favor of a connexion with England, and of the English constitution, gradually but rapidly wore off; and were succeeded by Republican principles and wishes for independence." Both sides, moreover, consistently underestimated the will of the other. "Each party counted too much on the divisions of the other, and each seems to have taken step after step, in the hope that its adversary would yield the point in contest without resorting to open force." Bloodshed may not have been inevitable, but open conflict could have been avoided only by the most statesmanlike policies. Since the English government underestimated the American will to resist, such policies were not forthcoming. "It ought to have been foreseen that with such a people, so determined, the conflict must be stern and hazardous. . . ."[17]

In successive chapters David Ramsay described how each crisis hardened colonial determination. The disputes over taxation created a false impression that the dependence of the British economy on American trade provided an infallible weapon against the mother country. "Elevated with the advantage they had gained, from that day forward; instead of feeling themselves dependent on Great Britain, they conceived that, in respect to commerce, she was dependent on them." These impressions were in turn reinforced by the ministry's contradictory policies. "In one moment the Parliament was for enforcing their laws, the next for repealing them. Doing and undoing, menacing and submitting, straining and relaxing, followed each other, in alternate succession." By 1773 both sides were entrenched in irreconcilable positions. Proud Britons refused to accept colonial defiance of Parliamentary authority, while Americans proclaimed with equal haughtiness, "Shall the petty island of Great Britain, scarce a speck on the map of the world, control the free citizens of the great continent of America?"[18]

To describe the interplay between events and the psychology of the participants was not to explain why the Revolution had occurred. There was built into these discussions, however, a set of assumptions that added up to an implicit if not clearly defined theory of historical causation. That American historians focused on the response to particular circumstances reflected their Enlightenment assumption that to explain historical causation in human terms represented an advance over older beliefs in blind chance, fate, or divine intervention. To construct a reasoned narrative some distinct principle of causation was required; yet when it came to translating that belief into an explanation of specific events the performance of eighteenth century historians was disappointing. They had no unified or explicit theory which could systematically explain historical change.[19]

When eighteenth century historians thought about causation at all they usually oscillated between several approaches.[20] For those who still followed a traditional Christian historiography, exemplified by Bishop Bossuet, history and the destiny of man were controlled directly by God.[21] Few if any American historians accepted in undiluted form the views of Bossuet. Those who tended in that direction, most notably Mercy Otis Warren, Benjamin Trumbull, and Isaac Backus, visualized God as acting not by direct intervention, but indirectly through human instruments. Like most contemporary writers, their thinking about causation was ill-defined and inconsistent. Ramsay, for example, could refer to the "inscrutable operation of Providence" while discussing the American Revolution entirely in terms of human motivations and choices. They seemed to come closest, then, to a Deist version of Bossuet's theory which affirmed their Christianity while replacing the personal God Jehovah, who intervenes directly in human affairs, with a distant, more impersonal Supreme Being or Providence. Since the Enlightenment the philosophy of history of Christian theology had been superseded by a succession of theories representing world history as the working out of some implicit principle or idea.[22] Americans liked to think that the Revolution represented the fulfillment of mankind's march toward a more rational, freer society. Providence's approval of the Revolution was frequently invoked by Deist and Christian historian alike, but the events were seen as the result of human imperatives.

An alternative, popular among some philosophes, was the great man theory of history, which tended to view development as the outcome of the impact of exceptional individuals. Borrowed from classical writers, it prevailed in the Encyclopedia and influenced the more mass-oriented Rousseau. While the adulation of Washington by American historians came close to this approach however they implicitly rejected great men causation. Republican theory and their conception of the Revolution as the united action of a united people ruled out glorification of individuals, especially of military men. American historians were not altogether consistent on this point. Still, if the figure of Washington dominated their narratives of the war, most writers placed far more emphasis on the nation's republican virtues as exemplified by the citizen soldier. Indeed, neither Washington nor any other Patriot leader dominated their accounts of the events leading up to the rupture with Great Britain. Historians used Washington much as Voltaire utilized prominent men to epitomize a period; in the American case, as a symbol of the efficacy of republican institutions.

There was a third approach, though it hardly deserves to be called a theory. Generally the works of eighteenth century historians were sprinkled with lists of causes, but offered no systematic interpretation to show how causes interacted or to determine their relative importance. American works shared this limitation. While building their version of the national past around the development of a republican society, historians were unable to co-ordinate or clearly differentiate the factors that had led to that development. Yet, in their efforts to explain the causes of the Revolution they possessed certain advantages. As contemporaries to the event they had observed the American participants at first hand. At the least, by generalizing from their own personal experience they could offer plausible if subjective explanations. More important, they had a polemical interest in determining which factors were causative. Their special purpose was to assign responsibility to Britain, show that the colonists had acted as a united people, and prove that the behavior of Americans demonstrated that they possessed the virtue essential to a republican society. Those goals made it imperative to develop a fairly clear theory of causation.

To explain the motives of the participants historians relied on a doctrine common to their philosophical environment: "the same causes will ever produce the same effects; and the things that have happened will ever happen again, in like circumstances."[23] This doctrine implies that there is in the mind of man a uniform play of motive and that the motives of men are the same for all times and places. Yet even within this rigid framework there was room for a certain variety of interpretation. Human nature did, after all, include different characteristics; by concentrating on specific traits writers gave their works important differences in emphasis. To account for the shift in colonial policy after 1763, for example, some insisted that the actions of the British government were a direct consequence of the corrupt state of English society. "Corruption was making gigantic strides in England," wrote Randolph, "and America was a field in which necessitous partisans might be pampered at the expense of American labor."[24]

By choosing human nature as their guiding principle of interpretation American historians reflected a doctrine central to Enlightenment historiography. More particularly, their views echoed the works of the English Whig writers who had a decisive influence on the ideology of the Revolutionary movement.[25] A preoccupation with corruption and the idea of conspiracy had deep roots in Anglo-American political culture. From the beginning of the imperial conflict the question of motivation had been discussed in conspiratorial terms. Writing in the early 1720s, John Trenchard and Thomas Gordon co-authored a series of essays in which they warned that "the liberty which England enjoys" was being undermined by "public corruption and abuses." It was in times of ripe corruption, they continued, that "ministerial vultures lunged for illegal power" by such means as the impoverishment of the people by costly wars, the preferment to office of "worthless and wicked men," and ultimately the deliberate provocation of "the people to disaffection" in order to create "an argument for new oppression."[26]

William Gordon's description of the imperial conflict, written at its height in characteristically Whig terms, described it as a gift in disguise. "Americans," he feared, "were falling off apace from their primitive manners, and debilitating themselves by luxurious habits; had these habits been thoroughly rooted by long continuance, and our managers been artful, they might have carried their point without difficulty; whereas by beginning too soon, they have revived your dying virtue and disconcerted their own projects." Gordon warned the colonists to arm themselves against the artful duplicity of a corrupt English officialdom. The "ministry may now possibly give up all thought of forcing you into an acquiescence . . . and may try the arts of soothing and chicanery, of negotiation and corruption. The colonies should especially beware of investing their agents with full powers to settle their differences; with a full treasury at their command and honors to bestow the ministry would become temptors too powerful for frail mortals."[27]

For Jeremy Belknap, England's effort to raise an American revenue was only symptomatic of a more ambitious scheme. Many Britons, he argued, had gained a false impression of colonial wealth from military men serving in America. A great but temporary influx of money into the colonies because of the French and Indian War created an illusion of affluence. Moreover, planters' and merchants' sons who went to England for their education seemed to confirm these opinions. Unfortunately, these false impressions excited the cupidity of a nation in the throes of corruption. "In no age, perhaps, excepting that in which Rome lost her liberty, was the spirit of venality and corruption so prevalent, as at this time in Britain." Therein lay the seeds of conflict. Greed inspired the passage of ill-considered revenue measures to which the American colonists could not help but react strongly. As "the true friends of constitutional liberty [they] now saw their dearest interests in danger, from an assumption of power in the parent state to give and grant the property of the colonists at pleasure. . . ." But, he went on, the colonists were not alarmed solely by the unconstitutionality of these acts: "It was our opinion, that the grand object was to provide for dependents and to extend the corrupt and venal principles of crown influence, through every part of the British dominions."[28] Belknap did not define precisely the nature of the conspiracy. He simply stated that if left unchecked the avarice of the ministry would have devoured American liberty.

In their attacks on the corruption of English officialdom American historians generally refrained from singling out specific individuals. Surprisingly, they avoided attacks on George III. Mercy Otis Warren provided the only exception. In her view the degeneration of English political life reached its nadir with a "misguided sovereign, dazzled with the acquisition of empire, nurtured in all the inflated ideas of Kingly prerogative. . . ." He and his Scottish advisor, Lord Bute, had turned Parliament into "the mere creature of administration, and appeared ready to leap the boundaries of justice, and to undermine the pillars of their own Constitution, by adhering steadfastly for several years to a complicated system of tyranny. . . ." Having established political hegemony, the Crown then "threatened the new world with a yoke unknown to their fathers" by sending hirelings from Britain to "ravish from the colonies the rights they claimed both by nature and by compact."[29]

Belknap's and Warren's interpretations rested on the traditional Whig idea that the inevitable victim of venality is liberty. They made no effort to analyze the nature or causes of corruption or its precise relationship to the policies of the British government. They simply assumed that corruption inevitably leads to policies that threaten liberty. William Gordon was in agreement, but he went a step further by charging a specific conspiracy. He recounted that, during a visit to

Portsmouth, New Hampshire in April 1764, the celebrated evangelist George Whitefield had told two Congregational ministers that "my heart bleeds for America . . . there is a deep laid plot against your civil and religious liberties, and they will be lost." Gordon reasoned that since the evangelist had not been in England for several years he must have learned of this conspiracy even before the plan for raising an American revenue had been laid. The Stamp Act must have been the first stage of a larger and more pernicious design. The alleged strategy of the plot was, first, to involve Parliament in American affairs and then, with Parliamentary approval, to alter the colonial governments by placing them entirely under royal direction. Control of government was to be followed by the establishment of episcopacy and the introduction of Bishops.[30]

By emphasizing avarice and the lust for power Belknap, Warren and Gordon pictured the Revolution as a moral drama, a conflict between a virtuous American citizenry and a corrupt British government. They infused the Whig ideology of the Revolution into historiography. Every American historian agreed that British officials had been motivated by a desire to make the colonies "subservient to their avarice and ambition."[31] Yet within the boundaries of their Whig ideology there was room for important differences of interpretation. By the simple concession that the officialdom was burdened with the complex problems of managing a vast and diverse empire, most historians produced studies that were remarkably free of moral extremes. Although they portrayed British leaders in an uncomplimentary light, by treating them as shortsighted rather than malicious they softened the effect of their criticism; it was easier to sympathize with human frailty. Plagued by new responsibilities that required additional revenue, they unwisely decided to tax the American colonies. The ministry foolishly raised the issue of taxation, declared Marshall, but the attempt was predictable since "in Britain it had always been asserted, that Parliament possessed the power of binding them in all cases whatsoever."[32]

Emphasizing pride as the chief characteristic of human nature, Ramsay observed that it was natural for the mother country "to wish for an extension of her authority over the colonies, and equally so for them, on their approach to maturity, to be more impatient of subordination, and to resist every innovation for increasing the degree of their dependence." There are no malicious ministers in his *History*, only shortsighted men trying to do a job that would have been difficult for the wisest of statesmen: "Great and flourishing colonies, daily increasing in number, and already grown to the magnitude of a nation, planted at an immense distance, and governed by constitutions resembling that of the country from which they sprang, were novelties in the history of the world." To have combined such colonies into a uniform system of government "required a knowledge of mankind, and an extensive comprehension of things." Perhaps an original genius "with just ideas of the rights of human nature, and the obligations of human benevolence" might have devised a scheme to secure the liberty of the colonies and still allow the mother country a degree of supremacy. "But the helm of Great Britain was not in such hands."[33]

If there were in the works of American historians important differences in emphasis, they all nevertheless wrote within the same framework and with the same ends in mind. Their basic assumption was the universality of human nature. While there was some confusion of terminology and difference of opinion about the motives for specific acts, they all emphasized characteristics that added up to ambition or pride. The lust for power, defined by Warren as a passion for "distinction," differed only slightly from Marshall's and Ramsay's references to "British pride," although in practice the differences did affect the tone of the accounts. The blunt truth is that there was no overriding interest in defining the circumstances that led British leaders to act as they did, so long as responsibility for the conflict was placed squarely on the mother country. American historians did not bother to spell out systematically whether they were describing the behavior of British leaders or the character of British society. Mason Locke Weems was unusually careful to point out that his quarrel was with the government, not the people. "Reader, if you be a Briton, be a Briton still. . . . I am not about to say one word against your nation." The threat to American liberty had come from the machinations of greedy men at the top. "I am about to speak of the ministry only, who certainly at that time, were a most ambitious and intriguing junto, that by *bad means* had *gotten* power, and by *worse* were endeavouring to extend it, even to the destruction of both *American and British liberty*. . . ."[34] But others generally made no such distinctions, for the actions of Britain were important to them chiefly as a backdrop for a portrayal of the American character.

In explaining the motives of the colonists there was basic unanimity. The classic Whig conflict between government and people became a weapon in the campaign to define American nationality. The theory of government that Americans gleaned from their reading of Whig writers held that politics involved a perpetual battle between the passions of the rulers and the united interests of the people.[35] But historians did not portray the Revolution as a simple battle between rulers and ruled. They gave Whig theory a nationalist tone by defining the conflict as a struggle between a united American citizenry and a corrupt British government. In Whig political theory, moreover, once the people were in control they could be as tyrannical as their leaders. In America historians were determined to demonstrate that not only were governors and governed indivisible but that the people could govern wisely.

What, then, distinguished the behavior of Englishmen from Americans? Since human nature is the same in all men, both sides were presumably guided by something akin to ambition or pride. "The study of the human character," observed Warren, reveals "a noble principle implanted in the nature of man, that pants for distinction." If a passion for "distinction" (i.e. ambition or pride) "operates in every bosom," it manifested itself differently in England than in America. In Warren's description the actions of British statesmen were anything but noble. "When the checks of conscience are thrown aside, or the moral sense weakened by the sudden acquisition of wealth or power, humanity is obscured, and if a favorable coincidence of circumstances permits, this love of distinction often exhibits the most mortifying instances of profligacy, tyranny, and the wanton exercise of arbitrary sway."[36] How was it that pride and ambition led to a lust for power in one and a defense of liberty in the other? The answer tendered by every American historian was the same: in America ambition and pride could be fulfilled honestly.

In these discussions of the causes of the Revolution the colonial past, the national character and the Revolutionary era were drawn together into a constant pattern. The formative element was the republican character of the people. From the beginning the process of settling a new land, the English heritage, and the circumstances of life in the New World had combined to plant "the germ of that general union of counsels and sentiments, which produced the American Revolution." In the New World the colonists had been transformed into men who knew their rights and were willing to defend them. During the Revolutionary struggle, wrote Warren, the colonists demonstrated "that manly spirit of freedom, characteristic of Americans from New Hampshire to Georgia." The crux of the matter is the reaction of the national character to the stimulus of British policy. "The love of liberty, or property, and an idea of their own strength," observed John M'Culloch, "spirited up the Americans to a determined resistance."[37]

Given the premise of the republicanism of the American character, it was logical to assume that in a test of will the colonists would vigorously defend their cherished liberties, and that once "the prejudices in favor of a connexion with England . . . wore off," to quote Marshall, they would be replaced by republican sentiments. But there was an intellectual problem: an inability to convincingly relate the republicanism of the national character to the events of the Revolution, for them republicanism was essentially a static concept. Most historians talked of development but were unable to demonstrate it; they simply detected a pattern and offered examples of its existence.

---

If American historians never quite integrated their long range explanation of the Anglo-American conflict with their narrative accounts, they were at their best when they discussed its meaning and consequences. The causes of the Revolution could not be discussed in isolation. It involved a wide range of social and political problems, and the serious historian could not help but enter into conceptualizations of American life. Americans had come to think of themselves as a special people, uniquely placed by history to capitalize on, complete and fulfill the promise of man's existence. Equal in importance to the issue of causation was that of the lessons to be drawn from the Revolution for the nature of American society. It is to the social and political problems raised by the Revolution, and its lessons, that we now turn.

# VII. Nationalizing the Revolution

The primary goal of the Revolutionary generation of historians was to establish a national past. From their vantage point, it appeared that the thirteen colonies had developed a common pattern of life which fulfilled the basic conditions for independence and a national consciousness. Yet the national consciousness itself had grown directly with and out of the Revolution. It was, therefore, from the perspective of the Revolution that historians read back into the past the existence of a distinct national society. The union, and the republican principles upon which it was founded, thus represented a logical fulfillment of American history. The Revolution was pictured as a unified effort of a united people, a community enterprise. Moreover, the conduct of Americans during the crisis proved they possessed the traits of character necessary to sustain a republican society. In short, the historians' goal was to show that the Revolution grew naturally out of the American past, and that it was a true revolution without the accompanying disorders usual in such upheavals.

The portrayal of motivation was designed to point to important conclusions about the nature of American society. The historians came close to giving the impression that the colonists had been of one mind. They attributed the same motives to practically every supporter of the cause and seldom alluded to factions or quarrels among the Patriot leadership. As one writer observed, the Revolution had been "remarkable" for "the fewness of apostacies in the capital characters; the fewness of desertions to the enemy; the sailors taken in the American service, have preferred the horrors of a prison ship, to fighting against the country who has employed them; men of every rank have generally felt and spoke alike, as if the chords of life struck in unison through the continent."[1] State historians, too, represented the Revolution as a common national effort. They either ended their works with its commencement or contented themselves with a summary of national events interspersed with local developments, resisting the temptation to claim a special niche for their states.[2]

The idea of a united national Revolution depended upon proving the Loyalists to be a small dissident minority out of touch with the overwhelming majority. One tactic was to discredit their motives. The Loyalists of Georgia, wrote Hugh McCall, consisted of "many of the most wealthy inhabitants" who "foresaw, that their pecuniary ruin would be the inevitable consequence of participating with the other colonies, in resistance to the aggression of the Crown." Along with the wealthy there was "another class composed of the dissipated and the idle, who had little or nothing to risk, [and] perceived their advantage in adhering to the royal government a wide field for pillage would be opened. . . ."[3] Most historians dismissed the Loyalists with a few derogatory comments. They are there but the canvas is large and they are absorbed in the picture of national unity.

David Ramsay, in his analysis of the motives of Patriots and Loyalists alike, displayed a sophistication unique in his generation. Most American writers depicted the Patriots as devotees of liberty and the Loyalists (when they considered them at all) as mean-minded, either too fearful or under "the influence of ministerial gold."[4] It would be more than a half century before an American historian would write of the Loyalists with some measure of sympathy. Not until the publication of Lorenzo Sabine's *Biographical Sketches of the American Revolution* (1847) would they be the subject of an extended and sympathetic account.[5] Ramsay's *History* was a striking exception. To be sure, he referred only to the few Loyalists who dissented "from principle"; most had done so "from love of ease . . . self-interest . . . fear of the mischievous consequences likely to follow." Although he usually refrained from singling out particular groups of Loyalists, as a South Carolina politician he uncharacteristically indulged his local partisanship by a bitter attack upon "a set of men called regulators." He described them as "disorderly persons, who had fled from the old settlements to avoid the restraints of civil government." On the whole, however, Ramsay was sympathetic to the plight of the American Loyalist: "that three million of such subjects should break through all former attachments and unanimously adopt new ones, could not reasonably be expected."[6]

To explain why some men could sever ancient attachments and others could not, Ramsay analyzed regional differences, ethnic and religious backgrounds, and private interests. New England's overwhelming support for the Patriot cause he attributed to its homogeneous population. True, a few were attached to the British interest, but "these were as the dust in the balance, when compared with the numerous independent Whig yeomanry." New Englanders were "so connected with each other by descent, manners, religion, politics and a general equality, that the killing of a single individual interested the whole, and made them consider it as a common cause." In less homogeneous areas the response was more varied. The Scotch-Irish, with few exceptions, were attached to the Patriot cause. Not only had they fled from oppression in their native land, but their predisposition to liberty was strengthened by their religious opinions as Presbyterians. "The Scotch, on the other hand, though they had formerly sacrificed much to liberty in their own country were disposed to support the claims of Great Britain." Their homeland had recently benefited from royal favor and they were offended by "the illiberal reflections cast by some Americans on the whole body of the Scotch. . . ." Still, many among them served the Patriot cause well.[7]

Often the politics of a group derived from the theology or material interests of its church. "The Presbyterians and Independents were almost universally attached to the measures of Congress. Their religious societies are governed on the republican plan. From independence they had much to hope, but from Great Britain, if finally successful, they had reason to fear the establishment of a church hierarchy." The laity and clergy of the Church of England in the northern provinces tended to support the parent state. Many of the clergy were pensioners of the British government. In contrast, in the Southern colonies, where the church was self-supporting, episcopal ministers were among the most ardent Whigs. Because of their religious beliefs the Quakers were usually against war, although the American cause was served by two Quaker generals. Moreover, the more affluent and politically powerful among them were adverse to independence, since "revolutions in government are rarely patronized by any body of men, who foresees that a diminution of their own importance is likely to result from the change."[8]

As for economic self-interest, Ramsay admitted that in some instances loyalties varied with changing circumstances. At times merchants were able to reconcile their economic interest with patriotism, for example, in their reaction to the Tea Act. "They doubtless conceived themselves to be supporting the rights of their country, by refusing to purchase tea from Britain but they also reflected that if they could bring the same commodity to market, free from duty, their profits would be proportionately greater." In general, however, very few wealthy persons in the northern and middle states were active in the Revolution. The reverse was true in the southern provinces: "There were in no part of America more determined Whigs than the opulent slaveholders in

Virginia, the Carolinas, and Georgia." Finally, there were places where
material interest, social attitudes, and family ties came together to
determine loyalties. In New York City "a large number" of people "were
attached to royal government."

> That city had long been headquarters of the British army in
> America, and many intermarriages, and other connections, had
> been made between British officers, and some of their first
> families. The practice of entailing estates had prevailed in New
> York to a much greater extent than in any of the other
> provinces. The governors thereof had long been in the habit of
> indulging their favorites with extravagant grants of land. This
> had introduced the distinction of landlord and tenant. There was
> therefore in New York an aristocratic party, respectable for
> numbers, wealth and influence, which had much to fear from
> independence. The city was also divided into parties by the
> influence of two ancient and numerous families, the Livingstones
> and Delanceys. These having been long accustomed to oppose
> each other at elections, could rarely be brought to unite in any
> political measures. In this controversy, one almost universally
> took part with America, the other with Great Britain.[9]

The impact of Ramsay's criticism of Loyalists was blunted by
the admission that some Patriots had also acted out of selfish
considerations. Yet even Ramsay's discussion of the Loyalists was almost
an afterthought. They were not a significant factor in his analysis of the
dynamics of the Revolution, and he isolated them from his narrative by
relegating discussion of their motives to an appendix. Their presence is
acknowledged mainly by way of comparison with the Patriots. While
conceding that some had acted selfishly, Ramsay affirmed his conviction
that for the vast body of Patriots, and of the nation, "the love of liberty
was their predominant passion."[10] By contrast, all but a few Loyalists
were characterized by such phrases as "lack of daring," "timidity," or
"old men attached to ancient forms and habits."

The belittling or ignoring of Loyalists left no doubt that the
Anglo-American conflict was one of nation against nation. The crisis may
have resulted from external circumstances, but the nature of the response
had been predetermined by the "temper and habits of the people."
Emphasis on a union of sentiment provided a convenient device for
affirming popular unity. The assumption that Americans were one
people before the Revolution made it easy to treat the whole era as one
of internal continuity. "The American Revolution," observed Samuel

Williams, "explained the business to the world, and served to confirm what nature and society before produced."[11]

The way historians periodized the past was also calculated to emphasize union as the fulfillment of a common history. Logically the colonial period could have been divided into distinct epochs, but the assumption that New World conditions stimulated the development of a republican society largely precluded the delineation of stages of growth. Given the belief that by 1763 Americans were one people in ideals and values, if not in political organization, there was a curious absence of any effort to describe how they arrived at that consensus. The crises that dotted the colonial period were used to show that the colonies had arrived individually at what they would be collectively when faced with a common crisis. The histories convey the determined impression that no alternative had ever been possible; the colonial era blends into the Revolution.

Similarly, the Revolution could logically have been divided into distinct periods, from 1763 to 1776 and from 1776 to 1783, for example; but historians chose to treat the entire span from 1763 to 1789 as a single epoch. Although they could hardly avoid emphasizing different issues at different moments, the net effect was to give the impression that the developing conflict, the negative act of independence, and the positive act of creating a political union were varying phases in the drive for nationhood. "The act of independence," declared Ramsay, "did not hold out to the world thirteen sovereign states, but a common sovereignty of the whole of their united capacity."[12]

More important than chronologically smooth continuity was ideological continuity with the past. To interpret the Revolution as a fulfillment of principles already accepted was to give it a special coloration; it suggested an orderliness not ordinarily associated with revolutions. American intellectuals were sensitive to charges that republics, especially those extending over large territories, were bound to fall prey to disorder. "The world," wrote Mercy Warren, "is now viewing America, as experimenting in a new system of government, a *Federal Republic*." But, she argued against the Montesquian view, "the practicability of supporting such a system, has been doubted by some; if she succeeds, it will refute the assertion that none but small states are adapted to republican government. . . ." Citing the United States and the French Republic as examples, Joel Barlow took issue with "Montesquieu, Voltaire, and many other respectable authorities, [who] have accredited the principle, that republicanism is not convenient for a great state."

Barlow contended "that the republican principle is not only proper and safe for the government of any people; but that its propriety and safety are in proportion to the magnitude of the society and the extent of its territory."[13]

Barlow's reflections were written before Robespierre and the Terror soured him on French politics. When the Revolution took a violent turn the dire predictions about the fate of republics seemed to have come true — the plunge into anarchy that led inevitably to despotism. The French fate fed the fear that the same deadly vices existed in American society. Did the decline in public virtue, asked Jeremy Belknap, prove "that the people of this country are not destined to be long governed in a democratic form?" The bitter party battles of the 1790s and the passionate pursuit of wealth appeared as danger signals that the virtue essential to a republic was crumbling. "The most important truth" to be found in the events of the French Revolution, Noah Webster warned his countrymen, "is that *party spirit* is the source of *faction* and *faction* is *death to the existing government.*" "The union of sentiments and interests that bind Americans together have appeared to be on the wane," observed Warren. "Let them never be eradicated, by the jarring interests of parties, jealousies of the sister states, or the ambitions of individuals."[14]

The French Revolution inevitably influenced the views of American historians. Not only did it invite comparison with the American Revolution; the politics of the 1790s significantly reflected the controversy it aroused. Whether one was a Federalist or a Republican often depended upon one's attitude toward France. The choice was not only ideological, for once war broke out in 1793 between Britain and France the United States had to face the unpleasant dilemma of choosing between its obligations under the French alliance and its own interest in friendly relations with Britain. Initially the response of American historians was favorable to Revolutionary France. As late as 1794 Ramsay linked the two Revolutions together and declared that the "eyes of the world are fixed on this country and on France."[15] Before long the excesses of the Terror effected a nearly complete reversal of American opinion. Although at first criticized for his opposition to the French Revolution, Edmund Burke was its most celebrated critic. It is difficult to say whether he directly influenced American historians, but his writings, especially the *Reflections on the Revolution in France* (1790), were widely distributed and reprinted in the United States.

No American historian agreed with Burke's claim that before 1789 France possessed the elements of a constitution nearly as good as historical circumstances allowed. But his contrast of the disorderly excesses there with the slow, orderly growth of English liberty was similar to the American attitude. The constant reiteration of American continuity served a dual purpose: as a logical device for structuring a national history and as a convenient way of contrasting the two Revolutions. John Marshall bitterly criticized "the revolutionists of France" for their "mad and wicked pursuit . . . through oceans of blood, [of] abstract systems for the attainment of some fancied untried good." But he argued that their pursuit was "mad and wicked" because they were "spreading their doctrines of equality" in a society in which "distinctions and prejudices" could be "subdued only by the grave." The implication of his writings and those of other Americans was not unlike Burke's belief that political values are to be judged in the context of the historical community to which they pertain. Marshall had no use for doctrines of absolute equality; but he was a republican who believed that experience and national character proved that no other system was practicable in the United States. In America history and circumstances laid the foundation for a natural evolution toward representative government and relative equality of condition, whereas in France such accomplishments could be achieved "only by the grave."[16]

American historians did not need the excesses of the French to remind them of the perils inherent in a republic; classical theorists had taught them the danger of disorder. Sensitive to the problem of instability, they hoped to demonstrate that their country was a "well balanced republic, which equally abhors the tyranny of irresponsible authority, the absurdity of hereditary wisdom, and the anarchy of lawless liberty."[17] They took special pains to show that apparent instances of "the anarchy of lawless authority" occurred only when those in power abused republican principles.

Naturally, in dealing with the Revolutionaries it proved difficult to adhere to a narrow definition of legality. Historians skirted the issue by appealing to a higher law: historical destiny. The actions of Britain they cast in terms of illegality; it was the British government that had violated constitutional liberty. England had been the beacon of liberty since the Glorious Revolution; now America had taken the mantle. This was not merely a parochial view; the idea was reinforced by powerful elements of Enlightenment thought. European illuminati identified America, as John Locke had done, as a special preserve of virtue and liberty. Voltaire had stated that America was the refinement of all that was good in England, writing, for example, that Penn and the Quakers had actually brought into existence "that golden age of which men talk so much and which probably has never existed anywhere except in Pennsylvania."[18] It was the colonists, then, fulfilling the dictates of their

history and special destiny, who had defended legality, albeit by
extralegal means. The American Revolution, wrote William Vans
Murray, was "not one of those events which strikes the public eye in the
subversions of laws which have usually attended the revolutions of
governments." The fight for independence, proclaimed Samuel Williams,
"was a war of all true Americans for their natural rights of life, liberty,
and property, carried on not by mobs, but an enlightened, virtuous,
substantial body of uncorrupted citizens."[19]

Admitting instances of mob violence and breakdowns of civil
authority,[20] Patriot historians strongly emphasized the commitment of the
overwhelming majority of Americans to orderly, legal procedures. "Some
licentious persons," wrote Belknap, "began to think that debts could not
be recovered, and that they might insult their creditors with impunity.
On the first appearance of this disorderly spirit, associations were formed
. . . to support the magistrates and preserve the peace." British authority
— that is, authority itself — had not been destroyed but replaced by
popular, extra-legal but not illegal bodies. Even though the Continental
Congress had only advisory powers, observed M'Culloch, "their
recommendations were as effectually carried into execution as the laws
of the best regulated states." Americans had "chosen to hazard the
consequences of returning back to a state of nature, rather than quietly
submit to unjust and arbitrary measures," wrote Warren, but the result
was not anarchy. "It is indeed a singular phenomenon in the story of human conduct," she continued, "that when all legal institutions were ab-
olished . . . the recommendations of committees and conventions, not
enforced by penal sanctions, should be equally influential and binding
with the severest code of law, backed by royal authority, and strengthened by the murdering sword of despotism."[21]

A credible case could be made for the Revolutionary movement
as a relatively orderly affair, but an episode such as Shays' Rebellion
posed a more difficult problem. One would suppose that political
affiliation would determine attitudes toward the Rebellion, with
Federalists taking a more uncompromising, harsher view than Republicans. Such was not the case: a zealous Republican like Warren exhibited
no more sympathy for the rebels than such Federalists as Webster and
Belknap. In fact no historian attempted to justify the Rebellion. There
was, however, an effort to dismiss it as an aberration, for if allowed to
stand as a classic example of the disorder inherent in a republican society
it would do violence to the carefully drawn portrait of a virtuous, law
abiding people.

The strategy of American historians was to treat the uprising as
a unique situation, created by the economic dislocation following the

Revolutionary war, in which a handful of demagogic leaders misled their followers into rash acts. There is a distinct condescension in the depiction of the Shaysites as the victims of devious men. Historians offered no clear conception of a republican society, much less of the relationship between leaders and citizens in a republic; but their treatment of the Rebellion suggests that their praise for the good sense of the private citizen was not entirely candid. To establish a national identity American intellectuals were inclined to magnify the elements that presumably made the nation unique. To overcome a sense of cultural inferiority they often rejected the premises of high culture in the mother country and lauded the values of their own culture on other grounds. Since they often portrayed these values as the property of ordinary citizens — most notably, an instinctive understanding of the principles of a free society — they stressed the superior moral worth of the common people. Their populist ideology, however, was not necessarily egalitarian.[22] In their histories, and from the internal evidence of the few historians who left private writings, there is an implicit assumption that the people need direction. Invariably when the people go wrong it is because they are misled by the wrong leaders.[23]

The primary purpose to be inferred from the historians' treatment of Shays' rebellion was to make the best of a bad situation. However uncharacteristic of the society, it could be used to prove that even under trying circumstances Americans still behaved with restraint. John Jay was no friend of the Shaysites, but when he compared them to English mobs he was impressed by their restraint. "These people bear no resemblance to an English mob, they were more temperate, cool and regular in their conduct — they have hitherto abstained from plunder, nor have they that I know of committed any outrages but such as the accomplishment of their purpose made necessary." Most American historians agreed.[24]

The only full-scale account of Shays' Rebellion reveals the difficult question posed by the uprising: how to condemn it without also condemning republican society and diminishing the nation's repute abroad. Its author, George R. Minot, was clerk of the Massachusetts House of Representatives and later probate judge of Suffolk county. His politics were Federalist, but moderate. "Their sentiments are undoubtedly the justest," he wrote of his party, "but they run into extremes."[25] When Minot published a *History of the Insurrections in Massachusetts* (1788) most readers praised his impartiality. While he did not skirt the difficult issues, he wrote a book that satisfied virtually everyone. The genesis of Minot's *History* provides a good example of the conflicting pressures, intellectual and personal, that determined how American historians would deal with the national past. For most of them one can only infer motivation, but Minot confided his thoughts to a diary.[26]

Trained as a lawyer, Minot disliked the day-to-day tensions and personal rivalries of law practice. By his own testimony he preferred to avoid extremes, was anxious to avoid public controversy, and was eager to have everyone think well of him. Moreover, he had literary and historical inclinations and exercised them to advance his country's fortunes and his own. When Minot published the first volume of his continuation of the history of Massachusetts he dedicated it to the president of the American Academy of Arts and Sciences, who happened to be John Adams, President of the United States. Self-advancement was not his only purpose. He was genuinely devoted to the proposition that the survival of the United States offered proof that man could govern himself.[27] This nation, he observed, was "an experiment to ascertain the nature of man; whether he be capable of freedom, or whether he must be led by the reins of tyranny."[28] Given Minot's temperament and patriotic sentiments, it is not surprising that his book appeared "impartial" to so many readers.

Since Minot began work on his *History* only a year after the event, the rebellion was still a simmering political issue. Moreover, the hostility between John Hancock and James Bowdoin, the two most powerful figures in Massachusetts politics, could not be ignored. Bowdoin had been governor during the uprising, but Hancock presided over its aftermath and was still in office when Minot's work was published in 1788. To further complicate matters, Lieutenant Governor Benjamin Lincoln, who had commanded the government troops against the rebels, was a Bowdoin supporter deeply resented by Hancock. Caught between two hostile factions and ambitious for appointive office, Minot had every reason to avoid antagonizing the rivals. He showed his manuscript to several of them so that, as he put it, "they might object to anything relative to their conduct, before it appeared in print."[29]

Ambition and timidity established the tone of Minot's treatment. He carefully avoided antagonizing any of the competitors. It was more difficult to resolve the problem of assessing the Shaysites. To describe them as selfish, unreasonable and ignorant would please the people he wanted most to impress and who were most likely to purchase his book: his Boston friends and the eastern businessmen and southern plantation owners who had been most alarmed by the Rebellion. Moreover, as a creditor, lawyer, and government official, he had feared the uprising. Nevertheless, instead of simplifying the rebellion as a contest between right and wrong, order and chaos, Minot attempted to understand why it had occurred. Though unwilling to justify the actions of the rebels, he did seek out the extenuating circumstances that would explain their behavior.[30]

Minot's practice of looking for reasons to explain even what he did not like tended to soften his denunciation of the Shaysites. Perhaps because of self-consciousness about his own motives, he was eager to comprehend the behavior of others. As early as 1784 he sought, in a long passage in his diary, to understand why people in the interior counties were having trouble paying taxes. He analyzed the problem in terms of the state's monetary system, the relative fluidity of capital invested in commerce and in land, and the emotional attachment of farmers to their land. He sought extenuating circumstances which would explain if not justify the behavior of the rebels. Minot was also anxious to dispel any impression that public order and republican government were incompatible. The revisions he made in his early drafts reveal a concern to justify the United States to a European, especially an English, audience. My aim, he explained to Washington, has been "a love of truth, and a wish to preserve the reputation of my country."[31]

The Rebellion, to Minot, was not a serious affair but a temporary product of temporary conditions, kept alive by the rebel leaders well after the rank and file realized their error. Although force had to be employed to suppress "a dangerous internal war," it was accomplished "by the spirited use of constitutional powers, in a manner that must attach every man to a constitution, which . . . governs its subjects without oppression, and reclaims them without severity." The insurgents had been misled, but were now ready to resume their place in a healthy and stable society. Here was a formula designed to promote the reputation of the United States in the eyes of Englishmen without alienating Massachusetts conservatives, and, at the same time, to allay agrarians who had participated in or sympathized with the rebellion.[32]

That American historians were willing to explain away disorder also may have reflected the nature of civil disturbances in eighteenth century America. Not all mobs were lawless; some used extra-legal means to enforce laws not otherwise enforceable or to support local authorities and provincial interests against imperial policy.[33] Hence the Revolutionary generation was not inclined to deny out of hand the legitimacy of popular upheavals. But to accept selected popular uprisings as legitimate political activity made it imperative to distinguish between the legitimate and the illegitimate.

In his discussion of Bacon's Rebellion, Edmund Randolph decried the fact that the Rebellion "has lately received a historical gloss, the object of which is to metamorphose it into one of those daring efforts which gross misrule sometimes suggests, if it may not strictly vindicate."

Randolph was referring to John Daly Burk's *History of Virginia*, which contained the only favorable account of Bacon's Rebellion written during the early national period. Burk was determined "to counter a universally received opinion . . . that Virginia was distinguished for her invariable loyalty, and her submissive and tractable temper, during the greater part of her colonial existence." He seized upon Bacon's Rebellion as evidence that "the conduct of Virginia . . . was exactly the opposite of what it has been represented." Randolph was no less sensitive to Virginia's place in the national past, but he preferred to rest the Old Dominion's reputation on the stability of its political system. He concluded the rebellion was illegitimate by applying a simple formula. "A legitimate government existed. It was honest in the measures of general defense." And he ended with the warning that merely because "the whole force of precedent [has] been already obtained in the successful resistance of the American colonies to Great Britain, we ought not to sanction a new case in which tyranny is less palpable or less clearly mediated. Let the transaction therefore be seen in its real chracter."[34]

After the American and French Revolutions it was no longer possible to disregard the impact of popular movements on modern history. A new epoch required a new historiography that took into account what the masses did and believed. Americans did not fully comprehend the new reality and they responded to it less from historical logic than from practical necessity, but they showed some perception. "The war was the people's war," concluded Ramsay, "and the exertions of the army would have been insufficient to effect the revolution, unless the great body of the people had been prepared for it. . . ."[35] Polemical necessity more than scholarly or sympathetic understanding impelled American historians to focus on the activities of the populace. Their intent was to prove that Americans possessed the indispensable republican qualities and to forge a popular national identification. In the process they ended up by treating the events that led to the creation of the United States as a popular movement: not the unleashing of popular discontents and hatreds such as had occurred in France but the action of an organic community defending and expanding institutions and liberties that had evolved naturally out of a common past.

Anxious to prove "that genuine republicanism is friendly to order," historians portrayed their countrymen as a reasoning people capable of responding sensibly to rational argument. Thomas Paine was singled out for special praise: however skilled as a propagandist, he appealed to reason and experience. "Learning their principles from the state of Society in America, Paine and other writers upon American politics met with amazing success," observed Samuel Williams. "Not because they taught the people principles, which they did not before understand; but because they placed the principles which they had learned of them, in a very clear and striking light, on a most critical and important occasion." In preparing "the minds of the people for independence," wrote John Marshall, "the pen of Thomas Paine stood pre-eminent. . . ." Even though Marshall strongly disagreed with Paine's politics, he urged that a "mantle" be "cast over" his "imperfections." To "his memory" should be paid "the tribute of your gratitude, for the services which he hath rendered in establishing the independence and happiness of yourselves, as a nation. . . ."[36]

The real heroes of the Revolution were "the well informed citizens," for "they had encouraged political inquiries, and the eyes of the people were opened." Public opinion, not the acts of statesmen, determined the outcome, and revolutionary organizations were important only as its conduits and organizers. "What the eloquence and talents of Demosthenes could not effect among the states of Greece," observed Ramsay, "might have been effected by the simple device of committees of correspondence." They provided means of communication indispensable to the success of a popular revolution: "It is perhaps impossible for human wisdom to contrive any system more subservient to these purposes, than such a reciprocal exchange of intelligence by committees." Many states had lost their liberty for want of such organizations, for "the few have been enabled to keep the many in subjection in every age, from the want of union among the latter."[37]

Because historians depicted the Revolution as a popular movement their narratives implied that the role of leaders was secondary to what the mass of men did and believed. The names of the prominent dot the pages of every history, but rather as agents of change than driving forces. In most accounts of the years preceding independence (Washington stands out as a wartime exception) leaders are remarkable for their anonymity. Even the two exceptions, Warren's *History of the American Revolution* and Randolph's *History of Virginia*, presented them chiefly as instruments of the popular will. The names of statesmen and generals often were mentioned only as matters of fact akin to dates, places, battles and manifestos. Take, for instance, Belknap's failure to credit Thomas Jefferson with the authorship of the Declaration of Independence. Since the Declaration was a reflection of the "minds of the people at large," who had "called upon their delegates in congress to execute the act which should save us from foreign dominion, and put us into a situation to govern ourselves," there seemed little point in mentioning the author. Similarly, in his discussion of the New Hampshire Constitution (1776) Belknap omitted the names of its authors, explaining that the document reflected "the sentiments of the people at that time."[38]

Such obvious omissions as the actions and names of famous men must have been calculated. But the emphasis on collective activity did not derive from a conscious theory of causation. Eighteenth century historians found it difficult to relate specific causes to specific events. Voltaire, for example, insofar as he attempted to explain causes, wavered between a great man theory and an insistence that great events result from minute and trivial causes. Taking the latter approach, some writers concluded that apparently insignificant causes like the length of Cleopatra's nose can have important results. At times Voltaire did maintain that what mattered was not kings and battles, but culture and scientific achievement; but he could not formulate a clear line of causation. Instead he often turned to a great man theory, e.g. when he attributed the French Renaissance to Frances I.[39]

When discussing the actions of the British government American historians were willing to treat individuals as causes. Of Governor Thomas Hutchinson, Warren wrote that "every historical record will doubtless witness that he was the principal author of the sufferings of unhappy Bostonians, previous to the convulsions which produced the revolution." But Americans were reluctant to apply either of Voltaire's alternatives to the Revolution. Trivial causes would make it appear an irrational or mundane event; and, without explicitly denying the importance of outstanding men, good republicans were reluctant to glorify individuals, especially the military. Moreover, in a republic it was especially important to understand what motivated the mass of men, and these in turn must be rational; the Revolution must appear to be a logical event that resulted from the actions of a community responding to rational arguments. Finally, these two types of causation, the trivial or accidental and the great man, have one thing in common: they both imply that important changes in the course of history occur by sudden events or actions intruding on society from the outside. For a group of historians determined to prove that the Revolution, or at least the response to British policy, grew out of a common national past, such an outlook was unacceptable.[40]

It was a practical rather than a scholarly calculation that inhibited a biographical emphasis. No matter how prominent a statesman may have been in national affairs, he was still identified with a particular state or section. Washington was the exception to this rule, but in the public mind John Adams, Samuel Adams, Thomas Jefferson, even Benjamin Franklin all had strong local identities. Thus, to stress the role of leaders could be self-defeating; it would give to their work the particularistic bias that historians were anxious to avoid. Given their goals — to promote union and republicanism — it seemed particularly appropriate to stress the role of the common citizen.

Another consideration may have influenced some historians who were elected or appointed office holders or seekers. Minot's history of Shays' Rebellion is only one example of the effect ambition could have on an historian's writing. As has often been the case in new nations, new leaders were particularly sensitive about their recent roles. Perhaps it is only coincidence, but the only critics of the Revolutionary leaders had no further political ambitions: Marshall with life tenure on the Supreme Court, Randolph in reluctant but permanent retirement, and Warren, whose sex disqualified her for public office. Warren's and Marshall's works provoked a storm of protest from offended public men and Randolph's manuscript went unpublished for nearly a century. Whatever the reasons — personal ambition, a desire to avoid divisive controversies, or both — the authors of biographical dictionaries included only the lives of deceased persons. That the issue was not one of historical theory is evidenced by the fact that historians did stress outstanding men in the colonial period. William Penn, John Winthrop, Roger Williams, John Smith, Christopher Columbus, Sir George Calvert were all portrayed as prime movers in an heroic mold.

---

Historians had no philosophical or methodological bias against biography as historical literature; practical considerations rather than theory dictated their approach to both narrative and biography. As in their narratives, they used biography to stress unity and to delineate the national character. They portrayed the actions and attitudes of both the community and the leaders as expressions of a republican society. Yet the historians did not repudiate the great men interpretation; they were never entirely clear on this point. The minor role they assigned to leaders in their narratives did seem to imply such a rejection; but their abiding interest in Washington belies this conclusion. Explicitly, the issue was neither posed nor resolved. Historians seemed to draw a vague, implicit distinction between the causes and the securing of independence. Washington, like other leaders, was seldom accorded a decisive role in the events leading up to independence. But in the war he was granted at least parity with the citizen-soldier.

As early as 1779 Belknap suggested to Ebenezer Hazard that he prepare a dictionary of American biography. Hazard pleaded that the magnitude of his own project of a documentary history of the United States precluded his taking on such a commitment, but he agreed that it was a good idea. Several years later Belknap responded to a request from William Spotswood, editor of the *Columbian Magazine*, to write a series of biographical sketches entitled "the American Plutarch." He prefaced the series with a quote from Lord Clarendon on the usefulness of the lives of great men as guides for the present, and continued:

> In deference to the judgement of such an attentive observer of mankind, and trusting that this country is capable of affording instances of such "heroic and virtuous men" as ought to be remembered and celebrated; we shall endeavour to present to the view of our readers, from time to time, some memoirs of the lives and character of the founders of the American states, and of such other persons as have made a principal figure in them, compiled from the best materials within reach.[41]

Belknap was encouraged by Spotwood's enthusiasm to undertake a dictionary of American biography. The first volume appeared in 1794; he died in 1798 with the second volume in press. He had planned to write sketches of outstanding men in American history from the age of discovery to the present. Unfortunately the completed volumes did not go beyond the seventeenth century. During the next two decades, however, other writers followed Belknap's example. Among the most widely read tomes were James Hardie's *New Universal Biographical Dictionary* (1801-04), which included an *American Remembrancer of Departed Merit*, compiled from a variety of secondary sources; A *Biographical Dictionary* (1809) of prominent New Englanders by John Eliot, a Boston Congregational minister and a founder of the Massachusetts Historical Society; and William Allen's *American Biographical and Historical Dictionary* (1809), a work of careful scholarship that remained a standard source until after the Civil War.[42] Although these biographical dictionaries varied in quality, they rested on similar stylistic and conceptual premises. The historians strove to transform the subject into a figure of national interest by passing over his interior experiences and portraying him as a personification of the nation's republican ideology, while they gave dramatic impact to his life by merging his personal history with that of the nation.

No better model existed than the New England tradition of spiritual biography, and it is no accident that the most ambitious projects were initiated by New Englanders.[43] The seventeenth century Puritan's conception of history was rooted in the conviction that religious progress depended on the individual. Whenever possible theological abstractions were related to personal experience. Since the Puritan was urged to judge each life by a spiritual measure, biography served the function of detailing the lives of those who seemed worthy of imitation. In his *Magnalia Christi Americana* (1702) Cotton Mather used individual lives to illustrate particular moral lessons and achievements. But if Mather and other New England writers weighted their work in favor of the spiritual life of the individual, the "Lord's Remembrancers" were not intended merely to record holy lives, nor only to point up the subject's interior experiences. Above all, they were not intended to extoll their subjects as singular individuals set apart from their fellows. Rather, each was viewed as part of a social and spiritual organism, his life indistinguishable from the life of the community.[44]

In this tradition the Revolutionary generation used biography to characterize the society. Writers broadened their appeal by the inclusion of subjects from every section of the country.[45] A few attempted to give American history universal importance. In his *American Biography* Belknap linked the nation's history to mankind's advance by adding the lives of the world's greatest scientists, geographers and explorers. Moreover, no clear distinction was drawn between history and biography. To study the lives of famous men, wrote William Allen, "it became necessary . . . to examine the whole of American history." His strategy was to merge the man with the nation "for the purpose of illustrating the history of this country." Like Cotton Mather before them, these writers depicted their subjects less as individual men with clearly defined personalities than as stylized reflections of American society. "In a word," explained Thomas Rogers, "here may the sons of America trace the lineaments of their fathers' glory, and by their example learn to imitate their deeds."[46]

The biographical sketches were intended to establish their subjects individually and collectively as personifications of American political and social principles and character. They were designed, in the words of one author, to strengthen "the attachment of Americans to their well balanced republic, which equally abhors the tyranny of irresponsible authority, the absurdity of hereditary wisdom, and the anarchy of lawless liberty." The names and the details differed; the qualities of character hardly varied. In his sketch of Samuel Adams, William Allen followed what had become a familiar pattern, using his public career to illustrate the ideal qualities of a republican leader: his love of liberty, devotion to public service, "incorruptible integrity."[47] Allen made only oblique references to the many quarrels that filled Adams's public life.

Even the very famous were stripped of uniqueness. Every biographical dictionary and general history included sketches of persons who could be readily identified with religious toleration. In his lectures on law James Wilson asked that if "immortal honors are bestowed on the name and character of Locke" for his enunciation of the principle of religious toleration, then "why should an ingracious silence be observed, with regard to the name and character of Calvert?" It should be made known, he concluded, that "before the doctrine of toleration was published in Europe the practice of it was established in America." Ramsay praised Calvert for laying "the foundation" of Maryland's "future prosperity on the broad basis of security of property, and of freedom in religion." Similarly, Isaac Backus credited Roger Williams with being a pioneer of religious liberty, while Morgan Edwards saluted Williams as "the first legislator in the world that fully and effectually provided for the established and free, full, and absolute liberty of conscience."[48]

Thus, for American historians biographical writing was a didactic exercise, a way of expounding the principles of a republican society. Usually the discussions involved only a general statement of principle, but Edmund Randolph devised a more elaborate scheme. In dealing with the Revolution in his *History of Virginia*, Randolph included fourteen biographical portraits of the state's outstanding leaders.[49] He maintained that the great Virginians of the epoch — Washington and Henry, Mason and Jefferson, Pendleton and the Lees — were less the product of individual genius than of a mature and sophisticated political system. To underscore this point Randolph drafted a series of thumbnail portraits of the dominant Virginia politicians. Although differences in personality and ability were not completely submerged, his purpose was to delineate the qualities common to the state's Revolutionary leadership. In varying degrees his pantheon of heroes possessed certain attributes: formal learning and oratorical skills, republican manners and force of character. These were the qualities Randolph considered indispensable to the ideal republican leader.

The qualities Randolph most admired were those that enabled one to influence others by winning their admiration and loyalty. "In official rank and ostensible importance," Peyton Randolph "stood foremost in the bands of patriots" largely because of his reputation as a man of decorum and moderation. The "frankness" of Benjamin Harrison, "though sometimes tinctured with bitterness, was the source of considerable attachment." "The propriety and purity" of Robert Carter Nicholas's life "were often quoted, to stimulate the old and to invite the young to emulation, and in an avocation thickly beset with seductions

[Nicholas was treasurer of Virginia], he knew them only as he repelled them with the quickness of instinct." George Wythe's "character, rather than his actions, rendered him a valuable resource to the infant Revolution." In each case force of character was the best resource for leadership. Since the ruling gentry molded public feelings by example, the people gained a greater confidence in the propriety of the struggle against Great Britain. Their leaders "had at stake fortunes which were affluent or competent and families which were dear to them; neither of these blessings would they have jeopardized upon a political speculation in which their souls were not deeply engaged."[50]

Finally, in Randolph's view Virginia society before the Revolutionary crisis tended to celebrate an aristocratic style of life, but the new circumstances of the Anglo-American controversy called for men of republican habits. George Mason had "an indifference for distinction, a disposition not averse from hospitality," and a "hatred for pomp" despite being endowed "with ability to mount in any line" and "a fortune competent to any expense." These attitudes were a product of "that philosophical spirit which despised the adulterated means of cultivating happiness." Edmund Pendleton "lived at home with the unadulterated simplicity of a republican; from abroad he imported into his family no fondness for show." For all Randolph's high regard for republican manners, however, he did not mean to weaken deference; he was merely suggesting an informality between classes characteristic of a stable social order in which everyone knows his place. Pendleton's "amiableness bordered on familiarity without detracting from personal dignity."[51]

Among Randolph's fourteen selected Virginia leaders Patrick Henry was the most dramatic but, revealingly, the most representative as well. It was Henry who, at the outset of the conflict with Britain, took command in the House of Burgesses: "They wanted a leader," and "at this critical moment, Patrick Henry appeared as a member from the county of Louisa." Randolph was quick to concede his shortcomings: as a scholar he had little training; he was more orator than thinker; "in black-letter precedents he was never profound." "Nor was he absolutely exempt from an irregularity in his language, a certain homespun pronounciation, and a degree of awkwardness in the cold commencement of his gesture." Nevertheless Henry abounded in qualities which were particularly suited to the crisis. "For grand impressions in the defense of liberty, the Western world has not yet been able to exhibit a rival. . . . In this embryo state of the Revolution, deep research into the ancient treasure of political learning might well be dispensed with. It was enough to feel, to remember some general maxims coeval with the colony and inculcated frequently afterwards." Since he was "identified with the people, they clothed him with the confidence of a favorite son."[52]

Considering Henry's record as a firebrand it seems odd that Randolph should cast him as the prototype of a ruling group celebrated for its decorum, moderation, and learning; but he recognized that despite the flamboyant behavior and seemingly radical tone Henry was an establishment man who played by the rules of the game. "From education he derived those manners which belonged to the real Virginia planter and which were his ornament, in no less disdaining an abridgement of personal independence than in observing every decorum interwoven with the comfort of society."[53] Even his vehement and often sarcastic tone was softened "by a demeanor inoffensive, conciliating, and abounding in good humor." In short, Henry differed from his fellows only in individual capabilities and personality, not in basic assumptions about the social order. Perhaps Randolph was also praising by inference the tolerance of a deferential society for upper class eccentrics like his nephew, Senator John Randolph.

Like his fellow historians, then, Randolph was not celebrating extraordinary men so much as the system that produced them. Indeed, although some of them — Washington, Patrick Henry, Richard Henry Lee — at one time or another had been his bitter political enemies, he exaggerated their virtues to show that the system required the politically ambitious to conform to a code. It was this theme that he developed dramatically in his portrayal of Patrick Henry, as in like manner other historians used the public lives of the great and near great to discuss broader historical themes. Randolph's inclusion of Washington in his republican pantheon may seem ironic considering that the first President had been the instrument of his political ruin. To be sure, his tribute — "I rejoice that I have lived to do justice to . . . Washington"[54] — was ironic. It was the pre-presidential Washington, yet to be infected by the spirit of faction, that he celebrated. Still, like Henry, Washington the Virginian was an embodiment of republican virtue and the effectiveness of the political system.

That Randolph did not directly criticize Washington may have been a consequence of his preeminence as the nation's most revered leader. No figure better symbolized the image of the national character or more nearly personified the ideal of national unity. As leader of the victorious Continental forces he was already widely admired, especially since he had protected the country from a rebellious army. With the adoption of the Constitution and establishment of the new government his reputation reached its apotheosis.[55] He was an ideal symbol. Since

Jefferson and Hamilton were combatants who represented polarity, biographical studies of them had to be partisan. But Washington appeared to be non-partisan, an image he had consciously propagated.

The first book-length life of Washington was Mason Locke Weems' highly successful filiopietistic biography. Serious scholars held Weems in low esteem, but certain basic themes in his *Life of Washington* (1800) were similar to those used by other historians: Washington as symbol of national unity, Washington as embodiment of the national character, Washington as emblem of American greatness. There were, however, more than scholarly differences between Weems and other biographers. Because he was interested in Washington's private character he recounted (or invented) details of his early life. But since other biographers wanted to portray Washington as an American, not a Virginian, they stripped him of local identity by omitting all but the most cursory references to his early life. Ramsay devoted less than three pages to the years before the French and Indian War, and in a 2,500 page work Marshall used only two pages.[56] They dwelt almost exclusively on the public man.

Even Marshall, who came closer than any other American historian to a great man causation, accepted the general premise of the leader as a reflection of the national character. He attributed victory in the Revolutionary War and much of the success of the national government to Washington's leadership. But in his narrative of the coming of the Revolution neither Washington nor any other individual dominated events. Marshall depicted Washington as a genius, but one who reflected his society, a point he underscored by opening with a volume on the colonial period in which his name appears only a half dozen times. He betrayed no interest in the private man, only in the symbol of two centuries of national history. In weaving the life of "America's greatest genius" into the fabric of the nation's past Marshall assumed the existence of a national tradition. "The history of General Washington," he explained, "is so much that of his country, that the work appeared to the author to be most sensibly incomplete and unsatisfactory, while unaccompanied by such a narrative of the principal events preceding out of the revolutionary war, as would make the reader acquainted with the genius, character, and resources of the people about to engage in that memorable contest."[57]

Biographers always celebrated Washington as the ideal republican leader. To a generation schooled in the classics his conduct readily stamped him as a modern Cincinnatus, an image that appealed to the deep distrust of the military and affection for heroes who submitted to popular government. Twice during his career, they contended, when he might have given way to ambition — at the end of the Revolutionary War and after eight years as President — he had voluntarily quit the life of power. "If Washington possessed ambition," wrote Marshall, "that passion was, in his bosom, so regulated by principles, or controlled by circumstances, that it was neither vicious, nor turbulent. . . . The various high and important stations to which he was called by the public voice, were unsought by himself; and, in consenting to fill them, he seems rather to have yielded to a general conviction that the interests of his country would be thereby promoted, than to an avidity for power." Americans took pleasure in advertising this image. Ramsay closed his biography by advising the world's leaders to "learn from Washington wherein true glory consists — Restrain your ambition — Consider your power as an obligation to do good."[58]

There were in this picture implications of the indispensable leader. To a degree historians idealized Washington in the way leaders in other new states have been idolized,[59] but they resisted the temptation to follow their contemporaries and turn him into a demi-god. Reluctant to criticize him, they came close to hero-worship, but their writings did not glorify him as much as their society. Because General Washington's "recommendation was law, and he was able to command the whole power of that people for any purpose of defense," wrote Joel Barlow, "the philosophers of Europe considered this as a dangerous crisis to the cause of freedom." They believed "that Washington would never lay down his arms, till he had given his country a master." When he belied their expectations they called it a "miracle," proclaimed "his virtue . . . to be more than human," and mistakenly concluded that Americans "enjoy their liberty at this day" because of "this miracle of virtue in him." In Barlow's view they missed the point. "To an American eye nothing extraordinary could appear in that transaction." The soldiers "were all citizens" and "their numbers were not the hundredth part of the citizens at large, who were all soldiers." Washington knew that neither he nor anyone else could impose his will on the American people. If "he was wise in discerning the impossibility of success in an attempt to imitate" past dictators, that "is to give him only the same merit for sagacity which is common to every other person who knows that country, or who has well considered the effects of equal liberty."[60]

Despite the emphasis of historians on the Revolution as a popular movement their interpretation had a decidedly conservative coloration. To them the Revolution was a non-charismatic mass movement: it involved the entire community, but was an affair of the intellect more than of passion, a remarkably orderly contest over constitutional issues. As such it had only been possible because of the distinctive national character and its continuity with the colonial past. In short, by representing the Revolution as a confirmation of what already existed American historians tinted their histories conservative. There is no hint of an internal upheaval pitting class against class, and little to suggest that independence brought anything more within the country than a change of the forms of government.

This traditionalist and legalist cast was not necessarily a repudiation of revolutionary change. So zealous a critic of the French Revolution as Noah Webster admitted that to some degree the differences between the two Revolutions could be explained by circumstance. He conceded that "much of the violence of their measures may be attributed to the combination of powers, formed for the most unwarrantable purpose of dictating to an independent nation its form of government."[61] Moreover, to emphasize order and continuity was not to say that there had been no Revolution. Enlightenment thinkers generally regarded progress as primarily the result of the removal of obstacles, such as tyranny, religious error or superstition. It was conceived of as an emancipation from restrictions, to be succeeded by the consequent achievement of the possibilities inherent in mankind. Every American historian pressed the same point: the Revolution had been revolutionary in the sense that it had removed barriers so that their countrymen could fully exploit their advantageous circumstances. To have established an independent national existence and government based on the sovereignty of the people seemed to be unchallengeably revolutionary. "The Revolution which called the democratic power into action," wrote Belknap, "has repressed the aristocratic spirit . . . [and] the people enjoy more equal privileges."[62]

# VIII. The Federal Union

Having provided a selective unity that made the Revolution and nationhood appear part of the logical flow of the common history, all that remained for the Revolutionary generation of historians was to incorporate the culminating act of nationhood into the pattern. David Ramsay in his *History of the American Revolution* (1789), the first such work published after ratification of the Constitution, established the accepted pattern of interpretation. Although he dwelled on the problems of forming an effective political union, his interpretation was based on the implicit assumption that Americans were one people. He minimized internal conflict, portraying the Constitution as the expression of a united people and the final, safeguarding act of the Revolution. Functionally, he saw it as an administrative charter designed to provide a national authority capable of dealing with the problems of its citizens and meeting the challenge of new problems.

Ramsay set the stage by describing how the American colonists had been transformed from a people united by sentiment alone into a political union. By 1763 the English "colonies in the new world, had advanced nearly to the magnitude of a nation," but they were "not sensible of it . . . Americans knew but little of one another. . . ." Not until the Anglo-American controversy did they come to fully realize their common bonds. "Men from all states by freely mixing together" in Congress and the army "were assimilated into one mass." As they returned home and mingled with the citizens of their states they "disseminated principles of union among them." Thus the Revolutionary crisis induced "men of liberal minds" to lead "in discouraging local distinctions, and the great body of the people, as soon as reason got the better of prejudice, found that their best interests would be most effectually promoted by such practices and sentiments as were favourable to union."[1]

The Revolution brought Americans to realize they were one people and "laid a foundation for the establishment of a nation," but independence raised practical problems that could only be met within the framework of a formal political structure. During the war enthusiasm for the cause and fear of British arms enabled a Congress lacking formal authority to perform the bare minimum of necessary national functions. As the war ended cohesion dissipated and the need for a central government became clear to many. Yet the first legally constituted government was ratified only with the greatest difficulty. "It was not easy to define the power of the State legislatures, so as to prevent a clashing between their jurisdiction and that of the general government."[2]

Critical as Ramsay was of the Confederation, he still regarded it as an essential way station on the road to a more perfect government. "The Articles . . . were proposed at a time when the citizens of America were young in the science of politics, and when a commanding sense of duty, enforced by the pressure of a common danger, precluded the necessity of a power of compulsion." Indeed, the Confederation had been responsible for some noteworthy achievements, especially the establishment of procedures for bringing new states "into the union on equal terms. By this liberal policy, the blessings of a free government may be gradually extended to the remotest bounds of the United States." Still, if all was not failure, "experience proved . . . that a radical change of the whole system was necessary to the good government of the United States."[3]

For Ramsay the Constitution was an administrative reorganization in response to the problems of conducting war and organizing a nation. "Some from jealousy of liberty were afraid of giving too much power to their rulers," but the central issue was the amount of power to be delegated by the states to the federal government, and how vested interests would be affected. Those "individuals who had great influence in State Legislatures" were opposed to a government which "would eventually diminish their own importance. . . ." By the same token, those who expected positions in the new government, "the mass of public creditors expecting payment of their debts," and those who favored prohibitions against "the issuing of paper money and all interference between debtor and creditor . . . had the same interested reason for supporting its adoption." Nevertheless the influence of vested interests was less decisive than "the great body of independent men." Seeing "the necessity of an energetic general government," they succeeded in effecting its establishment.[4]

The debate over the Constitution, then, was to Ramsay only incidentally a dispute over principles. In the years following the rejection of British sovereignty constitutions had been written in the newly independent states. During this period a mode of government suitable to "the genius of the Americans, their republican habits and sentiments," had been institutionalized. These governments, Ramsay concluded, "are miniature pictures of the community, and from the mode of their election are likely to be influenced by the same interests and feelings with the people whom they represent. . . . The assemblage of these circumstances gives as great a security that laws will be made, and governments administered for the good of the people, as can be expected from the imperfection of human institutions."[5] The Constitution was neither a revolution in first principles nor a break with the past. "The people of the United States gave no new powers to their rulers, but made a more judicious arrangement of what they had formerly ceded. They enlarged the powers of the general government, not by taking from the people, but from the State legislatures."[6]

The Constitution was potentially more controversial than the Revolution. Since the political battles of the beginning of the national period were fought largely on an ideological battleground with the participants divided by their interpretation of the Constitution, it would have been easy for historians to turn their discussions to partisan purposes. Yet from 1789 to 1794 the few works that dealt with the formation of the federal government interpreted it essentially as did Ramsay. He published his history in 1789, before the party battles of the 1790s. Jeremy Belknap (1792) and Samuel Williams (1794) were working on their histories before party lines had solidified. Jedidiah Morse (1789) omitted the Confederation period altogether, giving the impression that the Constitution had grown directly out of the Revolution.[7]

The historiography of the Constitution was related to the course of politics; the hotter party politics became, the less historians had to say. From 1795 to 1805, when national politics reached fever pitch, no historian accorded the Constitution more than cursory treatment. They described it simply as the final act of the Revolution. "The embarrassments and difficulties in carrying on the war were great," wrote John M'Culloch (1795). "But they were compensated and greatly overbalanced by the important advantages of the Revolution. . . . An opportunity was offered of establishing liberty on a broad basis, and of instituting governments on the authority of the people. . . . It was a prize worth contending for."[8]

Even though most historians held strong convictions or were active in politics, they rarely used their books as partisan platforms. The few who discussed the years after 1789 usually weighted their accounts with non-political subjects. For example Abiel Holmes, minister of the First Congregational Church of Cambridge and a devoted Federalist, lived in an environment where to mention Thomas Jefferson aroused anger; but Holmes, who corresponded with Jefferson,[9] was more distressed by the divisiveness of party politics. When he first published his *American Annals* in 1805 he intended to make periodic revisions to include subsequent events. Holmes refrained from controversy, and in the second edition of 1809 he merely noted the election of James Madison to the presidency without comment and turned to such matters as the establishment of Miami University in Ohio.

When Ramsay wrote his *History of the United States* (1816-17) he offered a more detailed account but essentially the same interpretation as in his earlier *History of the American Revolution*, with national unity as the central theme. In 1789 he had written of the Constitution as a logical fulfillment of the Revolution. In his later work he added specific examples to demonstrate that it signified the climactic stage "of a general tendency to union." This had been encouraged as far back as the Stuarts for defense against foreign enemies and "to increase their own power" but was also "aimed at the people of America . . . solely for their own defense and security." Ramsay cited the New England Confederation and the Albany and Stamp Act congresses as examples of this "general tendency to union."[10]

Although a Federalist, when Ramsay reached the year 1789 he abruptly switched to a bland recitation of events that avoided the divisive issues of the 1790s and early 1800s. In his *Life of George Washington* (1807) he dwelled on the war years; of some 350 pages only seventy-five were devoted to the presidency. Ramsay did mention the bitter partisan attacks on the president; but he elaborated on only one, the publication of a series of letters allegedly written by Washington in 1776, and did not specify the content of the letters, referring to those who had published them as "fellow citizens who differed from him [Washington] in politics."[11] As for Alexander Hamilton, that central and controversial figure is nowhere to be found; his economic policies are mentioned only in passing and are not specifically identified with him. To read the *History of the United States* and the *Life of Washington* one would think that the years after 1789 had been tranquil.

Not until Mercy Otis Warren (1805) and John Marshall (1807) published their histories did an American historian deviate from uncritical praise of the Constitution or favor one faction, and no others joined them. Unlike Ramsay, who had first published his *History* when the success of the new government was in doubt, Warren may have felt less constrained. Her version appeared when the Union had survived the party battles of the 1790s and a transfer of power. Where Ramsay had been a strong advocate of ratification, Warren's feelings were ambivalent. Actively opposed to ratification, once the Constitution had gone into effect she reacted with mixed apprehension and pleasure. "We now seem to have verged to the entrance of a permanent and I hope peaceful Government, an object which has long been the wish of every good man and woman in America."[12] Her ambivalence was reflected in a rambling, sometimes contradictory commentary on the genesis of the national government.

On one point Warren agreed with her predecessors: the success of the Revolution had been endangered by the Confederation's lack of "sufficient powers" to deal with such problems as the debt, disputes between the states over the national domain, internal disorders like Shays' Rebellion, and, most important, a general decline in private and public virtue. Faced with so dangerous a threat to "their internal felicity, the inhabitants of America were in general sensible, that the freedom of the people, the virtue of society, and the stability of their commonwealth, could only be preserved by the strictest union. . . ." Warren did disagree with Ramsay over the motives of the authors of the Constitution. "The greatest happiness of the greatest number was not the principal object of their contemplations. . . ."[13] For Ramsay the contest had not been over ideology, but between the states and the central government over the redistribution of sovereignty. He emphasized the politics of self-interest, economic and political. In Warren's account such motives played no conspicuous part. For her the issues were exclusively ideological, a struggle between republicans and monarchists.

There is in Warren's analysis a deceptive simplicity calculated to discredit the Federalists. She skillfully cast her account in the form of a moral drama in which true republicans are pitted against thinly disguised monarchists. Not that she ignored the difficult economic problems that plagued the nation, but she cited them only to illustrate that the question of reorganizing the national government had become inescapable. When it came to determining what form the central authority should take, the issue was for her exclusively ideological. Just as the Revolution had been a struggle between republican America and monarchist England, "soon after the organization of the new Constitution a struggle began to take place between monarchists and republicans. . . ."[14] The insinuation of an ideological coup d'etat is unmistakable.

By monarchism Warren meant political and social practices "that wore the appearance of regal forms and institutions." She singled out the members of the Society of Cincinnatus, who "panted for peerages in the shade of retirement," "ambassadors abroad, who had adopted a fondness for nominal distinctions, members of congress and of state legislatures, and many others who had acquired a taste for the external superiority that wealth and titles bestow. . . ." These men "threatened the annihilation of the darling opinion, that the whole sovereignty in the republican system is in the people. . . ." Standing against the monarchists were the general body of citizens who were committed to "the ideals of a free and equal participation in the privileges of a pure and genuine republicanism." They objected to "being precipitated, without due consideration," into "a system that might bind them and their posterity in the chains of despotism. . . ."[15]

Warren directed her heaviest fire at John Adams. His fall from grace had occurred during his residence in England, where he "became so enamored with the British constitution, and the government, manners, and laws of the nation, that a partiality for monarchy appeared, which was inconsistent with his former professions of republicanism."[16] That explanation of Adams' apostasy illustrates a fundamental weakness in Warren's analysis. Her implicit assumption was that a direct correspondence exists between what men believe and how they behave; but she offered no adequate explanation of why particular men believed and acted as they did. In Adams' case she could find no other rationale than his four year residence in England. A long-standing friendship did not prevent Warren from denouncing him as a monarchist. The reverence in which Washington was held probably prevented her from blaming him for the sins of the Federalists, but she did criticize his inaction while the monarchist element organized a party to control the government and introduced projects, such as Hamilton's funding system and Jay's Treaty, that were inimical to republicanism. Warren would not go so far as to accuse Washington of being a monarchist, but she attacked him for not checking "the aspiring ambition of some of his former associates."[17]

At first glance Warren's strictures against Adams and her oblique criticism of Washington give her *History* the appearance of a party tract. She did, after all, use the familiar Republican device of exposing the Federalists as monarchists who "creep under the mantle of federalism."[18] Yet her distaste for political parties in general kept her work from degenerating into overtly partisan propaganda. "Both history and experience have proved, that when party feuds have thus divided a nation, urbanity and benevolence are laid aside; and, influenced by the most malignant and corrupt passions, [men] lose sight of the sacred obligations of virtue, until there appears little difference in the ferocious spirits of men in the most refined and civilized society, or among the rude and barbarous hordes of the wilderness."[19] Warren's purpose was to discredit the Federalist party. But because she feared factional politics she did so by indirection, attacking individuals and policies rather than groups or organizations. She did not mention the parties by name or identify them with any particular class, section, or state, let alone openly endorse the Republican party. She did not even spell out the erstwhile opposition's views or policies; and Jefferson's name is conspicuous for its absence.[20]

Warren's belief that the new government was a threat to liberty did not deter her from praising the Constitution extravagantly. "Perhaps genius has never devised a system more congenial to their wishes, or better adapted to the condition of man, than the American Constitution. . . . On the principles of republicanism was this condition founded; on these it must stand."[21] Many of her doubts had been relieved by the passage of the Bill of Rights. But Warren was also an ardent nationalist, and by the time she published her *History* (1805) the Constitution had become the symbol as well as the reality of union. By then, too, the national government was in the hands of men she trusted. One suspects that the end results of the first fifteen years of the federal system, especially the election and re-election of Jefferson, eased her fears.

It is not surprising, therefore, that Warren advanced an ambiguous history of the Constitution, impugning the motives of its authors without repudiating the document. But if men who held views inimical to liberty seduced the nation into accepting a dangerous scheme of government, how could the Constitution be founded "on the principles of republicanism?" Warren offered no answer except to intimate that the Bill of Rights had set things right and that "the United States of America . . . may perhaps be possessed of more materials that promise success than have ever fallen to the lot of any other nation."[22] The republicanism of the American character had made for the successful Revolution. Fighting a war and organizing a nation led to a declension in republican morality, but the people still possessed the virtue to defend their liberties. Here was an optimistic assessment for a latter day Puritan who believed that "perfection in government is not to be expected from so imperfect a creature as man."[23]

Clearly Warren used historical narrative to discredit Federalists. Talented, self-confident, even egocentric, she had always been exceedingly outspoken. The author of plays, essays, and poems, she was a peer in the inner councils of Massachusetts Revolutionary leaders and had never flinched from powerful adversaries. In a series of plays during the 1770s she had attacked the British government and Governor Thomas Hutchinson with biting satire.[24] Later she and her husband became vocal partisans of Jefferson in their Federalist state. Yet when it came to writing history Warren displayed an uncharacteristic restraint. Though it was completed by 1791, she laid her work aside because, as she explained to a friend, "the virulence of party spirit shuts up the avenues of just information. Until *truth* has a chance for fair play, the annalist . . . may as well seclude her observations to the cabinet."[25] She even apologized for usurping the male prerogative of writing history: "It is true" that "there are certain appropriate duties assigned to each sex; and doubtless it is the more peculiar province of masculine strength . . . to describe the blood-stained field, and relate the story of slaughtered armies."[26] Given her background, achievements, and outspokenness (no other historian of the period dared criticize the "Great Washington"), one wonders why she wrote in so circumscribed and apologetic a manner.

Though they appear unrelated, there is an important connection between the restrained tone of Warren's *History* and the sexual apology. Despite her active public life, she seemed determined to discredit Mary Wollstonecraft — the most radical feminist of the day — and promote a model of soft, retiring, malleable American womanhood: "our weak and timid sex is generally but the echo of the other and like some pliant piece of clock-work the springs of our souls move slow or more rapid just as hope, fear, or fortitude give motion to the conducting wires, that govern all our actions. . . ." Warren often advised women to devote themselves to the softer duties of the hearth; these, not political matters, were the patriotic obligations of "our febler [*sic*] sex."[27] Her advice was radically at odds with her conduct.

This disparity, of which she was keenly aware, may provide its own key. It was a common device of nineteenth century female writers that she used in acknowledging that a woman was not properly an historian, politician, or even poet.[28] Ostensibly, her literary activities were born of mere chance circumstances; with no special skill or vocation, she wrote "for the amusement of solidtude, at a period when every active member of society was engaged, either in the field, or the cabinet, to resist the strong hand of foreign domination." Her "trembling heart . . . recoiled at the magnitude of the undertaking. . . ." But since "every manly arm was occupied" in the popular defense and unavailable for literary labors, it was her patriotic obligation to record "the new and unexperienced events exhibited in a land previously blessed with peace, liberty, simplicity, and virtue."[29]

Perhaps Warren was jealous of her position as first among women. Perhaps as a member of the prominent Otis and Warren families she drew back from disturbing the established social order.[30] Despite her avowed political radicalism, she recoiled from taking stands that might disturb social relationships. When Abigail Adams suggested petitioning Congress to liberalize common-law restrictions on married women, she disapproved. Whatever her personal reasons, Warren's strategy reflected a concern common to historians of her generation. Like them she felt compelled to emphasize what Americans had in common and minimize or ignore what divided them. The intent was not only to close political ranks; it reflected a larger fear that the stability of the union was in jeopardy. She dedicated her *History* to helping cement "a union of interests and affection."

Warren was reluctant to arouse antagonisms that might endanger the nation's and the society's fragile cohesiveness. As a woman in the male world of politics and letters, she implicitly felt that no public figure of either sex could afford to be too critical of a weak and embryonic new nation or to openly challenge the existing order in families. The Revolution and nation-building had been difficult and emotional experiences, and even with Jefferson in power success was not assured. There was, too, an ever-present sense of foreign danger in a world dominated by the hostilities of maritime-imperial England and Continental-imperial Napoleonic France. For a former colonial people there was always the nagging fear that the former metropolis would attempt to regain its ascendancy. Moreover, Whig political theory taught that republics were particularly vulnerable to foreign influence. In this situation the historian must allay internal political turmoil and promote a unified national morale. Like overtly partisan political history, a partisan sexual commentary would be disruptive. A woman of the established order, Mercy Warren doubtless believed that more would be lost than gained by a public display of partisanship on either count. For a woman on the inside, who had gained the substance if not the recognition of equality, national cohesion took precedence over the more "provincial" interests of the Republican party or the female sex.

Where Warren stressed moral issues and had only a passing interest in practical politics, John Marshall made no such distinctions. His *Life of Washington* (1804-07) is less a biography than a general history of the United States, a hardheaded though partisan assessment of the early years of the national government. It is a work of considerable importance for Marshall's interpretations, and apart from his judicial opinions it is the best source for his political and legal philosophy.[31] The theory of history and politics that emerges from his writings rests on the belief that the past could be used to demonstrate the superiority of practical experience over abstract reasoning. The success or failure of a public policy must be judged by its ability to meet the demands of a given situation. For example, in discussing the Sedition Acts he did not deny their constitutionality, but he attacked them as foolish and inflammatory; instead of encouraging national unity they undermined it. "I should have opposed them," he told the voters in the district where he was running for Congress, "Because I think them useless; and because they are calculated to create unnecessary discontents and jealousies at a time when our very existence as a nation may depend on our union."[32]

In assessing Washington, Marshall never failed to mention his superior judgement; but he placed particular emphasis on his ability to win popular support and inspire public trust. Marshall praised the policies of the first Federalist administration because they worked, not because they fit a particular philosophy. Even his championing of the Constitution was not simply out of patriotism; he gave to it and to the Union neither the aura of a mystique nor an unquestioning loyalty, but a practical adherence based on its success and popularity. Marshall sought to demonstrate that only a strong national government could serve the nation's interests and that Washington's administration had faithfully provided this service.

Marshall's belief in the historical superiority of experience over abstract reasoning has much in common with the ideas of Edmund Burke. It is difficult to say whether he was directly influenced by Burke. On more than one occasion he expressed admiration for him, and he wholly subscribed to the Burkean notion that "the science of constructing a commonwealth, or renovating it, or reforming it, is like every other experimental science, not to be taught *a priori*."[33] Like Burke, he believed that political values should be judged in their relation to the historical community, and he would have heartily agreed that the British Constitution was not the product of speculative sagacity. Marshall was always suspicious of abstract schemes of government, such as John Locke's Fundamental Constitutions of Carolina. Though he regarded the Federal Constitution as the work of a handful of wise individuals, their wisdom lay in having derived a formula organically out of the historical community, one suited to the character of the American people.

Burke's ideas probably represented little more to Marshall than confirmation of a perspective he had already acquired from his personal experience, most notably during the Revolutionary War. "I partook largely of the sufferings and feelings of the army, and brought with me into civil life an ardent devotion to its interests."[34] His account of the war emphasized the hardships and the accomplishments of the Continental Army. In a work that is, as literature, a monument to dullness, the author's passion broke the bonds of literary rigidity only when he described the plight of the men in the field.[35] They are the real heroes of the Revolution. Despite inadequate pay and provisions the army persevered; only their devotion and Washington's leadership averted disaster and brought triumph.

In politics Marshall's views were colored by his wartime experience.

> My immediate entrance into the state legislature [he wrote in his autobiography] opened to my view the causes which had been chiefly instrumental in augmenting those sufferings, and the general tendency of state politics convinced me that no safe and permanent remedy could be found but in a more efficient and better organized general government. The questions, too, which were perpetually recurring in the state legislatures, and which brought annually into doubt principles which I thought most sound, . . . gave a high value in my estimation to that article in the constitution which imposes restrictions on the state.[36]

It is not surprising that he deplored the Confederation government's inability to meet pressing problems. Like every American historian, he treated the 1780s as a critical period in which the survival of the nation hung in the balance. Without an adequate national authority the disinterested patriotism characteristic of the early days of the war disintegrated and Americans retreated rapidly into parochial loyalties and private concerns. Everywhere strong local interests opposed the delegation of important powers to the national government and advocated measures favorable to debtors. A process of "national degradation had already commenced," and the republican character of society could be preserved only by a government invested with powers adequate to its obligations.[37]

Having set the stage, Marshall turned to an analysis of how a weak government was transformed into an effective national authority. Because he regarded the Constitution as predetermined — the only possible route to national salvation — Marshall accorded the Philadelphia convention only the most cursory treatment. Instead he was preoccupied with the reasoning behind the debates over the Constitution. Like Ramsay, Marshall identified the primary issue as a conflict over the proper distribution of sovereignty. Wedded to the ideal of local authority were "a numerous class of honest men . . . , many of whom possessed no inconsiderable share of intelligence" but lacked the foresight to envision a government that was republican and yet exercised powers across state boundary lines. Operating on the supposition "that an opposition of interests existed between different parts of the continent," they "could not consider" the national legislature "as safely representing the people" unless it consisted of "a majority from their particular state."[38] Although Marshall did not question the sincerity of their opposition, he conveyed no doubt concerning the quality of their judgement. Their error lay in an inability to transcend parochial interests or learn from experience. By contrast, the supporters of a strong national government were "enlightened individuals" who, like Marshall, had profited from "the repeated lessons of a severe and instructive experience."

> Men of enlarged and liberal minds who, in the imbecility of a general government, by which alone the capacities of the nation could be efficaciously exerted, could discern the imbecility of the nation itself; who, viewing the situation of the world, could perceive the dangers to which these young republics were exposed, if not held together by a cement capable of preserving a beneficial connexion; who felt a full value of national honour, and the full obligation of national faith . . . the officers of the army, whose local prejudices had been weakened by associating with each other, and whose experience had furnished lessons on the inefficacy of requisitions which were not soon to be forgotten, threw their weight almost universally into the same scale.[39]

To this point Marshall's account differed from Ramsay's only in emphasis, the latter's version being cast in more muted tones. They parted company in their assessments of the divisiveness of the process of ratification. Ramsay conceded that "almost every passion which could agitate the human breast, interested States and individuals for and against adoption. . . ." Yet, with his bent for minimizing conflict he implied (without explicitly stating) that the great majority of Americans either supported or acquiesced in ratification. Marshall made no effort to mask deep divisions of opinion. "Indeed, it is scarcely to be doubted," he admitted, "that, in some of the adopting states, a majority . . . were in the opposition." The Constitution was nevertheless ratified only because of the skill of its advocates, for "had the influence of character been removed, the intrinsic merits of the instrument would not have secured its adoption." For Ramsay ratification signalled the end of the battle and "was celebrated in most of the capitals of the States with elegant processions, which far exceeded any thing of the kind ever before exhibited in America." In Marshall's view the battle only served to increase bitterness. "The intensity of the debate over ratification had a necessary tendency to embitter the dispositions of the vanquished, and to fix more deeply, in many bosoms, their prejudices against a plan of government, in opposition to which all their passions were enlisted."[40]

As his account suggests, political divisiveness was a major theme of Marshall's history. All the more remarkable, then, was the success of the new government. He urged the reader "to glance his eye at the situation of the United States in 1797, and to contrast it with their conditions in 1788." In the space of eight years "the authority of the government was firmly established," the agricultural and commercial wealth of the nation had risen "beyond all former example," and "the numerous tribes of warlike Indians . . . had been taught, by arms and by justice, to respect the United States, and to continue in peace. . . ." In foreign affairs the administration could claim some notable achievements, especially normalization of relations with Great Britain, "free navigation of the Mississippi," "the use of New Orleans as a place of deposit," and access to the Mediterranean for American vessels. The only cloud was relations with France, but Marshall supported Washington in arguing that "these discontents" could have been avoided only by "surrendering the real independence of the nation. . . ." Not "that this beneficial change in the affairs of America is to be ascribed exclusively to the wisdom which guided the national councils;" but "their successful operation was facilitated . . . by the system which was adopted. . . ."[41] However, Marshall left little doubt that the system would not have functioned so well as it had without "the wisdom" of Washington and his advisors.

The *Life of Washington* is party history. The Constitution had become the symbol as well as the substance of the Union. By identifying the Federalists as the party of the Constitution and arguing that the success of the government depended upon the implementation of their policies, it followed that opposition to those policies threatened the survival of the Union. Marshall went so far as to label the Republicans the "party opposed to the constitution." Perhaps it was fear of that stigma that led Mercy Warren into the logical gymnastics of praising the Constitution while criticizing its authors. Marshall's strategy of placing Washington above party was designed to identify the President and his Federalist supporters with national, supra-partisan interests. What especially irritated Republicans was the implied connection between the combatants to the controversies of the 1780s and the political parties of the 1790s. Marshall's portrayal suggested that one group stood for viable national authority and the honest payment of debts, while the defenders of states rights were the same people who had stood for repudiation of debts and against effective national government. "In describing the first by their views and motives," Jefferson complained, "he implies an opposition to those motives in their opponents which is totally untrue."[42]

Still, the *Life of Washington* was much more than narrow party history. Although Marshall, with Warren, alone used history as a partisan weapon, he adopted a practical tone which served to soften his bias. In some ways Marshall was unique among the historians of the Revolutionary generation. He exhibited little interest in the larger sweep of history, paying no more than lip service to the American past as the grand culmination, or grand beginning, of an epoch of western history. Unlike his fellows, he did not invoke Providence to demonstrate that American history was part of a cosmic design for the future improvement of mankind. For Marshall the only question worthy of extended consideration was the Union and the effectiveness of the government designed to preserve it. Consequently, his partisanship was pragmatic in tone and appearance — an effect that gained from dullness — rather than heatedly ideological. Indeed, he did not produce an explicitly identifiable Federalist philosophy of history or government. He avoided broad philosophical generalizations, limiting himself to a pragmatic espousal of the specific policies of Washington's government. The ultimate test of their worth was less a matter of a philosophy of government than of success in meeting the nation's needs. Conversely, if his bias led him to accuse the Republicans of weakening the government by their opposition to the administration's economic policies and by their devotion to France, their failure lay in an inability to learn from experience, not just from differences in philosophical perspective.[43]

The personifications of opposing viewpoints were, as to so many others, Thomas Jefferson and Alexander Hamilton. Although he favored Hamilton, Marshall honored his cousin Jefferson, who had deservedly "been placed by Americans amongst the most eminent of her citizens, and had long been classed by the President with those who were most capable of serving the nation." Each possessed unquestionable talent, but they differed "in the original structure of their minds, and, in some measure, in the situations in which they had been placed."[44] It was to this "difference" in their "situations" that Marshall attributed their differing views.

Through personal experience Hamilton had learned that the nation's survival depended upon the creation and maintenance of a strong unified government. Service in the army brought "perpetually before his eyes . . . the danger to which the independence of his country was exposed from the imbecility of the government." In like measure, his years in the Congress 'forcibly directed his attention" to "the loss in the government's" reputation and the "sacrifice of its best interests." Like others with similar experiences, including Marshall himself, Hamilton understood "the mischiefs produced by the absolute sovereignty of the states, and by the control which they were enabled and disposed separately to exercise over every measure of general concern . . . , which he, probably, believed was to be the more dreaded, because the habits and feelings of the American people were calculated to inspire state, rather than national prepossessions." Hamilton's political philosophy, his struggles for the Constitution, his policies as Secretary of the Treasury, were all founded on a conviction "that American liberty and happiness had more to fear from the encroachments of the great states, than from those of the general government."[45]

In contrast, Jefferson always seemed to be in the wrong place. He had not served in the army, and he "had retired from Congress" in favor of the governorship of Virginia "before the depreciation of the currency had produced an entire dependence of the general on the local governments. . . ." At the close of the war he was "employed on a mission to the court of Versailles." Absent from the country at a critical juncture, "he did not feel so sensibly, as those who had continued in the United States, the necessity of the new Constitution." Jefferson "seems to have entertained no apprehension from the debility of the government; no jealousy of the state sovereignties; and no suspicion of their encroachments." Rather, "all his precautions were used to check and limit the exercise of the powers vested in the government of the United States, especially the executive department."[46]

Thus, in the careers of Hamilton and Jefferson, Marshall symbolized the dynamic of party conflict in the early national period. The issue was posed less as a contest over philosophical predilection than a perception of practical problems, less a matter of class, economic, or sectional division than of individual experience.

There is in the histories of Marshall and Warren a sense of restraint that can only be understood in the context of the politics of history in Revolutionary America. If they alone used history for partisan purposes, they did so with restraint. Like their fellows, neither argued that the divisions in American society had resulted from deep-seated economic, class, ethnic, or sectional differences. At a time when much of the nation's press was violently political, American historians restrained their partisanship. Even John Daly Burk and James T. Callender, who both had escaped punishment for seditious libel under the Sedition Act by fleeing to Virginia and England respectively, set aside overt partisanship in their histories.[47] Perhaps they regarded historical writing as a permanent record of national unity that transcended the temporary divisions of contemporary politics. History as a record of the national consensus provided a useful vehicle for demonstrating to Americans and Europeans that the United States possessed the unity essential to the

maintenance of a republican society. Consequently, neither Marshall and
Warren nor their colleagues wrote party history in the English tradition.
Unlike the Whigs and Tories, they did not use the whole of American
history to prove the correctness of their party's philosophy. Both were
committed to republican government and both expressed that republicanism so vaguely that it is difficult to tie it to a party program.

Marshall's principles were implied in his characterization of
Washington's beliefs.

> In speculation, he was a real republican, devoted to the
> constitution of his country, and to that system of equal political
> rights on which it is founded. But between a balanced republic
> and a democracy, the difference is like that between order and
> chaos. Real liberty, he thought, was to be preserved, only by
> preserving the authority of government. Scarcely did society
> present two characters which, in his opinion. less resembled each
> other, than a patriot and a demagogue.

There is a tinge of aristocratic republicanism in this vision. Yet Marshall
clearly supported popular representative government, although one in
which the desires of ordinary citizens were filtered by representation and
checked by a balanced government with a division of powers. Like other
historians, he undoubtedly assumed that in practice such difficulties as
time away from home and little or no pay would limit public office to
the well- to-do and better educated. In this context, his portrayal of
Washington as a man of moderation with a practical concern for the
interests of the whole community was as well suited to a popular
republic based on an assumed equality as to a society based on the
activities and prerogatives of superior men. In Marshall's view the
American experience and character proved that no other system was
practicable in the United States. Washington represented the ideal
republican leader, one who by placing the public interest above
popularity and personal power afforded "the highest example of
moderation and patriotism."[48]

Like Marshall, Warren never defined precisely what she meant
by a republican society. She did, however, lay down a number of
precepts, such as sovereignty of the people, the protection of personal
liberty, private property, and freedom of conscience, and the separation
of powers.[49] With these maxims Marshall was in full accord; there is
nothing in his history to suggest that he questioned popular sovereignty
as the foundation of government. His criticism of democracy rested on
what he regarded as the Republicans' sacrifice of the ideal of leadership

to demagoguery. The final arbiter in the contest was popular consent. Marshall disparaged the Republicans as the "party that called itself The People." Though at times they might gain the upper hand he preferred to find their true calling in their support of Washington.

The division between Warren and Marshall was predominantly over specific policies and individual motives. So far as their histories are a gauge of party differences, they indicate the Federalists' preoccupation with devising an instrument to meet practical problems and the Republicans' concern for safeguards against the power generated by that instrumentality. But these differences are minor compared to a common bias in favor of the national government as the expression of American nationality. Like their colleagues, they depicted a self-defeating parochialism under the Confederation and a revival of nationalism under the Constitution. Standing back from the partisanship of the 1790s, their conceptions of a republican society, at least as expressed in their histories, were not far apart. If Marshall had not been a prominent Federalist and Warren a known Republican, or if neither had dealt with the years after 1789, it would have been difficult to discover marked differences between them. In this they were characteristic of their fellow scholars; allegiance to national unity tended to minimize differences even among the most partisan of the historians.

# IX. The Revolutionary Generation and After

As in Europe, interest in history increased in the American colonies as the eighteenth century progressed. Newspapers, magazines and almanacs published an increasing number of historical items. American authors shared only incidentally in the boom. Before the Revolution the most widely read historical works were British and European; some were popular enough to be reprinted in the colonies.[1] Colonials preferred the best that Europe had to offer because their own writers seldom provided the excitement of great men, grand events and exotic places, and books by transatlantic authors were a cultural bridge to the cosmopolitan world. Form often counted for as much as thought, and American men of letters could not compare with such accomplished stylists as Gibbon, Hume, Voltaire and Robertson.

The imbalance in demand for works of European and American writers continued after the Revolution. The hope that the establishment of a republican society would stimulate a renaissance of letters proved unfounded. Few historians wrote history for profit, at least not after the disappointment of their first publication. Little writing of any kind was profitable to American authors: the buying public was small, printing expensive, and copyright laws ineffective. When David Ramsay published *The History of the Revolution of South Carolina* (1785) he expected financial success, believing the nationalism of the age would acclaim a native product. But Ramsay was severely disappointed. Despite critical acclaim he sold no more than 825 copies and lost over $1,500. Anticipated profits from abroad never materialized. In England publication was aborted because the publisher feared possible suits by the Crown and insisted on revisions; in France a translation fared poorly, clearing only $133.33.[2]

The absence of copyright agreements usually aborted foreign profits, not to mention the threat of pirated foreign versions being shipped to the United States to compete with American editions. Authors were expected to bear the costs of publication. and most lost money. Even the biography of Washington by the prominent John Marshall sorely disappointed the debt-ridden Chief Justice. The only substantial financial success of the period was Mason Locke Weems' *Life of George Washington* (1800). Furthermore, there was a dearth of good libraries, archival collections, and printed records. And since the study and writing of history was the private affair of learned men, not an academic discipline, they had to subsidize their own research. For all but a few this meant historical scholarship had to be secondary to the more pressing concerns of earning a living. It is a measure of their commitment that a number of historians continued to write and publish after losing money. Though in debt and troubled by the needs of a growing family, Ramsay spent more than thirty years publishing a series of historical works.[3]

The impact of the Revolutionary generation on American historiography cannot be measured simply in terms of sales. It did not depend solely upon professional appeal, but more upon the appeal of the ideas to the general and intellectual public. Many Americans could not read; among those that did possess rudimentary reading skills, few were regular readers of books. But in the libraries, public and private, that served the small audience, the histories won a prominent place. The early nineteenth century was the golden age of the social library; it has been estimated that in 1803 there were a hundred library societies in Massachusetts alone. Invariably Jeremy Belknap, David Ramsay, and to a lesser extent their colleagues found their way into these collections. *The Farmer's Almanac* of 1793 recommended "as books worthy of the perusal of every American — Ramsay's *History of the Revolution;* Morse's *Geography;* and Belknap's *History of New Hampshire.*" Two decades later the *Almanac* continued to proclaim it "all important that every man should know the history and geography of his own country," adding Williams's *History of Vermont* and Marshall's *Life of Washington* to its list.[4]

Many Americans learned their history through newspapers and magazines. The early publications of the Massachusetts Historical Society, for instance, appeared in the weekly *American Apollo,* the Massachusetts *Spy* serialized William Gordon's *History of American Independence,* and the *Columbian Magazine* printed Ramsay's *History of the Revolution* and Belknap's "American Plutarch," which he later expanded into an *American Biography* (1794-98). Through these media the Revolutionary generation's view of history affected the present and future. The school books of the early decades of the Republic, which established the pattern for those to follow, echoed the attitudes of the first national generation.[5] Works like John M'Culloch's *Concise History of the United States* (1795) and Noah Webster's *Elements of Useful Knowledge* (1804) were written specifically as school texts. Finally, in important ways the works of later historians, although different in spirit and emphasis, transmitted much of the outlook articulated during the years from 1784 to the 1820s.

Aside from their future influence, the Revolutionary generation's writings won an important place in American historiography. Although their primary interest is as an unconscious reflection of society, they are also of independent and continuing interest on their own terms. Despite their shortcomings they compose a respectable body of literature that includes works of enduring value. Belknap's *History of New Hampshire* (1784-92), Ramsay's *History of the Revolution* (1789) and Williams' *History of Vermont* (1794) can still be profitably read. Each made an important contribution.

Belknap's *New Hampshire* was a work of original scholarship by a conscious literary craftsman. A pioneer collector of historical materials and the founder of the nation's oldest historical society, he was more than an archivist. He strove to clothe his facts and ideas with style and form. Apart from the skillful manner in which he handled the standard themes of the period, Belknap wrote a work rich in the details of frontier life. What made his *New Hampshire* a readable, even an exciting book was the ability to capture a quality of first-handedness in his treatment of Indian wars, tales of captivity, the simple heroism of taming a rude frontier. The first American after the Revolution to publish a major historical work, his *New Hampshire* was welcomed by an intellectual community eager for evidence of a cultural renaissance. But Belknap also won wide acclaim outside the United States. Brissot de Warville, in his *New Travels in the United States* (1792), cited "the precious *History of New Hampshire* as an instance of American genius." From Hamburg the German historian Christopher O. Ebeling wrote Belknap that "your excellent *History of New Hampshire* meets with due applause in Germany. . . . In the Gottingen Review . . . it has been reviewed with great applause, as well on account of the materials as the true elegance of historical style." Some years later Alexis de Tocqueville, in his effort to find out what was an American, relied on Belknap's insights.[6]

While Belknap demonstrated the possibilities of primary historical research, Ramsay was less an original scholar than a collector of ideas. In his *History of South Carolina* (1809), the most original of his many histories, he still relied heavily on the works of Alexander Hewatt and George Chalmers, even though they were both Loyalists. Ramsay's achievement lay primarily in an ability to bring into sharp focus and synthesize the major themes that would dominate the writings of the Revolutionary generation. His basic ideas were not novel, but never before had they been developed systematically with such clarity and logic. The American reading public found his approach to history to its tastes. He expressed a set of ideas about American history in general and the Revolution in particular that were common currency in the United States. But he expressed them for the first time in the form of a well-reasoned and documented historical narrative: a work that was suitably pro-American, yet judicious in its treatment of Britain, that made a strong case for American uniqueness while maintaining the ideal of the United States as a model for the world.

While he was a successful popularizer, Ramsay studied the Revolution with a remarkably detached spirit. Despite his commitment to a special historical truth, he looked at diverse men and events in a sympathetic manner. He was far less impassioned than many combatants who took up their pens in later generations. At the same time Ramsay made a convincing and ably written case for the existence of a common national character that suited the nation's republican institutions and confirmed the necessity and desirability of union. As a result he became the nation's favorite historian, and his *History of the American Revolution* the most influential work of the period. From 1789 to 1865 it went through six American editions, including a serialized version in the *Columbian Magazine*, as well as two English, one Irish, two French, and one Dutch edition, and received generally favorable reviews.[7] Ramsay's facts may not be impeccable, but his judgements are sensible and his evaluation of causation surprisingly perceptive and even penetrating.

It is impossible to say whether Williams was one of Belknap and Ramsay's wide circle of friends, correspondents and collaborators, but they admired his *History of Vermont*. Lacking Belknap's literary craftsmanship or Ramsay's instinct for popularizing ideas, Williams' *Vermont* nevertheless has a magisterial quality of its own. Montesquieu would no doubt have appreciated him, for no American of the time more skillfully pursued the relationship between the physical environment and human society. Where Belknap's artistry lay in personalizing the human drama in the development of a frontier community, Williams' achievement was his demonstration that the distinctive character of American society could be attributed to the interplay of human nature and a unique environment. Yet, as he pursued this theme he argued for the United States as a model to the world. Building on the commonplace assumption of the constancy of human nature, he observed that the same state of society, anywhere and at any time, would produce the same forms of government, manners, customs, habits, and pursuits.

Belknap, Ramsay and Williams were the ablest practitioners of their generation. Their colleagues were equally committed but more uneven in the quality of their work. Mercy Warren's *History* suffered from too many digressions and prose that is often rhetorical and at other times flat. John Marshall's *Life of Washington* is written in a turgid style and its central figure appears wooden and lifeless. Benjamin Trumbull's general history is an artificial attempt to merge an account of the colonies into a single chronological narrative. Despite important insights, Edmund Randolph's *History of Virginia* is an incomplete, sometimes poorly written account distorted by a disproportionate emphasis on the colony's first seventeen years. John Daly Burk's history of the Old Dominion suffers from an unconvincing effort to prove that the colony resisted every attempt by the British government to encroach on local rights.

Collectively, however, their record is impressive. Given the problems of research and publication, their output was a considerable accomplishment. Men and women of differing political and sectional loyalties thought and acted in sympathy to write a national history. A generation of American historians agreed on a basic approach to the American past, differing only in emphasis and the routes they chose. Individual attitudes and ambitions gave a certain variety; political differences caused some difficulties and sectional jealousies more, but the major consensus obscured if it did not entirely eliminate disagreements. Together these historians laid the basis of a national history.

It is not difficult to explain the near unanimity among this varied group. Nationalism was the strongest force binding Americans of their generation together. It held those in conflict on speaking terms, let alone helping to overcome or minimize differences. Behind the histories of Ramsay, Warren, Marshall, Belknap, Randolph, James Sullivan, Noah Webster, Ebenezer Hazard, George R. Minot and others lies the conviction that the historian should be a man of affairs carrying out a patriotic duty to serve the national interest. Before writing a line of history nearly every one of these writers had won a modest place in the political world. As men and women of affairs they could not help but be influenced by events at home and abroad. The political turmoil triggered by Hamilton's financial program and the disputes with Great Britain and Revolutionary France, which led to the formation of political parties and sometimes domestic disorder, were regarded by them as a threat to the stability and the existence of the republic.

That historians of varying backgrounds and perspectives would define the meaning of these events in a uniform manner can best be explained by their common acceptance of the dominant republican ideology. From this viewpoint they perceived a pattern menacing to the life of the republic. The Revolutionary generation viewed the world through the lens of political ideology and found meaning in its

experience from the perspective of republican theory. This emerges
clearly from the pamphlet literature of the 1760s and 1770s, the debates
in the new states and over the Federal Constitution, and the public and
private writings of historians. Historians may have differed on the
specifics of republican theory, although their deliberate avoidance of
particulars make this difficult to ascertain; but they shared a common
body of assumptions about republican society and about the problems
involved in its establishment, maintenance and survival. Theory taught
that republics were frail structures vulnerable to internal decay, external
threat, and subversion. No wonder historians devoted so much space to
demonstrating that by virtue of environment and heritage Americans
possessed the qualities of character to maintain a republic. In John
M'Culloch's words, "the colonies from their first settlement, were
nurseries of freemen. The inhabitants were devoted to liberty, and grew
up in an acquaintance with, and attachment to their rights."[8]
Fortunately, observed James Sullivan, "the freedom of thinking, with
which our ancestors began to cultivate society . . . grew with their
growth."[9]

Few notions were more widely held by the Revolutionary
generation than the belief that faction, the internal splintering of society
into selfish and competing political groups, was the chief enemy of
republican society.[10] The near if not complete obscurity of historians
about politics in the 1790s, the aggressive insistence on the political
unity of the colonial and revolutionary periods, and the oft-stated repug-
nance for factionalism testify to a concern with the threat faction posed
to the life of the republic. This fear influenced Ramsay to explain
that in his *History of the United States* (1816-17) he had "lightly passed
over the squabbles in Congress but dwelled on the happy effects of a
good government wisely administered. . . . I write not for a party but
for posterity."[11]

An aspect of the problem of faction in the historian's lexicon of
fears was the divisiveness of sectional and state loyalties, for politics to a
considerable extent reflected those loyalties and interests. Contained in
the introductions to many histories and in the surviving correspondence
between historians is a constant refrain: their writing must bring
Americans of all classes and sections together, for nothing, to quote again
from John Quincy Adams, "is so likely to have a decisive influence as
historical works, honestly and judiciously executed."[12] Since American
historians regarded their writings as weapons in the struggle to unite the
nation, it is not surprising that they tended to ignore or gloss over local
and sectional differences, almost to the point of losing sight altogether of
the diversity of American life. They treated the Revolution not as a

sudden, cataclysmic event but as a gradual, natural, organic development out of a common past. Even local historians focused on a state or section as a microcosm of national development rather than as a distinct entity. Social and economic differences between locales, such as in labor systems, farming methods, commerce, urbanization, and social structure received little or no attention.

The sources of the Revolutionary author's historical views were not new, although they refashioned them to suit their own needs. Most conspicuous was the New England heritage, the source of a sense of mission and example, a conviction that the founders of the colonies had come to the New World with the conscious goal of establishing a society based on civil and religious liberty. New England historiography also provided a factual basis for one of the central themes: early America as a battleground between arbitrary British authority and colonial devotion to liberty. These basic themes were modified, secularized and nationalized to fit the needs of a new identity.

Equally influential were the ideas and attitudes of Enlightenment rationalism, the rationalism of both liberal reform and enlightened conservatism. Only infrequently did American historians acknowledge their debt to specific authors, but from style, phraseology, and implicit philosophic assumptions the influence of British and Continental writers can be inferred. Phrases from David Hume, William Robertson, and Montesquieu, to name three of the most famous, recur regularly. The similarities are familiar: the constancy of human nature, the universality of human experience, the existence of general laws that order the histories of every society, history as a phase of philosophic inquiry. Enlightenment historians and philosophers provided a general theoretical framework, with the works of English Whigs being of special importance. Whig theoreticians, especially as their ideas were filtered through American writers of the Revolutionary era, contributed a fundamental view of politics and conflict.[13] They viewed history as an eternal conflict between government and people. Americans reversed that perspective to demonstrate that the historical cycle had been broken with the creation of a harmonious society.

This cluster of ideas, important as it was, did not compose a coherent intellectual pattern; there were incongruities and contradictions. What brought the strands of Puritan, Whig, and Enlightenment historiography together and wove them into a coherent fabric was the conviction that the entire span of American history revealed a basic unity. That conviction determined the configuration of the works, the themes they emphasized and those they ignored or muffled. So strong was the theme of unity that even writers not usually given to hyperbole lost control of their pens when they discussed national feelings. Ramsay, for example, could write that "the differences among nations are not so much owing to nature as to education and circumstances," but his *History* gave the impression that national unity had been predetermined by nature and God. Hugh Williamson, first of all a naturalist, was not a simple environmental determinist, but in his eagerness to demonstrate an inherent unity he argued that the temperate American climate was a unifying influence: "There is, and ever will be, in America, a much greater similarity of form and complexion, among the human race, than is to be found upon the other continents. That similarity may produce a more friendly intercourse and general communication of sentiment."[14]

The related themes of national unity and uniqueness helped to create a genre new to America and to the Western world, a mode characterized by the subjugation of history to the service of the nation-state. There is a nationalistic bias that the philosophes would no doubt have found distasteful: an intimation that the unique national past required a special kind of history which only an American could properly write. A European, wrote Ezra Stiles, cannot "do justice to the history of the American provinces."[15] The new historical writing was new to the extent that it was directed primarily at establishing a national identity. It was not the historiography of an elite, or class, or movement for reform, but the secular ideology of a whole nation. The Revolutionary historians differed in crucial ways, then, from Enlightenment historiography, most notably in the way they refashioned commonplace eighteenth century assumptions to emphasize the distinctive qualities of American society.

Religious attitudes illustrate the different perspectives of American and European historians and the effects of national bias. Voltaire and Hume vented their antagonism toward church and religion, but most American historians did not reject their Christian past nor fully embrace Enlightenment skepticism. Many began their careers as clergymen (Belknap, Eliot, Backus, Morse, Holmes, Parish, Trumbull, Weems, Williamson, Williams) or were devout laymen (Warren, Ramsay, Proud, Adams, Randolph). Even avowed deists like John Daly Burk and James T. Callender enlisted God in the service of nationalism. Not that they were uncritical of bigotry; but religion as such was not at fault, only its perversion.

Like the philosophes, American historians defined progress as the advancement of humanity by the removal of obstacles to the fulfillment of man's rational powers. In the American setting that meant the progressive development of a republican spirit. But where the philosophes saw the Reformation as a battle between two false religions, American historians regarded it as the beginning of a vast intellectual transformation that led to the discovery and settlement of the New World. To them the planting of colonies in North America and the Protestant Reformation were part of the same historical development. This view did not imply Protestantism as a formal religious doctrine, but a secular view of the Reformation as the catalyst of a progressive increase of civil and religious liberty. The virtue of this formulation was that it invested the first settlers with a special significance as the crucial link in a chain of causation that improved the human condition.

If American and Enlightenment historians diverged in their assessments of organized religion, their attitudes toward the role of God in history were not far apart, although Americans disliked the religious skepticism of the philosophes. They seldom if ever attributed specific events to Providence and their view of America as part of the advancement of human knowledge and liberty was a secular concept. Nevertheless, practically every American historian made use of the role of God in ways that the philosophes undoubtedly would have disapproved. They offered a secularized version of the seventeenth century Puritan's city upon a hill. Their intimations of Providential favor were extensions, in secular form, of Puritan covenant theology. Salvation was not earned by individuals by their own merit alone. When they devoted themselves to living a holy life, God had contracted with them for their prosperity and glory.[16] The historical glory was America's destiny to enlighten mankind. In the context of world history the founding of the colonies marked a significant epoch. What better way to convince a devout people already fond of portraying themselves as an example to the world that there was purpose and unity to the national past?

Americans did not diverge from Enlightenment historiography out of conscious intellectual pioneering. But while the elements of their thought were ordinary, the emphasis they placed upon them and the use they made of them were not. Like their foreign contemporaries, didactic motives actuated much of their work. They shared the conviction that historical knowledge was valuable for present and future progress. But, while Enlightenment historians were reformers working to change society by exposing the follies of warriors, monarchs and priests, American historians were of the establishment. A handful held major offices and most were close to centers of power. Although they did not ignore past injustices or present difficulties, they accentuated positive achievements and were determined to justify and preserve, not change their society. Their task was clear. To preserve the nation Americans must think as a nation with a unified national past. It was in pursuit of this goal that American historians drifted away from Enlightenment cosmopolitanism.

American historians transformed the relativistic strain in eighteenth century historical writing into an important — if egocentric — element where it had previously been minor. True, Enlightenment historians had led the way toward a new awareness of the diversity of historical phenomena. While the concept of an unvarying human nature gave them a homogeneous vision of the past, it also encouraged them to make comparisons among civilizations and periods, each with its distinctive characteristics. But relativism remained for Europeans only a secondary element, the servant of polemical necessity. Different epochs and civilizations were used chiefly to prove the deficiencies of the past and promote contemporary reform. Polemical motives also influenced the works of Americans. There is always present in their histories a sense of contrast with other societies and ages. But, unlike the philosophes, the comparisons the Revolutionary generation drew betwen American institutions and those of other nations or peoples were seldom made explicit. In fact, there usually was no reference whatever to nations other than the United States. Behind an apparent self-preoccupation lay the need and desire to justify and celebrate America and only secondarily to understand the generality of mankind or promote reform, not to mention the need to avoid unfavorable comparisons with the superior cultural achievements of Europe. What American historians meant by change was simply the vague ideal of a world following the national example. What they meant by universalism was the nebulous notion that the world of the future would resemble the American example. Above all, American historians founded their case for national unity and particularity on the concept of national character, which they used to show that the inhabitants possessed the qualities indispensable to, and inevitably tending toward, a republican political and social order.

The perception of national identity was shaped by ambiguity toward the mother country. As nationalists, historians stressed the unique elements; yet the concept of national character allowed them to express a sense of uniqueness without wholly repudiating their English heritage. Americans could be regarded as Englishmen who had been transformed by the distinctive physical and social environment of the New World. Paradoxically, that formula also incorporated Enlightenment cosmopolitanism into a parochial frame of reference. If human nature was the same in all times and places, Americans were different by virtue of their unique civil and natural environment. Given similar circumstances, all mankind would develop in a similar manner; but American circumstances were so exceptional that it was difficult to comprehend how any other nation could experience a similar development.

Americans were hardly the first to discover national sentiment or the related idea of national character. Enlightenment historians conceded diversity in the character of nations and peoples, although they tended to emphasize what human beings had in common. Montesquieu had placed special emphasis on environment as the determinant of a people's character. In the eighteenth century, if not earlier, Englishmen in particular showed a distinct national consciousness in their attitude toward history. They tended to be less cosmopolitan in choice of subject than their contemporaries on the Continent, where there was less satisfaction with existing institutions. Even Bolingbroke, an enthusiastic cosmopolitan (and a particular favorite among Americans), was a philosopher turned patriot. He believed that God had planted in human beings the impulses that constituted distinct nationalities. The forms of government should vary according to the national spirit, and governments once constituted should devote themselves to national rather than class or dynastic interests. From this theory Bolingbroke went on to characterize the national genius of the British and to extoll their history.[17]

Yet there is a significant difference between Bolingbroke's nationalism and that of Americans. From the former we have a few scattered ideas and a thin line of patriotic sentiment incidental to the main line of thought. But for American historians, motivated by a passion for distinctiveness and the practical necessity of finding a basis for national unity, nationalism was basic. In an early and somewhat ambiguous form, they gave an unaccustomed emphasis to national feeling and put it to new uses. They explained a unique national character in the familiar terms of eighteenth century historical environmentalism. What they began was developed and carried out more systematically, when it was not altered, by later scholars.

Following in the footsteps of Montesquieu and the Scottish Enlightenment, American historians conceived of environment not only as geography but as a wide range of social factors as well. Montesquieu's view of the relationship between human nature and environment, physical and social, nicely complemented their own. But there is a further equation in their mixture of environmentalism, social factors, and heritage that suggestively anticipates the thinking of nineteenth century historians. Behind their explanation of the republicanism of the American character is an intuitive element that cannot be explained by geography and heritage alone, one that is suggested when Samuel Williams refers to the American's ability to "at once discern and understand the voice of nature," or David Ramsay to the "simple creed of an American,"[18] and when Ramsay, Marshall and other historians emphasize that American republicanism was not the product of abstract logic or utopian dreams but of the average individual's implicit understanding.

It would be too much to interpret these nebulous hints as more than dim anticipations of major elements in Romantic thought. Still, it is intriguing to hear overtones of some of the ideas important to the nineteenth century, especially Herder's spirit of the nation or, closer to home, George Bancroft's conviction that the "spirit of the colonies demanded freedom from the beginning."[19] Unlike the Romantics, the Revolutionary generation never argued that behind change lay feeling, emotion, yearning. Republican advocacy induced them to argue that Americans were rational men who would respond to rational arguments. That is one reason why their writings lacked emotional intensity. Yet despite the logic of their explanation of the American republican spirit, based as it was on social and physical environment, English heritage, a moderate colonial policy, there is an implicit element, an almost mystical belief in a special capacity to "at once discern and understand the voice of nature."

There is no direct evidence that American historians were influenced by Rousseau; but like him they supplanted Voltaire's enlightened despot with an enlightened people. They did not parallel, however, his concept of the general will. A patronizing tone toward the people in discussions of such issues as Shays' Rebellion and the dispute over the Constitution hint at ambivalence toward the dogma of self-government. Coupled with the lionization of Washington, these doubts give the appearance of a sympathy for enlightened despotism. But these are minor and inconclusive touches in an almost uniformly favorable picture of a republican society. Washington's career, like those of other leaders, was intended to personify the virtue and good sense of a people experienced in directing their own affairs.

Neither Europeans nor Americans recognized the Revolutionary generation as precursors of Romantic history. That role was assigned, generally, to Herder in Germany and Rousseau in France. What notice Europeans took of American historical writings was to confirm preconceived political and social ideas. The avowed purpose of Chevalier de Langeac's *Anecdotes anglaises et americaines* (1813) was to applaud the merits of absolute monarchy and reveal "how vile is that English constitution, half royal and half popular and always oppressive." Ironically, for this purpose he culled, out of a variety of sources but principally from David Ramsay, a long list of incidents of the American Revolution to illustrate the cruelties and injustices inflicted by the

English on the simple, virtuous, courageous Americans.[20] Claims that America was purer and freer than England, that special preserve of virtue and liberty, were not merely parochial; they were reinforced by powerful currents in Enlightenment thought from John Locke to the Illuminati. European friends of the United States found confirmation of these views in American works. Although Ramsay's *History of the Revolution* (1789) was widely read in France, it is doubtful that anyone took seriously his hope that it would be used as a textbook of revolution. Following a brief interest in American affairs, French readers turned their attention to exotica like William Bartram's *Travels* in 1799 and Henry Timberlake's *Memoirs* in 1797 (in translation), or to special topics, such as a work of Robert Fulton on canals and John Paul Jones's *Memoirs*.[21]

In Britain the writings of American historians, when they were noticed at all, served as ammunition in the continuing recriminations over responsibility for loss of the colonies or in debates over the character of revolutions. But there were parallel developments in the two countries. Changes in the political atmosphere of the United States as a result of the French Revolution were not unlike those occurring in Britain. There a new phase of nationalism bloomed, marked by Edmund Burke's contrast of the slow, orderly growth of English liberty with the disorderly excesses across the channel.[22] American writers, too, were affected by the events in France, which impelled them to distinguish their Revolution from the French. Like Burke's, their writings took on a new emphasis on national differences.

---

By the 1820s the tide was running out on the Enlightenment view of history. After William Robertson and Edward Gibbon in the 1780s there came a pause in outstanding historical writing, except perhaps in Germany, until the flowering of literary historians in the second and third decades of the nineteenth century. Critics found even the old giants out of date. "Hume, Robertson and Gibbon are no longer acceptable," observed one reviewer in 1815. "It is time," said another, "that we have a more worthy school."[23] In America too there was an increasing demand for a new, more stylish approach. Most historians of the Revolutionary generation were dead or had left the field. The exceptions, Marshall, Morse and Webster, issued revisions of earlier works. The older histories came to seem stale, their preoccupation with politics and political institutions too narrow. The first national generation possessed at least the virtue of first-handedness, of being eyewitnesses and participants. As they retired from the scene the works that followed were dull copies with little to recommend them to a reading public increasingly susceptible to Romanticism. Though dissatisfaction with the Revolutionary historians was directed at their literary inadequacies, art and subject matter cannot be neatly segregated from each other. Their style, what the eighteenth century referred to as conjectural history, reflected their use of subject matter primarily for analytic and didactic purposes. The new Romantic literary techniques not only appealed to a growing mass audience but expressed the rhetoric of democratic nationalism and new ideas of causation, stages of development, and the role of great men in history.

In part the emergence of a new historiography was the result of improvements in the commercial prospects of serious writing. The years between 1830 and 1860 witnessed the genesis of a mass audience. Improvements in transportation and communication and the "Cheap Postage Law" of 1851, which permitted books to be sent through the mails at very low rates, contributed to rapid growth in the publishing business.[24] While these factors made it possible to reach a growing mass audience, historical writing was still a relatively unprofitable enterprise; but, unlike the early years of the republic, it was passing increasingly into the hands of men of means. With the rise of Jacksonian democracy, the United States developed a class of displaced patricians who found few attractive outlets for their energies in political leadership. It was this group that produced historical writers.[25]

The task of writing national history, moreover, was facilitated by a growing accumulation of accessible source materials. In the 1820s the first great compilers began to work. Hezekiah Niles brought out his *Principles and Acts of the Revolution in America* in 1822, Jonathan Elliot his useful edition of the debates over the ratification of the Constitution during 1827-30, Jared Sparks his *Diplomatic Correspondence of the American Revolution* during 1829-30, and Peter Force his *American Archives* beginning in 1837. The few historical societies of the 1790s became some two dozen by 1830. Documents and personal papers were beginning to pass into accessible public repositories. It was becoming increasingly possible to write the nation's history from authentic sources.[26]

There was also a new political mood. For the men and women of the Revolution the primary task was to make the past conform to the idea of nationhood. They felt the need to bolster national unity in a time of particularist passions. Bancroft's generation enjoyed a more comfortable perspective. Nationhood was an established fact; the United States had become a viable enterprise and writers could afford the luxury of exploring new questions. The difference is reflected in the types of authors who were drawn to history. In the first national generation they were intensely political; a specific political event — the Revolution — led them into historical writing. In various ways — as legislators, soldiers, propagandists — most had participated in it. That involvement continued after the war, in the debates of the 1790s and early 1800s.[27] By contrast, Romantic historians were gentlemen scholars engaged in a labor of love who usually avoided personal involvement in politics. Bancroft stood alone among the major writers of his age in his eagerness to enter the political game. In other respects, however, he had much in common with Prescott, Parkman and Motley. All were men of letters who had tried poetry, fiction or criticism. They possessed the literary skills their new audiences demanded. To be sure, there were those among the Revolutionary generation who also had literary ambitions. Warren, Belknap and Burk wrote poetry and plays. But their efforts were primarily another form of political weaponry and only secondarily literary.

Where Warren, Belknap and Burk brought politics to literature, Bancroft, Parkman and Prescott brought literature to history. Avid readers of Scott and Cooper, Wordsworth, Coleridge and Byron, they were the American counterparts of the Romantic historians of Europe. For them the purpose of historical writing was to establish an imaginative relation with the past, not to analyze but to re-create it. History was a literary art whose main objective was to recapture experience. Not that the Revolutionary generation lacked concern for its architecture. Edmund Randolph, for example, spoke of "the dignity of history," a phrase borrowed from William Robertson which was meant to include beauty of language and construction. Yet the results were disappointing, the prose often stilted and dull. If the Revolutionary writers passionately defended a movement that had dominated their formative years, their works do not reveal that passion. The Enlightenment idea of style was to be rational and to organize in a rational manner. When eighteenth century writers did display a degree of passion it was muted.

American Revolutionary historians portrayed the participants in the conflict as motivated by the strongest of human passions — vanity, greed, lust for power, love of liberty. They believed that the Revolution represented a unique event in world history: the creation of a nation based on principles that would lead to "the progressive increase of human happiness." Human passions and a world-shaking event: surely these were the ingredients for a drama of unparalleled magnitude. But contemporaries organized their works in a manner that made it difficult to convey drama. It was not simply that they lacked literary sophistication and skill. They adopted an impersonal, analytical style that suited their purposes, but lacked the Romantic's impulse toward the unusual and the mysterious. To treat leaders as representative of abstract political ideals was to present them in the most mechanistic terms, without personalities and human interest. Determined to give to a diverse nation the appearance of uniformity, they ignored the unusual. Because they regarded the Revolution as the act of a united people their accounts lack the dramatic internal clash of personalities and interests. True, there are always the ongoing conflict with Britain and the contrasts between the character and institutions of nations and peoples. But the drama was diluted because the Anglo-American clash, even during the Revolution, served primarily to display the American character, while the contrasts among peoples and nations were seldom made explicit.

A Gibbon or a Voltaire could operate within similar constraints with outstanding results, but no American of the time could approach their experience or talent. The Americans were chiefly professionals who, lacking independent means or a profitable market for their writings, could not devote themselves entirely to literary pursuits. They were amateurs deficient in practiced technique. Even Jeremy Belknap, the most artful of the group, was incapable of full control of his invention. In its time and place, the theme of his *History of New Hampshire* was magisterial — America as a model to the world and New Hampshire as a microcosm of America — and he exhibited a talent for ordering the facts of frontier life into a meaningful pattern. Yet at times his points are lost in a maze of detail that often resembles the jottings of an antiquary.

In extenuation it should be noted that the Romantic taste and talent for the exotic and the mysterious flowed more easily from the pens of historians like Prescott and Parkman who took their readers into primitive tribes, strange civilizations and clashing empires. Bancroft was an exception, an accomplished stylist, whose concern with domestic politics was less suited to Romantic literary theory than Prescott's or Parkman's forests. When the first volume of his *History of the United States* (1834-74) appeared critics were ecstatic: "He is the instrument of Providence"; "He is worthy of his country and his age"; "we have come of age!"[28] His subject matter and his nationalism, which was perhaps more aggressive, however, gave him a closer substantive kinship with the Revolutionary generation than the work of Prescott, Parkman, and Motley. But these were the outstanding historians of the period. For hundreds of others Romantic literary theory was little more than an ideal. Compared with most nineteenth century historians, the historians of the first national generation do not fare badly.

While the Revolutionary generation of historians looked unde-signedly toward a new genre of writing, its approach differed in crucial ways from those that followed. Their styles contrasted not only because of the superior literary quality of the best Romantic historians, but also because style reflected substantive differences in philosophy. The Enlightenment approach was naturalistic and rationalistic; every-thing in history reflected cause and effect relationships. The Americans were particularly fascinated by the interplay between civil and natural history. They related history to philosophy in an attempt to integrate facts into a larger scheme, making history, in Bolingbroke's phrase, "philosophy teaching by example." The conclusions they drew from their data were fixed before they began; they knew what they believed and they made sure that the facts fell into place. The Romantic school was by contrast mystical and obscurantist. Its basic doctrine was a belief in the gradual development of a distinct and unique national spirit, a unified and organic development of traditions, customs, laws, and culture which formed the essence (or Zeitgeist) peculiar to a people. It was an emotional approach to history, for it made no other rational attempt to explain the development of these national peculiarities than simply terming them the results of a mystic national spirit.[29]

Preeminent to Romantics were heroic characters. The hero was the embodiment of the people. "In the Netherland story," wrote Motley, "the people is ever the true hero." Even in the works of Bancroft, the most aggressively "Popular" of the historians, the common people remained in the background. They were a perceptible force only in crisis, and even then, usually, they acted through their agent, the great man. He, the mystic instrument of progress, represented quintessentially the virtues of his people.[30] The Revolutionary generation also depicted the hero as representative, but with a subordinate role. For Romantics, representative individuals were the organizational center of their work. Though the Revolutionary generation's attitude toward great men, especially Washington, was often ambiguous, generally leaders were treated as agents of the popular will rather than driving forces in their own right. Indeed, leaders are often conspicuous only by their absence. Even in biographies of Washington, with the notable exception of that by Weems, there was little interest in personal attributes of character.

Romantics, fascinated with the personality of the hero, portrayed him as the personification of highly individual moral characteristics such as simplicity, naturalness, loftiness of motive, directness, spontaneity, self-reliance, piety, industry. Such characteristics were not wholly lacking in the Revolutionary generation's portrayals, but they were clearly subordinate to political character. Bancroft was attracted by the balance of Washington's personality, the "faultless proportion" of his qualities: "He was all order, all proportion, all completeness. . . . His mind resembled a well ordered commonwealth."[31] What interested the Revolutionary generation was the republicanism of Washington's character, his recognition and acceptance of the limitations of power in a republican government.

However different their philosophies of history, the two generations had much in common. For all his originality as a scholar and talent as a writer, Bancroft expressed a set of ideas that had been turned into common currency by his predecessors.[32] Every one of his interpretations of the Revolution had been advanced by earlier writers,[33] although unlike them he wrote with an exuberant rhetoric that reassured his readers that these ideas were true and enduring, and he documented their origin and existence with what seemed undeniable and exact evidence.[34] Like the Revolutionary generation, he was interested in the colonial period primarily as a backdrop for the Revolution and as a vehicle for exploring the national character. (Five of eight volumes deal with the period after 1748.) In phrases that were novel primarily in rhetorical flourish, Bancroft described Americans as a "liberty-loving" and a "freedom-loving" people. To him the Revolution came "out of the soul of the people, and was an inevitable result of a living affection for freedom, which actuated harmonious efforts as certainly as the beating of the heart sends warmth and color and beauty to the system."[35] The first national generation would have disagreed at most with the word "inevitable" and would have been unfamiliar with the tints and colors of his prose.

Like his predecessors, Bancroft placed the Revolution, and American history, in a universal context. History, he explained in his preface, must have a theme, some "great principle of action" to lend unity and significance to the narrative. He chose two. The first was liberty: "the spirit of the colonies demanded freedom from the beginning." Though Bancroft wrote with more precision and gave less emphasis to the environment and the English heritage, his theme of liberty was fully shared by the earlier historians. Although with greater skill and evidence, and perhaps national unity, like them he traced how the United States grew out of infant colonies to become the most free, just, and harmonious society in the world, one dedicated to "the practice and defense of the rights of man" and offering a haven for liberty.[36]

The second controlling theme of Bancroft's *History* was the United States as the creation of Divine Providence. In American history one could clearly discover "the mysterious influence of that power which enchains the destinies of states . . . and which often deduces the greatest events from the least commending causes."[37] Bancroft's personal inclination (he had studied for the ministry) and the New England historiographic tradition made this outlook natural for him.[38] Though fond of declaring America to be part of a grand design, the Revolutionary generation was on the whole ambiguous about the role of Providence. For some, like Mercy Otis Warren, Isaac Backus, and Benjamin Trumbull, it was reasonably clear, although they never established a causative relationship between God and specific events. Others showed less interest in a Providential view than in demonstrating that American history deserved universal attention and as a polemical tool for convincing their countrymen that there was a purpose and unity to the national past. Still, in practice if not always in theology, there was a family resemblance in the uses of the idea of Providence by the two generations. Bancroft's deeply religious conception of God's role was shared by only a few of his immediate predecessors, but most agreed in assigning to America a special, universal significance.

Perhaps the most important element of continuity between Bancroft and the Revolutionary generation was their often strident patriotism and emphasis on national unity. True, there were important differences. As contemporaries the first national generation did not, for example, hold the Federal Constitution in the mystical awe of Bancroft. For them it was primarily a much needed administrative reorganization that completed the work of the Revolution, not a sacred tablet brought down from Mount Zion. Their accounts of its drafting and ratification are notable for the absence of rhetorical enthusiasm. They contain few details and less praise. They did, like Bancroft, treat it as a logical fulfillment of a history that was marching inexorably toward nationhood and unity. The theme of unity, developed by the Revolutionary generation and carried further by Bancroft, dominated American historiography until the civil war made it difficult to maintain.

A central concern of the Revolutionary generation was the emergence of a national character upon which to base their thesis of unity and uniqueness. Despite important differences, their views were suggestive of the racism implicit in the Romantic concept of national essence. Few nineteenth century historians offered a coherent theory of race, but they did adopt a racial scale to explain national differences. At the top stood the Americans. It was assumed that the religious basis of settlement, pioneer life, and widespread ownership of land reinvigorated the virtues originally acquired in the ancient forests of northern Europe. Above all, Americans loved liberty, hated oppression, were democratic, and possessed the moral qualities of industry, temperance, and self-reliance. Along with the Americans stood the other Teutonic peoples, Germans, Dutch and English. Stereotypes of the Spaniards, Italians, French, and Irish were reinforced by religious emotions. Hatred of Roman Catholicism colored the histories. At the bottom of the racial scale was the African, with the Indian only slightly higher, each characterized as inferior beings though the Indian conjured up contradictory images of the noble savage and the complete barbarian.[39]

Strategic considerations usually limited the Revolutionary writers' discussion of national character to abstract ideas. They maintained that Americans were united by common devotion to republican principles. The national characteristics were those toward which all mankind naturally strived, though paradoxically the circumstances that brought the American character into being appeared unique to the United States. Despite this superficial and often inconsistent allegiance to the Enlightenment ideal of the universality of mankind, the earlier writers exhibited ideas of national distinctiveness that foreshadowed those of the nineteenth century. Unlike the Romantics, they did not regard American liberty as having been born in the forests of Northern Europe. They emphasized the physical environment as a determinant of American republicanism. At the same time they did not disavow their English heritage. There is the clear implication, even in the works of such natural historians as Samuel Williams and Hugh Williamson, that the English were best suited to take advantage of the opportunities afforded by the environment of the New World. By contrast they drew invidious comparisons with the Indian's and Spaniard's inability to exploit that setting to create prosperous, free societies. Neither the Revolutionary nor the Romantic generation had a racial theory of American liberty. But their national pride had enough of vanity to prepare the way for later acceptance of such an interpretation.

---

As the nineteenth century progressed tastes changed and the writings of the first national generation came to seem archaic and dry. Yet their scholarship if not their style continued to be respected and their works were sometimes reprinted. The contributors to Justin Winsor's cooperative *Narrative and Critical History of America* (1884-89) praised Ramsay for having "brought an ardent patriotism to the task, and a literary skill hardly surpassed among his compatriots."[40] But in the early years of the twentieth century the Revolutionary generation of historians fell into disrepute. Their decline coincided with the growth of professionalism and the spread of scientific history in the late nineteenth century. The new school valued scholarly objectivity, reportorial detachment, and verifiable evidence more than generalized theory. Its attack centered upon the charge of plagiarism. In a series of articles between 1899 and 1902, Orin Grant Libby denounced the older writers as plagiarists who had copied or paraphrased large portions of Dodsley's *Annual Register*, a Whig-oriented English journal that had published a day by day account of the Anglo-American conflict. Libby clearly implied that they had deliberately misled their readers and that their plagiarized works were useless as history.[41]

The Revolutionary generation would have been puzzled by the attack, for they had never claimed to be original in their use of sources or secondary materials. It was common and open practice to excerpt from the works of others without specific attribution. William Gordon wrote in the preface to his history that "the *Register* and other publications have been of service to the compiler of the present work, who has frequently quoted from them, without varying the language, except for method and conciseness."[42] Gordon's frankness was echoed by others. Not everyone, of course, borrowed thus. Warren avoided the *Annual Register* or any other secondary source in her *History of the American Revolution*. State historians usually managed to do basic research from nearby resources. Belknap and Williams expended much time and energy gathering colony and town records, corresponding with local ministers, and compiling statistics.

Actually, the Revolution stimulated interest in the collection and use of source materials. The fact that Ebenezer Hazard was able to solicit for his *Historical Collections* (1792-94) the support of influential persons, among them Thomas Jefferson, Benjamin Harrison and Edmund Randolph, is indicative of a general awareness of the need for documentary evidence in the writing of history. The Massachusetts Historical Society assigned large portions of its *Collections* to the reprinting of source materials. Some historians published documentary appendices in their books. Despite these efforts, it was beyond the means of most who wrote national history to do a thorough job of primary research. In an age when reference materials were virtually non-existent, the only available day by day account was in the *Annual Register*. Furthermore, a remarkable freedom from scholarly rivalry and a strong sense of being part of a cooperative venture caused most historians to be flattered to have their writings borrowed by others. When portions of David Ramsay's work were incorporated without quotation but with slight improvements in Gordon's *History*, he accepted the improved version in his next publication.[43] The only embarrassment felt over borrowing from the *Annual Register* was the chagrin of nationalists who had to rely on a foreign source, however sympathetic its interpretation.

Such practices, innocent as they were, gave the appearance of "scissors and paste history," a kind of history which depends altogether upon the testimony of authorities.[44]

The low regard in which the early Revolutionary historians were later held was not simply a matter of scholarly practice. Historians and public alike, by the end of the nineteenth century, had rejected most of the assumptions on which they based their works. The pivotal emphasis of the Progressive historians upon economic and political conflict was uncongenial to early national writers. On the assumption that men are moved primarily by economic forces, the Progressives stressed the growing competition between rival capitalist systems and the intracolonial conflict generated by lower class demands for greater economic and political roles. John Marshall, it is true, alone among his contemporaries exhibited a degree of kinship with the Progressive view of conflict, at least in his discussions of the Constitution and the 1790s. Charles Beard praised him as an "authority, whose knowledge of the period and whose powers of judgement and exposition will hardly be denied by the most critical" and an "historian of great acumen" whose "masterly" *Life of Washington* is a "great" work.[45] But it would be stretching a point to see in Marshall a basic theory of economic class conflict. Since the Progressives regarded the Patriot Constitutional and philosophical arguments as masks for deeper motives, they had little use for their histories.

Yet there are certain parallels between the generations. The Progressives tended to look upon the Revolution as the product of impersonal and inexorable forces deeply rooted in the colonial past. Because the Revolutionary generation was determined to counteract the rival contemporary view that the Patriots had sought independence from the outset, they were reluctant to openly acknowledge the inevitability of nationhood. But their dissertations on the national character, the unique physical and social environment, and destiny belied their own disclaimers. Their basic philosophical assumptions may have been radically different, but like the later Progressives their discussions of maturing colonial institutions and attitudes strongly implied that it was virtually impossible for Americans to continue in a subordinate status.

Even before the Revolution, from the early Puritan "city upon a hill," there existed among Americans a sense of uniqueness. The first national generation translated it into a nationalist doctrine which has formed an important part of the American historical consciousness ever since. The philosophical and scholarly bases for Frederick Jackson Turner's frontier thesis, for example, differed from the Revolutionary generation's interpretation of American society; concepts such as individualism and democracy had different meanings for them. They attributed much greater significance to the English heritage than Turner, who came close to arguing that in America people began anew, wiping clean the slate of inherited tradition. But the environmentalism of Samuel Williams, Jeremy Belknap, Hugh Williamson, to name a few, although theoretically imprecise, still bespeaks a line of descent to Turner. Like him, they emphasized nature and the availability of land (among other factors) in the formation of the American character. "The distance of America from Great Britain," David Ramsay suggestively concluded, "generated ideas in the minds of the Colonists favourable to liberty. . . . The wide extent and nature of the country contributed to the same effect. The material seat of freedom is among high mountains and pathless deserts, such as abound in the wilds of America."[46]

More recently the ideas of the Revolutionary generation have come back into vogue. Many of its works have been reprinted and treated as reliable sources of contemporary opinion. One reason for this modest revival is the reaction that began in the 1950s against the Progressive historians. Unlike them, the neo-Whig school does not regard the ideology of the Revolution as a mask for deeper and more dubious motives and ambitions; it begins with the assumption that the revolutionists meant what they said and were accurate in saying it. It is the contention of the neo-Whigs that the Revolution was essentially a conservative movement, a defense of existing American rights and liberties against provocations by the mother country. They have emphasized domestic harmony — the absence of serious social or class conflict — and harmony with Britain before 1763. The colonists as a whole were happy subjects, contented with the existing order before the imperial authorities shortsightedly adopted policies that fundamentally challenged American rights and property. It is not difficult to see the general similarity of this outlook to that of the Revolutionary generation.

---

By the conventional standards of modern scholarship the writings of the Revolutionary generation of historians have serious shortcomings. In spite of them they represent a well defined interpretation. Their authors refashioned American historical thinking in light of the Revolution and nationhood. It is easy to emphasize their limitations; they posed more problems than they solved, and their data and ideas seem fragmentary and unsystematic. Nevertheless, however imprecise and eclectic, their writings brought a new understanding to the American past.

# Notes

## Preface

1. Cited in Page Smith, *The Historian and History* (New York, 1964), p. 37.
2. For the party battles of the early national period see Richard Buel, Jr., *Securing the Revolution: Ideology in American Politics, 1789-1815* (Ithaca, 1972).
3. John R. Howe, Jr., *The Changing Political Thought of John Adams* (Princeton, 1966), p. 194. For discussions of attitudes toward political parties see Richard Hofstadter, *The Idea of a Party System: the Rise of Legitimate Opposition in the United States, 1780-1840* (Berkeley and Los Angeles, 1969), pp. 40-121.
4. Peter Gay, *Style in History* (New York, 1974), p. 7.
5. Richard Hofstadter, *The Progressive Historians: Turner, Beard, Parrington* (New York, 1968), p. 3.

## Chapter I

1. William Stoughton, *New England's True Interest* (Cambridge, Mass., 1670), p. 4.
2. William Stith, *The History of the First Discovery and Settlement of Virginia* (Williamsburg, 1747), p. vii; Alden T. Vaughan, "The Evolution of Virginia History: Early Historians of the First Colony," in *Perspectives on Early American History: Essays in Honor of Richard B. Morris,* ed. Alden T. Vaughan and George A. Billias (New York, 1973), pp. 31-36; Benjamin T. Spencer, *The Quest for Nationality: An American Literary Campaign* (Syracuse, 1957), pp. 1-7.
3. Patricia U. Bonomi, "The Middle Colonies: Embryo of the New Political Order," in *Perspectives on Early American History,* pp. 63-94.
4. David Ramsay, *Oration on American Independence* (1794), in Robert L. Brunhouse, ed., "David Ramsay, 1749-1815: Selections From His Writings," *Transactions of the American Philosophical Society,* new ser., LV (1965), pt. 4, 191.
5. Cf. Thomas Prince, *A Chronological History of New England in the Form of Annals* (Boston, 1736); Stith, *History of Virginia;* Samuel Smith, *The History of the Colony of Nova-Caesaria, or New Jersey* (Burlington, N.J., 1765); George Chalmers, *Political Annals of the Present United Colonies: from their settlement to the peace of 1763* (London, 1780); Alexander Hewatt, *An Historical Account of the Rise and Progress of the Colonies of South Carolina and Georgia* (London, 1779).

6. Lewis P. Simpson, "Literary Ecumenicalism of the American Enlightenment," in *The Ibero-American Enlightenment*, ed. A. Owen Aldridge (Urbana, 1971), pp. 317-32.

7. David Ramsay, *Oration*, "Ramsay . . . Writings," p. 191.

8. For discussions of the development of cultural nationalism see Spencer, *Quest for Nationality;* Russel B. Nye, *The Cultural Life of the New Nation, 1776-1830* (New York, 1960); Bert James Loewenberg, *Historical Writing in American Culture* (Mexico City, 1968), pp. 211-36; William J. Free, *The Columbian Magazine and American Literary Nationalism* (The Hague, 1968); Howard Mumford Jones, *O Strange New World: American Culture; The Formative Years* (New York, 1964), esp. pp. 312-50.

9. Quoted in Paul W. Conner, *Poor Richard's Politicks: Benjamin Franklin and His New American Order* (New York, 1965), p. 106.

10. Samuel Williams, *The Natural and Civil History of Vermont* (Walpole, N.H., 1794), p. xii; James Sullivan, *Thoughts Upon the Political Situation of the United States* (Worcester, Mass., 1788), p. 21.

11. Quoted in Spencer, *Quest for Nationality*, p. 15.

12. Hans Kohn, *American Nationalism: An Interpretive Essay* (1954; New York, 1961), p. 40.

13. Quoted in Norman Risjord, *Forging the American Republic, 1760-1815* (Reading, Mass., 1973), p. 245.

14. By public policy I do not mean here the policies of particular administrations, political parties, or interest groups, but what these men and women regarded as the public good, although no doubt some confused the public good with partisan fortunes.

15. John R. Howe, Jr., "Republican Thought and the Political Violence of the 1790s," *American Quarterly*, XX (1967), 147-48.

16. Ramsay to Jedidiah Morse, Aug. 12, 1807, "Ramsay . . . Writings," p. 160.

17. Mercy Otis Warren, *History of the Rise, Progress, and Termination of the American Revolution* (Boston, 1805), III, 392-95; Adams to Warren, Aug. 8, 1807, Massachusetts Historical Society, *Collections*, 5th ser., IV (1878), 432.

18. Quoted by Merle Curti, *Roots of American Loyalty* (New York, 1946), p. 58.

19. David D. Van Tassel, *Recording America's Past: An Interpretation of the Development of Historical Studies in America, 1607-1884* (Chicago, 1960), p. 82.

20. Adams to Warren, Aug. 8, 1807, as n. 17 above.

21. Isaac Kramnick, *Bolingbroke and His Circle: The Politics of Nostalgia in the Age of Walpole* (Cambridge, Mass., 1968), p. 153. For a discussion of the distaste for political parties during the early national period see Hofstadter, *Idea of a Party System.*

22. For the relationship between state and national history see Arthur H. Shaffer, "John Daly Burk's *History of Virginia* and the Development of American National History," *Virginia Magazine of History and Biography*, LXXVII (1969), 336-46.

23. Williams, *History of Vermont*, p. viii. John W. Campbell maintained that while the "history of Virginia is on many accounts of more importance than that of her sister colonies," his work would not "be confined to Virginia alone, whose

history is interwoven with that of the other states . . ." *A History of Virginia* (Philadelphia, 1813), p. 5.

24. Ramsay to Jeremy Belknap, March 11, 1795, "Ramsay . . . Writings," p. 140.

25. Cited in Michael Kraus, *The Writing of American History* (Norman, Okla., 1953), p. 57.

26. Arthur W. Zilversmit, *The First Emancipation: The Abolition of Slavery in the North* (Chicago, 1967), p. 157; Samuel A. Eliot, "Jeremy Belknap," Mass, Hist, Soc., *Proceedings*, LXVI (1942), 99-100.

27. Jeremy Belknap, *The History of New Hampshire* (1784-92), intro. by John Kirtland Wright (New York, 1970), I, 3.

28. For biographical information see Robert L. Brunhouse's intro. to "Ramsay . . . Writings," pp. 12-48.

29. Ramsay to Benjamin Rush, Dec. 29, 1788, ibid., p. 122.

30. Edmund Randolph, *History of Virginia*, ed. with intro. by Arthur H. Shaffer (Charlottesville, Va., 1970), p. 3.

31. For an analysis of Randolph's career see Shaffer, intro., ibid., pp. xi-xvii.

32. Ibid., pp. xi-xvi.

33. Ibid., pp. 157-178.

34. Ibid., pp. 24-25.

35. Jared Sparks, "Review of Jonathan Elliot, ed., *Debates, Resolutions and Other Proceedings in Convention on the Adoption of the Federal Constitution*," **North American Review**, XXV (October, 1827); quoted in Gerald A. Danzer, "America's Roots in the Past: Historical Publication in America to 1860" (Ph.D. dissertation, Northwestern University, 1967), pp. 202-03.

36. Ramsay to Rush, Feb. 17, 1788, "Ramsay . . . Writings," p. 19; John Quincy Adams to William Plumer, Aug. 16, 1809; quoted in Van Tassel, *Recording America's Past*, p. 83.

37. Belknap to Ebenezer Hazard, March 9, 1786, Mass. Hist. Soc., *Collections*, 5th ser., II (1877), 431-32; Marshall to James Wilkinson, Jan. 5, 1787, quoted in Robert K. Faulkner, *The Jurisprudence of John Marshall* (Princeton, 1968), p. 149.

38. Ramsay to Rush, July 11, 1783, "Ramsay . . . Writings," p. 75.

39. Ramsay to Thomas Jefferson, April 7, 1787; Ramsay to Rush, Aug. 6, 1786, ibid., pp. 105, 110.

40. Cf. Brunhouse, ed., "David Ramsay on the Ratification of the Constitution in South Carolina, 1787-1788," *Journal of Southern History*, IX (1943), 549-55; *An Oration on the Advantages of American Independence* (Charleston, 1778), "Ramsay . . . Writings," pp. 183-90.

41. "To the Governors of Certain States," Jan. 31, 1786; Ramsay to Rush, Feb. 11, 1786, ibid., p. 98.

42. Ramsay to Jefferson, April 7, 1787, ibid., p. 110.

43. *An Address to the Freemen of South Carolina on the Federal Constitution . . . By Civis* (Charleston, 1788); in Paul Leicester Ford, ed., *Pamphlets on the Constitution of the United States . . .* (Brooklyn, 1888), pp. 371-80.

44. Brunhouse, "Ramsay on Ratification," p. 553.

45. Shaffer, intro. to Randolph, *History of Virginia*, p. xii.

46. Ibid., p. 3; Warren, *History of the American Revolution*, III, 423.
47. Joel Barlow, *The Columbiad* (1807), book viii, pp. 97-80, quoted in Loewenberg, *Historical Writing in American Culture*, p. 224.
48. Barlow to Warren, Dec. 29, 1810; cited in Van Tassel, *Recording America's Past*, p. 83n.
49. John C. Miller, *The Federalist Era, 1789-1801* (New York, 1960), pp. 1-2.
50. Randolph, *History of Virginia*, p. 156; Robert A. Feer, "George Richards Minot's *History of the Insurrections:* History, Propaganda, and Autobiography," *New England Quarterly*, XXV (1962), 216; David Ramsay, *The History of the American Revolution* (1789; 2d ed., London, 1793), II, 323.
51. Noah Webster, *Sketches of American Policy* (1785), ed. Harry R. Warfel (New York, 1937), p. 30.
52. Warren, *History of the American Revolution*, I, vii-viii; Benjamin Trumbull, *A General History of the United States of America* (Boston, 1810), p. iii.
53. For semons and orations see Benjamin Trumbull, *A Century Sermon* (New Haven, 1801); Jeremy Belknap, *An Election Sermon, Preached Before the General Court of New Hampshire* (Portsmouth, N.H., 1785); John Daly Burk, *An Oration, Delivered to Celebrate the Election of Thomas Jefferson, and the Triumph of Republicanism* (Petersburg, Va., 1803); David Ramsay, *An Oration in Commemoration of American Independence* (Charleston, 1794); Ezra Stiles, *The United States Elevated to Glory and Honour* (Worcester, 1783); Samuel Williams, *A Discourse on the Love of our Country* (Salem, 1775). For plays see John Daly Burk, *Bunker-Hill; or, the Death of General Warren* (New York, 1817); Jeremy Belknap, *The Foresters* (Boston, 1792); and Mercy Otis Warren, *The Group* (Boston, 1775). For popular histories and textbooks see John M'Culloch, *An Introduction to American History* (Philadelphia, 1787); Jedidiah Morse, *The History of America in Two Books* (Philadelphia, 1790); Hannah Adams, *A Summary History of New England* (Dedham, Mass., 1799); Samuel Williams, *History of the American Revolution* in the *Rural Magazine; or, Vermont Repository* (Burlington, Vt., 1795), reprinted thirteen times from 1824 to 1831; John Marshall, *The Life of George Washington, written for the use of the Schools* (Philadelphia, 1838); David Ramsay, *A Chronological Table of the Principal Events which have taken Place in the English Colonies, Now United States, from 1607, Till 1810* (Charleston, 1811) and *Historical and Biographical Chart of the United States* (N.p., n.d.); Noah Webster, *American Selection of Readings* (3d ed., Philadelphia, 1787).
54. Richard Snowden, *The History of America* (Philadelphia, 1805, 1813), p. iii; Campbell, *History of Virginia*, p. 3.

**Chapter II**

1. David Ramsay, *History of South Carolina, from Its First Settlement in 1670 to the Year 1808* (1809; Newberry, S.C., 1858), I, v; and *Oration*, "Ramsay . . . Writings*," p. 196; Campbell, *History of Virginia*, p. 4. On this issue John Marshall took a different position. While not denying the importance of public opinion, he took the traditional view that history should be written for the

"useful lessons" it could "furnish the discerning politician." *Life of George Washington* (1804-07; New York, 1925), I, xv. For a discussion of his attitudes see William R. Smith, *History as Argument: Three Patriot Historians of the American Revolution* (The Hague, 1966), pp. 119-23; and Faulkner, *Jurisprudence of Marshall*, passim.

2. Among the harshest critics has been R. G. Collingwood, *The Idea of History* (1946, New York, 1956), pp. 76-85. For a more sympathetic assessment see Trygve R. Tholfsen, *Historical Thinking: An Introduction* (New York, 1967), pp. 93- 126.

3. Quoted in R. N. Stromberg, "History in the Eighteenth Century," *Journal of the History of Ideas*, XII (1951), 297. In the use of documentation American historians were most influenced by its best eighteenth-century practitioners: the Englishman, Edward Gibbon, and the Scotsmen, David Hume and William Robertson.

4. John Lendrum, *A Concise and Impartial History of the American Revolution* (Philadelphia, 1795), p. 99; Belknap, *History of New Hampshire*, I, 1; Abiel Holmes, *American Annals; or a Chronological History of America* (Cambridge, Mass., 1805), I, iii. Practically every American historian expressed a similar view.

5. These remarks appeared in Hazard's pre-publication proposal and are reprinted in Julian P. Boyd, ed., *The Papers of Thomas Jefferson* (Princeton, 1950), I, 144-49.

6. Smith, *Historian and History*, p. 38.

7. Lester J. Cappon, "American Historical Editors before Jared Sparks," *William and Mary Quarterly*, 3d ser., XXX (1973), 387-90; Stephen W. Haycox, "Jeremy Belknap and Early American Nationalism: A Study in the Political and Theological Foundations of American Liberty" (Ph.D. dissertation, University of Oregon, 1971), pp. 183-88.

8. Massachusetts Historical Society, *Collections*, I (1792), 1, II (1793), 1-2.

9. Peter Gay, *The Enlightenment: An Interpretation* (New York, 1969), II, 378-84; Hugh Trevor-Roper, "The Historical Philosophy of the Enlightenment," *Studies on Voltaire and the Eighteenth Century*, ed. by Theodore Besterman, XXVII (1963), 1676-80.

10. Isaac Backus, *History of New England, with Particular Reference to the Denomination of Christians called Baptists* (Boston, 1777-97), I, preface; Hugh Williamson, "On the Benefits of Civil History," New York Historical Society, *Collections*, II (1814), 27.

11. William Gordon, *History of the Rise, Progress, and Independence of the United States of America* (London, 1788), I, preface.

12. Jefferson, quoted in Loewenberg, *Historical Writing in American Culture*, pp. 201-02.

13. Backus, *History of New England*, I, preface.

14. Cf. Chapter VI, below.

15. *The Monthly Review Enlarged*, V (1791), 177-80.

16. "Ramsay . . . Writings," pp. 223-24.

17. Cf. Chapter VIII, below.

18. Cf. Chapter IV, below.
19. Cf. Danzer, "America's Roots in the Past," pp. 83-116.
20. J. B. Black, *The Art of History: A Study of Four Great Historians of the Eighteenth Century* (New York, 1965), p. 20.
21. Randolph, *History of Virginia*, pp. 3-4.
22. Black, *Art of History*, p. 31.
23. Quoted in Jane Belknap Marcou, *Life of Jeremy Belknap* (New York, 1847), pp. 47-48.
24. Trevor-Roper, "Historical Philosophy of the Enlightenment," p. 1676.
25. David Hume, *An Enquiry Concerning Human Understanding* (1748), in *David Hume: Philosophical Historian*, ed. David F. Norton and Richard H. Popkin (Indianapolis, 1965), p. 54; and "Of Eloquence," in *The Philosophical Works of David Hume*, ed. T.H. Greene and T.H. Grose (London, 1882), III, 163.
26. Gay, *The Enlightenment*, II, 382.
27. Ibid., pp. 380-85; Tholfsen, *Historical Thinking*, pp. 94-101.
28. Williams, *History of Vermont*, p. 376.
29. Quoted in William H. Nelson, "The Revolutionary Character of the American Revolution," *American Historical Review*, LXX (1965), 1006.
30. Stiles, *United States Elevated*, p. 22.
31. Trevor-Roper, "Historical Philosophy of Enlightenment," p. 1680.
32. Warren, *History of the American Revolution*, I, 1.
33. Trevor-Roper, "Historical Philosophy of the Enlightenment," p. 1686.
34. Three historians were political leaders of first rank: John Marshall, Chief Justice of the Supreme Court; Edmund Randolph, governor of Virginia and Attorney-General and Secretary of State in Washington's cabinet; and James Sullivan, governor of Massachusetts.
35. David Hume, *Enquiry Concerning the Human Understanding* (1748), quoted in Black, *Art of History*, p. 13; Marshall to Gouverneur Morris, Oct. 3, 1816, quoted in Faulkner, *Jurisprudence of Marshall*, p. 145; Warren, *History of the American Revolution*, I, iii.
36. Noah Webster, "On the Education of Youth in America," in *Collection of Essays and Fugitiv Writings* (Boston, 1790), p. 23.
37. The most favorable estimate of Ramsay's place in the historiography of the Revolution is in Page Smith, "David Ramsay and the Causes of the American Revolution," *William and Mary Quarterly*, 3d ser., XVII (1960), 51-77. See also Smith, *History as Argument*, esp. pp. 42-72; Elmer Douglass Johnson, "David Ramsay: Historian or Plagiarist?" *South Carolina Historical Magazine*, LVII (1956), 189-98; and Merle Curti, *Human Nature in American Historical Thought* (Columbia, Mo., 1968), pp. 46-52.
38. Free, *Columbian Magazine*, pp. 73-74, 108-11.
39. Cited by Charles G. Sellers, Jr., "The American Revolution: Southern Founders of a National Tradition," in *Writing Southern History: Essays in Historiography in Honor of Fletcher M. Green*, ed. Arthur S. Link and Rembert W. Patrick (Baton Rouge, 1965), p. 42.
40. Ramsay to John Eliot, Aug. 11, 1792, "Ramsay . . . Writings," p. 133.
41. *Oration*, ibid., p. 195.

42. Hannah Adams, *A Memoir of Miss Hannah Adams* (Boston, 1832), p. 22; Ramsay to Jedidiah Morse, Nov. 13, 1813; Ramsay to Belknap, March 11, 1795, "Ramsay . . . Writings," pp. 177, 140.
43. Ramsay to Jefferson, May 3, 1786, ibid., p. 101. See Merle Curti, "The Reputation of America Overseas, 1776-1860," in *Probing our Past* (New York, 1955), pp. 191-218; William B. Cairns, *British Criticism of American Writings, 1783-1815* (Madison, 1918); and Jones, O Strange New World, pp. 273-311.
44. Risjord, *Forging the Republic,* pp. 256-58.
45. Kohn, *American Nationalism,* pp. 15-18.
46. Ramsay to Eliot, Aug. 11, 1792, "Ramsay . . . Writings," p. 133.
47. *Oration* (1794), ibid., p. 193.
48. Ramsay, *History of the Revolution,* I, 31.
49. Ramsay, *History of South Carolina,* I, 43.
50. Ibid., pp. 74, 86, 90.
51. Ibid., p. 70.
52. *Oration,* in "Ramsay . . . Writings," p. 195.
53. Ramsay to Jefferson, May 3, 1786, ibid., p. 101.
54. Ramsay to Rush, April 8, 1777, ibid., pp. 54-55.
55. Ramsay, *History of the Revolution,* II, 315-23; *Oration,* in "Ramsay . . . Writings," p. 192.
56. Quoted in Free, *Columbian Magazine,* p. 15.
57. Spencer, *Quest for Nationality,* pp. 22-23. For French writers see Durand Echeverria, *Mirage in the West: A History of the French Image of American Society to 1815* (Princeton, 1957), passim.
58. Ramsay to Ashbel Green, Oct. 4, 1791, "Ramsay . . . Writings," p. 130.
59. Ramsay to Jefferson, May 3, 1786, ibid., p. 101.
60. As Seymour Martin Lipset has pointed out, the populist ideology of intellectuals in new nations results from their situation vis-a-vis the former metropolis and within their own country; it does not necessarily lead to an egalitarian attitude. *The First New Nation: The United States in Historical and Comparative Perspective* (Garden City, New York, 1967), pp. 76-85.
61. *Oration,* in "Ramsay . . . Writings," p. 191; *History of the Revolution,* I, 355.

## Chapter III

1. Richard Price, *Observations on the Importance of the American Revolution* (Boston, 1784), p. 5.
2. Quoted in Adrienne Koch, *Power, Morals, and the Founding Fathers: Essays in the Interpretation of the American Enlightenment* (Ithaca, 1961), p. 128.
3. David Ramsay, *Oration* (1794), in "Ramsay . . . Writings," pp. 191-92.
4. For much of my discussion of New England historiography I am indebted to Wesley Frank Craven, *The Legend of the Founding Fathers* (Ithaca, 1965), esp. pp. 18-32. For further discussion of Puritan historiography see Kenneth B. Murdock, *Literature and Theology in Colonial New England* (New York, 1963), pp. 67-97; "Clio in the Wilderness," *Church History,* XXIV, (1955), 221-38; and "William Hubbard and the Providential Interpretation of History," *Proceedings*

*of the American Antiquarian Society,* LII (1942), 15-37; Edward K. Trefz, "The Puritan View of History," *Boston Public Library Quarterly,* IX (1957), 115-36; Peter Gay, *A Loss of Mastery: Puritan Historians in Colonial America* (Berkeley and Los Angeles, 1966); Daniel B. Shea, *Spiritual Biography in Early America* (Princeton, 1968); and Cecelia Tichi, "Spiritual Biography and the Lord's Remembrancers," *William and Mary Quarterly,* 3d ser., XXVIII (1971), 64- 85.

5.  Stoughton, *New England's True Interest,* p. 199.
6.  Cited in Gay, *Loss of Mastery,* pp. 55-70.
7.  Craven, *Legend of the Founding Fathers,* pp. 18-22.
8.  Cf. for example John Barnard, *The Throne Established by Righteousness* (1734), reprinted in *The Wall and the Garden: Selected Massachusetts Election Sermons, 1670-1775,* ed. with intro. by A.W. Plumstead (Minneapolis, 1968), p. 230.
9.  Prince, *History of New England,* cited in Craven, *Legend of the Founding Fathers,* pp. 23-24; Thomas Hutchinson, *The History of the Colony and Province of Massachusetts Bay* (1764), ed. Lawrence S. Mayo (Cambridge, Mass., 1936), I, 82.
10. Amos Adams, *A Concise, Historical View of . . . the Planting and Progressive Improvement of New England* (Boston, 1769), p. 27. Cf. also Samuel Cooke, *A Sermon Preached at Cambridge . . .* (1770), reprinted in Plumstead, *Wall and Garden;* Judah Champion, *A Brief View of the Distresses, Hardships and Dangers our Ancestors Encountered in Settling New England* (Hartford, 1770).
11. For example, see Ramsay, *History of the Revolution,* I, 13; George Richards Minot, *A Continuation of the History of Massachusetts Bay* (Boston, 1798-1803), I, 17-18.
12. John Adams, *A Dissertation on the Canon and Feudal Law* (1765), reprinted in *The Works of John Adams,* ed. Charles Francis Adams (Freeport, N.Y., 1969), III, 451.
13. Ibid., pp. 451-56.
14. Jedidiah Morse and Elijah Parish, *A Compendious History of New England* (1801; 2d. ed., Newburyport, Mass., 1809), p. 107.
15. Trumbull, *History of the United States,* pp. 105, 108; Belknap, *History of New Hampshire,* I, 43, 47.
16. Warren, *History of the American Revolution,* I, 15-16. Warren attributed the Puritans' intolerance to the weakness of human nature; she had nothing but praise for Pennsylvania and the Quakers.
17. Morse, *History of New England,* p. 106; Adams, *A Dissertation,* in *Works,* III, 452; Minot, *History of Massachusetts,* I, 18; Backus, *History of New England,* I, passim.
18. Trumbull, *History of the United States,* pp. xi, 199.
19. Marshall, *Life of Washington,* I, 74, 127. The first volume was a history of the colonies. Cf. also Ramsay, *History of the Revolution,* I, 8-10.
20. Robert Proud, *The History of Pennsylvania in North America . . .* (Philadelphia, 1797-98), I, 5-8, 13.
21. Chalmers, *Political Annals of the United Colonies,* pp. 218-219; Robert Green McCloskey, ed., *The Works of James Wilson* (Cambridge, Mass., 1967), I, 71.

22. John Leeds Bozman, *The History of Maryland, Its First Settlement in 1633, to the Restoration in 1660* (1837), intro. by Richard Parsons (Spartansburg, S.C., 1968), I, 1-8. The first volume of the 1837 edition was a reprint of *An Introduction of the History of Maryland,* originally published in 1811.

23. Bozman, *History of Maryland,* I, 194, 222-32; Craven, *Legend of the Founding Fathers,* pp. 88-89.

24. Bozman, *History of Maryland,* I, 242, 194; II, 86. Bozman was critical of writers like Chalmers who contended that Calvert's primary aim had been to establish an asylum for Catholics in America.

25. John Daly Burk, *The History of Virginia, from its First Settlement to the Commencement of the Revolution* (1804-05; 2d ed., Petersburg Va., 1822), I, i, 160.

26. Ibid., pp. 160-300. See also Shaffer, "Burk's *History of Virginia* and American National History," pp. 336-46.

27. For discussions of historical writing in colonial America see Van Tassel, *Recording America's Past,* pp. 1-30; Jarvis N. Morse, *American Beginnings* (Washington, 1952); and Curti, *Roots of American Loyalty,* pp. 3-20.

28. Non-New England state histories by natives include Bozman, *History of Maryland;* Campbell, *History of Virginia;* Hugh McCall, *History of Georgia* (Philadelphia, 1811-16); and Randolph, *History of Virginia.*

29. Ramsay to Belknap, Aug. 11, 1792, Ramsay to Eliot, April 7, 1810, "Ramsay . . . Writings," pp. 133, 166.

30. Hannah Adams, *A Memoir of Miss Hannah Adams written by Herself with Additional Notices, by a Friend* (Boston, 1832), p. 22; Abiel Holmes, *American Annals,* I, 200.

31. Ramsay, *Oration,* in "Ramsay . . . Writings," p. 196.

32. Gay, *The Enlightenment,* II, 385-87.

33. Among clergymen who wrote history were Isaac Backus, Jeremy Belknap, Morgan Edwards, John Eliot, Abiel Holmes, Jedidiah Morse, Elijah Parish, Ezra Stiles, Benjamin Trumbull, Mason Locke Weems, Samuel Williams, and Hugh Williamson. Laymen who clearly displayed strong religious convictions include Hannah Adams, Robert Proud, David Ramsay, Edmund Randolph, Richard Snowden, and Mercy Otis Warren. While not anti-religious, John Marshall made no reference to Providence.

34. Trumbull, *History of the United States,* p. x.

35. Belknap, *History of New Hampshire,* I, 84-85. For a discussion of Belknap's historical and literary views see Sidney Kaplan, "*The History of New Hampshire:* Jeremy Belknap as Literary Craftsman," *William and Mary Quarterly,* 3d ser., XXI (1964), 18-39.

36. Backus, *History of New England,* I, preface; Williams, *A Discourse on the Love of our Country,* p. 1.

37. Warren, *History of the American Revolution,* I, 16, III, 64; Gay, *The Enlightenment,* II, 387.

38. Ramsay, *History of the Revolution,* I. For another interpretation of the role of Providence in Ramsay and Warren see Smith, *History as Argument,* (1966), esp. pp. 42-45, 72, 73-75, 116-19, 174-79, 201-04.

39. Joseph Priestley, *An Essay on the First Principles of Government and on the Nature of Political, Civil and Religious Liberty* (London, 1768), p. 1.
40. Burk, *History of Virginia,* I, 160.
41. Belknap, *History of New Hampshire,* I, 326; Ramsay, *Oration* (1794), in "Ramsay . . . Writings," p. 191. Jefferson's quote is from Daniel Boorstin, *The Lost World of Thomas Jefferson* (New York, 1960), p. 228. For the emergence of the idea of America's millennial role see Ernest Lee Tuveson, *Redeemer Nation: The Idea of America's Millennial Role* (Chicago, 1968), esp. pp. 1-25.
42. John H. Plumb, *The Death of the Past* (Boston, 1971), p. 93.
43. Jeremy Belknap, *A Discourse Intended to Commemorate the Discovery of America by Christopher Columbus* (Boston, 1792), pp. 28-31.
44. Tuveson, *Millenium and Utopia: A Study in the Background of the Idea of Progress* (New York, 1964), pp. ix, 137-39.
45. Belknap, *Discourse to Commemorate the Discovery of America,* pp. 7, 36-37; and *History of New Hampshire,* I, 3.
46. Gay, *The Enlightenment,* II, 522-28; Black, *The Art of History,* pp. 48-50, 103-08.
47. Trumbull, *History of the United States,* p. 107.
48. Ramsay, *History of the Revolution,* I, 29; Trumbull, *History of the United States,* pp. 177-78.
49. Adams, *A Dissertation,* in *Works,* III, 451.
50. Belknap, *History of New Hampshire,* I, 34-37.
51. Adams, *A Dissertation,* in *Works,* III, 452; Benjamin Trumbull, *A Complete History of Connecticut, Civil and Ecclesiastical* (New Haven, 1797-1818), I, 17.

### Chapter IV

1. Marshall, *Life of Washington,* I, 3-4; Williams, *History of Vermont,* p. vii.
2. For the debate over the nature of the American environment see Gilbert Chinard, "Eighteenth Century Theories on America as a Human Habitat," *Proceedings of the American Philosophical Society,* XCI (1947), 27-57; Ralph N. Miller, "American Nationalism as a Theory of Nature," *William and Mary Quarterly,* 3d ser., IX (1955), 74-95; Henry Steele Commager and Giroandetti, Elmo, eds., intro. to *Was America a Mistake? An Eighteenth Century Controversy* (New York, 1967), pp. 11-46; and Nye, *Cultural Life,* pp. 54-56.
3. Corneille DePauw, *Research on the Americans* (1768), quoted in Nye, *Cultural Life,* p. 56n.
4. Comte de Buffon, *Natural History, General and Particular,* in *Was America a Mistake?,* p. 60.
5. Miller, "American Nationalism as a Theory of Nature," pp. 74-76.
6. DePauw, *Research on the Americans,* in *Was America a Mistake?,* p. 77.
7. Abbé Raynal, *Philosophical and Political History of the Settlements and Trade of Europeans in the Two Indies* (1770), ibid., pp. 14-15.
8. Thomas Paine, *A Letter to the Abbé Raynal* (London, 1782), pp. 3-17.
9. William Robertson, *History of America,* in *Was America a Mistake?,* p. 89.
10. Quoted in Miller, "American Nationalism as a Theory of Nature," p. 82.

11. Belknap, *History of New Hampshire*, II, 172. For the impact of this debate on American science see Nye, *Cultural Life*, pp. 54-69.

12. American writers were not alone in denouncing the works of Buffon, DePauw, and Raynal. Europeans such as Condorcet, Chastellux, and Von Gentz joined them. See Commager and Giorandetti, *Was America a Mistake?*, pp. 34-46, 185-231.

13. Cf. Morse, *History of America;* James Callender, *Sketches of the History of America* (Philadelphia, 1798); Lendrum, *History of the American Revolution;* and Jeremy Belknap, "Has the Discovery of America Been Helpful or Hurtful to Mankind?," *Boston Magazine*, I (1784).

14. Thomas Jefferson, *Notes on the State of Virginia* (1784), intro. by Thomas Perkins Abernethy (New York, 1964), p. 64; Belknap, *History of New Hampshire*, II, 172.

15. Jefferson, *Notes on Virginia*, p. 90.

16. Ibid., pp. 62-63.

17. Ibid., pp. 64-65.

18. For Morse's geographical works see his *Geography Made Easy* (New Haven, 1784), which went through twenty-five editions, *The American Geography; or a View of the Present Situation of the United States of America* (Elizabethtown, N.J., 1789), and *The American Universal Geography* (Boston, 1793). See also Jeremy Belknap, "A Description of the White Mountains," *Transactions of the American Philosophical Society*, II (1786), 42-49.

19. Hugh Williamson, "An Essay on Comets," *Transactions of the American Philosophical Society*, I (1771). His paper, "Experiments and Observations on the Gymnotus Electricus, or Electrical Eel," was read before the Royal Society and published in its *Transactions* (1775). For this essay Williamson was awarded an honorary Doctorate of Law from the University of Utrecht. He was appointed to the chair of mathematics and natural philosophy at the College of Philadelphia, but inadequate funds prevented him from accepting the post.

20. Besides *The History of Vermont*, Williams wrote a *History of the American Revolution* which appeared in his journal, *The Rural Magazine; or Vermont Repository* (1795) and became a popular textbook, going through thirteen editions from 1824 to 1831. Cf. Ralph N. Miller, "Samuel Williams' *History of Vermont*," *New England Quarterly*, XXII (1949), 73-84; Merle Curti, *Human Nature in American Historical Thought*, pp. 54-59.

21. For Montesquieu's views on the importance of climate see his *Spirit of the Laws* (1748), intro. by Franz Neumann (New York, 1962), pp. 221-91.

22. Ramsay, *History of the Revolution*, I, 20; *History of South Carolina*, II, 215-20. Cf. Montesquieu, *Spirit of the Laws*, pp. 221-25, 271-73.

23. Hugh Williamson, *Observations on the Climate in Different Parts of America* (New York, 1811), p. 174. Cf. Montesquieu, *Spirit of the Laws*, pp. 221-24.

24. Cf. Williams, *History of Vermont;* Williamson, *History of North Carolina* (Philadelphia, 1812); Belknap, *History of New Hampshire;* James Sullivan, *History of the District of Maine* (Boston, 1795); and John Filson, *The Discovery, Settlement, and Present State of Kentucke* (Wilmington, 1784).

25. Williams, *History of Vermont*, pp. vii, 366; Benjamin Rush, *Essays, Literary, Moral and Philosophical* (Philadelphia, 1798), p. 78.
26. Belknap, *History of New Hampshire*, II, 171-90; Williams, *History of Vermont*, pp. 360-66; Williamson, *History of North Carolina*, I, 65-66. For the use of statistics in early America see John Kirtland Wright, "Notes on Measuring and Counting in Early American Geography," in *Human Nature in Geography* (Cambridge, Mass., 1966), pp. 205-49.
27. Belknap, *An Election Sermon*, p. 47.
28. Howe, *Political Thought of Adams*, p. 133. For further discussion of the cyclical view of history and the idea of progress see Stow Persons, "The Cyclical Theory of History in Eighteenth Century America," *American Quarterly*, VI (1954), 147-64; Gay, *The Enlightenment*, II, 98-125; and Charles Frankel, *The Faith of Reason: The Idea of Progress in the French Enlightenment* (1947, New York, 1969).
29. Proud, *History of Pennsylvania*, I, 5.
30. Gordon S. Wood, "Republicanism as a Revolutionary Ideology," in *The Role of Ideology in the American Revolution*, ed. John R. Howe, Jr. (New York, 1970), p. 85.
31. Ramsay, *History of the Revolution*, I, 197.
32. Quoted in Miller, "Williams' *History of Vermont*," p. 76n.
33. Williams, *History of Vermont*, p. 376; Sullivan, *History of Maine*, pp. vi-vii.
34. For discussions of late eighteenth-century American views on human nature see Leon Howard, "The Late Eighteenth Century: An Age of Contradictions," in *Transitions in American Literary History*, ed. Harry Hayden Clark (Durham, N.C., 1953), pp. 61-73; Nye, *Cultural Life*, pp. 17-28; and Curti, *Human Nature in American Historical Thought*, pp. 36-59.
35. Ramsay to Rush, Feb. 3, 1779, in "Ramsay . . . Writings," p. 59; Warren, *History of the American Revolution*, III, 415.
36. Ibid., I, 2-3; III, 400. I have used Warren because her assessment of human nature was more pessimistic than those of other American historians.
37. Ramsay, *History of the Revolution*, I, 348; John M'Culloch, *A Concise History of the United States of America* (Philadelphia, 1795), p. 189; Williams, *History of Vermont*, p. 375.
38. Douglass Adair, "The Politics May Be Reduced to a Science: David Hume, James Madison, and the Tenth *Federalist*," in *The Reinterpretation of the American Revolution, 1763-1789*, ed. by Jack P. Greene (New York, 1968), p. 489.
39. Douglas Sloan, *The Scottish Enlightenment and the American College Ideal* (New York, 1971), pp. 61n, 78-81.
40. Adam Ferguson, *An Essay on the History of Civil Society* (1767), ed. with intro. by Duncan Forbes (Edinburg, 1966), pp. 62, 210-14; Samuel Stanhope Smith, *Lectures on the Subjects of Moral and Political Philosophy* (Trenton, N.J., 1812), I, 77-78; Sloan, *Scottish Enlightenment*, p. 174. The best general discussion of the Scottish Enlightenment is Gladys M. Bryson, *Man and Society: The Scottish Inquiry of the Eighteenth Century* (Princeton, 1945).

41. Montesquieu, *Spirit of the Laws*, pp. 120, 2. On Montesquieu's political and sociological theories see Werner Stark, *Montesquieu: Pioneer of the Sociology of Knowledge* (Toronto, 1961); and Henry J. Merry, *Montesquieu's System of Natural Government* (West Lafayette, Ind., 1970).

42. Williamson, "On the Benefits of Civil History," p. 31; Williams, *History of Vermont*, p. 360; Stark, *Montesquieu*, pp. 122-28.

43. Williams, *History of Vermont*, p. 361; Ramsay, *History of the Revolution*, I, 34, 32.

44. Stark, *Montesquieu*, pp. 124-28; Gordon S. Wood, *The Creation of the American Republic, 1776-1787* (Chapel Hill, 1969), pp. 46-48, 119; Ramsay to John Eliot, Sept. 26, 1787, "Ramsay . . . Writings," p. 115.

45. Montesquieu, *Spirit of the Laws*, pp. 19-22, 34, 40-42.

46. Ramsay, *Oration* (1794), "Ramsay . . . Writings," p. 191; Williams, *History of Vermont*, p. viii; Ramsay, *History of the Revolution*, I, 29.

47. Williams, *History of Vermont*, p. 371; Lendrum, *Concise and Impartial History*, p. 201.

48. Warren, *History of the American Revolution*, I, 20-21; Ramsay, *History of the Revolution*, I, 34; Belknap, *History of New Hampshire*, II, 251.

49. Howe, *Political Thought of Adams*, p. 136. For the increasing concentration of wealth and social differentiation in American society see Lawrence A. Cremin, *American Education: The Colonial Experience, 1607-1783* (New York, 1970), pp. 271-571; James A. Henretta, "Economic Development and Social Structure in Colonial Boston," *William and Mary Quarterly*, XXII (1965), 75-92; Kenneth A. Lockridge, "Land, Population and the Evolution of New England Society, 1630-1790," *Past and Present*, No. 39 (1968), 62-80; James T. Lemon and Gary B. Nash, "The Distribution of Wealth in Eighteenth-Century America: A Century of Change in Chester County, Pennsylvania, 1693-1802," *Journal of Social History*, II (1968), 1-24; and Jackson T. Main, *The Social Structure of Revolutionary America* (Princeton, 1965).

50. Belknap, *History of New Hampshire*, I, 88-89.

51. Ramsay, *History of the Revolution*, I, 17-18, 34; *History of the United States* (Philadelphia, 1816-17), I, 231, 232.

52  Warren, *History of the American Revolution*, III, 251-52.

53. Thomas Reid, *Inquiry into the Human Mind* (1764), quoted in Bryson, *Man and Society*, p. 133.

54. Frankel, *The Faith of Reason*, pp. 68-74; Howard, "The Late Eighteenth Century," pp. 72-73.

55. Williams, *History of Vermont*, p. vii.

56. Howard, "The Late Eighteenth Century," pp. 61-79.

57. Marshall, *Life of Washington*, I, 43, 77-79. For a similar argument see Hugh McCall's discussion of the decline and fall of the Georgia proprietorship: *History of Georgia* (Atlanta, 1909), pp. 3-171.

58. According to M. Eugene Sirmans, authorship of the Fundamental Constitutions belongs to Baron Anthony Ashley-Cooper, the leading Carolina proprietor and Locke's patron, although Locke did assist him. Sirman's account contains a convincing attack on the long-standing view that the Fundamental

Constitutions was an unrealistic, utopian scheme which had little effect on the colony's subsequent development. *Colonial South Carolina: A Political History, 1663-1763* (Chapel Hill, 1966), pp. 7-16.

59. Marshall, *Life of Washington*, I, 155. "The operation and fate of Mr. Locke's system," wrote William Gordon, "may convince us of this truth, that a person may defend the principles of liberty and the rights of mankind, with great abilities and success, and yet, after all, when called upon to produce a plan of legislation, he may astonish the world with a signal absurdity." *History of the Independence of the United States*, I, 78. For a similar view see Williamson, *History of North Carolina*, I, 111-12, 122-26.
60. Williams, *History of Vermont*, pp. 343-44.

**Chapter V**

1. Winthrop Jordan, *White over Black: American Attitudes Toward the Negro, 1555-1812* (Chapel Hill, 1968), p. 336.
2. J. Hector St. Jean de Crevecoeur, *Letters from an American Farmer and Sketches of Eighteenth-Century America* (New York, 1963), pp. 62-64. For a discussion of the concept of national character and its subsequent history see Thomas L. Hartshorne, *The Distorted Image: Changing Conceptions of the American Character Since Turner* (Cleveland, 1968).
3. Maldwyn Allen Jones, *American Immigration* (Chicago, 1960), p. 40; Jordan, *White over Black*, pp. 337-340. For the argument against immigration by two noted Republicans see Jefferson, *Notes on Virginia*, pp. 82-84; and Warren, *History of the American Revolution*, III, 250-51.
4. Jordan, *White over Black*, p. 339.
5. Randolph, *History of Virginia*, pp. 166-176.
6. Proud, *History of Pennsylvania*, I, 20-100; Craven, *Legend of the Founding Fathers*, pp. 125-27.
7. Morse and Parish, *History of New England*, p. 329.
8. Burk, *History of Virginia*, II, 333-334. For Burk's career in Ireland and America see Joseph I. Shulim, "John Daly Burk: Irish Revolutionist and American Patriot," *Transactions of the American Philosophical Society*, new ser., LIV, pt. 6 (1964), 5-52.
9. Ramsay, *History of South Carolina*, I, 12-13; Jordan, *White over Black*, p. 337.
10. M'Culloch, *History of the United States*, p. 26; Randolph, *History of Virginia*, pp. 96, 202, 193, 216.
11. William W. Freehling, "The Founding Fathers and Slavery," *American Historical Review*, LXXVII (1972), 82-83.
12. Randolph, *History of Virginia*, p. 253.
13. Jordan, *White over Black*, pp. 340-341.
14. Ramsay to Jefferson, May 3, 1786, Ramsay to Eliot, November 26, 1788, in "Ramsay . . . Writings," pp. 101-123.
15. Cf. Belknap, *History of New Hampshire*, esp. I; and Trumbull, *History of Connecticut*, esp. I.
16. Williams, *History of Vermont*, p. 208.

17. Jefferson, *Notes on Virginia*, p. 90.
18. Roy Harvey Pearce, *Savagism and Civilization: A Study of the Indian and the American Mind* (Baltimore, 1967), pp. 160-61.
19. Randolph, *History of Virginia*, p. 259.
20. Ramsay, *History of the United States*, II, 302; *History of the Revolution*, I, 18-19.
21. For the Saxon myth see H. Trevor Colbourn, *The Lamp of Experience: Whig History and the Intellectual Origins of the American Revolution* (Chapel Hill, 1965), passim.
22. David Hume, *An Enquiry Concerning Human Understanding* (1748), quoted by Douglass Adair, "That Politics may Be Reduced to a Science: David Hume, James Madison, and the Tenth *Federalist*," *Huntington Library Quarterly*, XX (1957), 345-46.
23. Ferguson, *Essay on Civil Society*, pp. xxiv, 169.
24. Nathan Hale, "Review of Benjamin Trumbull, *A Complete History of Connecticut*," *North American Review*, VIII (Dec., 1818), 72-73, cited by Danzer, "America's Roots in the Past," pp. 1-2.
25. Marshall, *Life of Washington*, I, 103; Ramsay, *History of the Revolution*, I, 29.
26. Williams, *The Natural and Civil History of Vermont* (2d ed., Burlington, Vt., 1809), I, 493-503.
27. Williams, *History of Vermont*, p. 371.
28. Ramsay, *History of the United States*, I, 53; M'Culloch, *Concise History of the United States*, p. 35.
29. Wood, *Creation of the American Republic*, pp. 18-28; Bernard Bailyn, *The Ideological Origins of the American Revolution* (Cambridge, Mass., 1967), pp. 34-54; Colbourn, *Lamp of Experience*, passim.
30. Minot, *History of Massachusetts Bay*, I, 52-53.
31. Wood, *Creation of the Republic*, pp. 18-28.
32. Ramsay, *History of the Revolution*, I, 355; Belknap, *History of New Hampshire*, II, 201; Williams, *History of Vermont*, p. 342.
33. Ramsay, *History of the Revolution*, I, 355-56; Williams, *History of Vermont*, pp. 344, 372; Randolph, *History of Virginia*, p. 177.
34. Marshall, *Life of Washington*, I, 85, 226-37.
35. Ibid., pp. 96, 97, 100, 137.
36. Ibid., p. 184. Marshall allotted only five pages to the settlement of Pennsylvania, most of which was devoted to a discussion of the colony's boundary dispute with Maryland.
37. Cf., for example, Marshall's discussion of early Virginia, South Carolina, and Georgia. Ibid., pp. 22-71, 151-59, 252-56.
38. Burk, *History of Virginia*, II, 233, 307.
39. Randolph, *History of Virginia*, pp. 12, 147, 158.
40. Ibid., pp. 153, 157, 160-61, 163.
41. Ibid., pp. 24-25.
42. Burk, *History of Virginia*, II, 334.
43. Randolph, *History of Virginia*, p. 158.
44. For Stith see Van Tassel, *Recording America's Past*, pp. 26-27.
45. Burk, *An Oration*, p. 7.

### Chapter VI

1. Cf. William Henry Drayton, *Memoirs of the American Revolution, From Its Commencement to the Year 1776* (1779), ed. with additions by John Drayton (Charleston, 1821); Gouverneur Morris, *Observations on the American Revolution* (Philadelphia, 1779), written at the request of the Continental Congress; and John Adams, *Twenty-Six Letters* (1780; 2d ed., New York, 1789), a narrowly defined legal brief written ostensibly to explain the American case to a Dutch friend.

2. Gordon to John Temple, March 15, 1786, Massachusetts Historical Society, *Proceedings*, LXIII (1929-30), 610. It is difficult to ascertain what portions of Gordon's *History of the Rise, Progress, and Independence of the United States of America* would have given offense. In its published form it is an unblinking justification of the American cause, despite his claim that he toned it down because his publisher was fearful of prosecution under British libel laws. Cf. Merrill Jensen, *The New Nation: A History of the United States During the Confederation, 1781-1789* (New York, 1965), pp. 96-99; and Van Tassel, *Recording America's Past*, pp. 36-40.

3. Ibid., p. 34.

4. Cf. William Allen, *A Biographical Dictionary* (Boston, 1813); Jeremy Belknap, *American Biography* (Boston, 1794-98); John Eliot, *A Biographical Dictionary* (Boston, 1809); James Hardie, *New Universal Biographical Dictionary and America Remembrances of Departed Merit* (New York, 1801); John Kingston, *New American Biographic Dictionary* (Baltimore, 1810); and Thomas J. Rogers, *A New American Biographical Dictionary* (Philadelphia, 1812). The only exception is the biographical sketches Edmund Randolph included in his *History of Virginia*, pp. 176-93.

5. Andrew A. Lipscomb and Albert E. Berg, eds., *The Writings of Thomas Jefferson* (Washington, 1905), XVI, 126. For Jefferson's support of historical writing and his efforts to recruit Joel Barlow see Van Tassel, *Recording America's Past*, pp. 76-86; and John Dos Passos, *The Ground We Stand On: Some Examples from the History of a Political Creed* (New York, 1941), pp. 366-67. Jefferson helped Francois Soule write his *Histoire des troubles de l'Amerique anglaise. . . .* (Paris, 1787) and along with Thomas Paine attacked what he regarded as gross inaccuracies in the Abbe Raynal's *Revolution of America*. Cf. E. Millicent Sowerby, ed., *Catalogue of Thomas Jefferson's Library* (Washington, 1952), I, 223-24; and Van Tassel, op. cit., p. 77. For Adams' difficulties with Warren see the "Correspondence between John Adams and Mercy Warren relating to her 'History of the American Revolution,' July-August, 1807," Mass. Hist. Soc., *Collections*, 5th ser., IV (Boston, 1878), 317-491; and Warren, *History of the American Revolution*, III, 392-95. For a scurrilous attack on the Adams administration see John Wood, *The History of the Administration of John Adams* (New York, 1802).

6. Quoted in Broadus Mitchell and Louise Mitchell, *Biography of the Constitution of the United States* (New York, 1964), p. 21.

7. Ebenezer Hazard to Jeremy Belknap, April 10, 1782, Mass. Hist. Soc., *Collections*, 5th ser., II (1877), 126.

8. Paine, *A Letter to Abbé Raynal*, pp. 3-7.

9. Callender, *History of America*, p. 34; Burk, *History of Virginia*, I, 279, 281.

10. Ramsay, *History of the Revolution*, I, 19; Marshall, *Life of Washington*, II, 272; Belknap, *History of New Hampshire*, I, 327.

11. Trumbull, *History of the United States*, pp. 241, 338.

12. Randolph, *History of Virginia*, p. 166; Gordon, *History of the Independence of the United States*, I, 195.

13. Ibid., pp. 41, 127.

14. Tholfsen, *Historical Thinking*, pp. 286-87.

15. M'Culloch, *History of the United States*, p. 36; Randolph, *History of Virginia*, pp. 175-76, 199

16. McCall, *History of Georgia*, p. 257; Ramsay, *History of the Revolution*, I, 87.

17. Marshall, *Life of Washington*, II, 399, 217, 109.

18. Ramsay, *History of the Revolution*, I, 74-75, 87.

19. Black, *The Art of History*, pp. 37-38; Gay, *The Enlightenment*, II, 387-88.

20. For eighteenth century attitudes toward historical causation see ibid., II, 386-96; J. H. Brumfitt, *Voltaire, Historian* (London, 1958), pp. 104-11; and N. N. Schargo, *History in the Encyclopedie* (New York, 1947), passim.

21. Bishop Jacques Bossuet, tutor to the young Louis XIV, was the author of the influential *Discourse on Universal History* (1681).

22. Frederick J. Teggart, *Theory and Process of History* (Berkeley and Los Angeles, 1962), p. 48; Keith Thomas, *Religion and the Decline of Magic: Studies in Popular Beliefs in Sixteenth and Seventeenth Century England* (London, 1971), pp. 80-82.

23. Williamson, "Benefits of Civil History," p. 32. Williamson took these and other remarks without citation verbatim from David Hume's *An Enquiry Concerning Human Understanding* (1748).

24. Randolph, *History of Virginia*, p. 167.

25. Cf. Bailyn, *Ideological Origins*, pp. 33-52.

26. Bailyn, *The Origins of American Politics* (New York, 1968), pp. 42-43.

27. Gordon to James Bowdoin, May 18, 1770, "The Letters of the Reverend William Gordon, Historian of the American Revolution," Massachusetts Historical Society, *Proceedings*, LXIII (1929-30), 309.

28. Belknap, *History of New Hampshire*, I, 328.

29. Warren, *History of the American Revolution*, I, 22-23.

30. Gordon, *History of the Independence of the United States*, I, 143. For approval of Gordon's version of the Whitefield episode see Carl Bridenbaugh, *Mitre and Sceptre: Transatlantic Faiths, Ideas, Personalities, and Politics, 1689-1775* (New York, 1967), pp. 244-45.

31. Ramsay, *History of the Revolution*, I, 333. The same conspiratorial tone also characterized the accounts of loyalist historians such as Thomas Hutchinson, Johnathan Boucher, Peter Olver, and Thomas Jones.

32. Marshall, *Life of Washington*, II, 74.

33. Ramsay, *History of the Revolution*, I, 44, 54-55. For similar views see Drayton,

*Memoirs of the American Revolution;* Randolph, *History of Virginia;* and M'Culloch, *Concise History of the United States.*

34. Mason L. Weems, *The Life of Washington* (1800), ed. with intro. by Marcus Cunliffe (Cambridge, Mass., 1962), p. 59. The Cunliffe edition is a reprint of the 1809 version (Weems' italics).

35. For discussions of Whig political theory in the American context see Wood, *Creation of the American Republic,* pp. 3-45; Bailyn, *Ideological Origins,* pp. 55-93.

36. Warren, *History of the American Revolution,* I, 2.

37. Nathaniel Chipman, *Sketches of the Principles of Government* (Rutland, Vermont, 1793), p. 241; Warren, *History of the American Revolution,* I, 52; M'Culloch, *Concise History of the United States,* p. 35.

## Chapter VII

1. "An Historical Journal of the American War," Massachusetts Historical Society, *Collections,* II (1793), 246.

2. Edmund Randolph was an exception. In his account the Revolution did not become a wholly national movement until 1774. Up to that date he focused almost exclusively on events in Virginia. That state's response he regarded as a continuation of long standing opposition to intrusions on its rights by royal authority. *History of Virginia,* esp. pp. 149-75.

3. McCall, *History of Georgia,* p. 258.

4. Warren, *History of the American Revolution,* I, 301.

5. Actually the first sympathetic account of a Loyalist was Henry C. Van Schaack's filiopietistic *The Life of Peter Van Schaak . . .* (New York, 1842), But, unlike Sabine's work, it dealt with only a single individual. Sabine, a Maine politician, was no doubt sympathetic toward the Loyalists because of his contact with their descendants on the border of Maine and Canada, but his interest was also politically motivated. While the Revolutionary generation found it expedient to ignore the Loyalists or minimize their importance, they became a useful weapon in the hands of later historians who were involved in the growing sectional conflict. Sabine wanted to dispel the popularly held belief that the colonists had risen as one people against the British. He emphasized the patriotism of the people of New England by pointing out that "the adherents of the crown were more numerous at the South and in Pennsylvania and in New York, than in New England." His primary purpose was to attack the reputation of South Carolina, the fountainhead of nullification: "It is hardly an exaggeration to add that more Whigs of New England were sent to . . . [South Carolina's] aid, and now lie buried in her soil, than she sent from it to every scene of strife from Lexington to Yorktown." Van Tassel, *Recording America's Past,* p. 135. For a discussion of why American historians have tended until recently to ignore the Loyalists see Douglas Adair and John Schutz, eds., *Peter Oliver's Origins of the American Rebellion: A Tory View* (San Marino, Calif., 1965), pp. vii-ix.

6. Ramsay, *History of the Revolution,* I, 126, 312; II, 310.

7. Ibid., I, 125, 189; II, 310-311.

8. Ibid., II, 312-314.

9. Ibid., I, 95; II, 310-11, 314.

10. Ramsay, *History of South Carolina*, II, 214.

11. Burk, *An Oration*, p. 7; Williams, *History of Vermont*, p. vii.

12. Ramsay, *History of the Revolution*, I, 355.

13. Warren, *History of the American Revolution*, I, vii-viii (Warren's italics); Joel Barlow, *Advice to the Privileged Orders in the Several States of Europe Resulting From the Necessity and Propriety of a General Revolution in the Principle of Government* (1792), intro. by David Brion David (Ithaca, 1956), p. 3.

14. Belknap to Ebenezer Hazard, March 3, 1784, Mass. Hist. Soc., *Collections*, 5th ser., II (1877), 314; Noah Webster, *The Revolution in France Considered in Respect to Its Progress and Effects by an American* (New York, 1794), p. 41; Warren, *History of the American Revolution*, I, vii (Warren's italics).

15. David Ramsay, *Oration* (1794), p. 196. For America and Revolutionary France see Paul A. Varg, *Foreign Policies of the Founding Fathers* (Baltimore, 1972), passim.

16. Marshall, *Life of Washington*, V, 367-68. For Burke see Thomas P. Peardon, *The Transition in English Historical Writing, 1760-1830* (New York, 1933), pp. 107, 163-64, 174-75; and Hedva Ben-Israel, *English Historians on the French Revolution* (Cambridge, England, 1968), pp. 15-18.

17. Allen, *Biographical Dictionary*, p. viii.

18. Bailyn, *Ideological Origins*, pp. 83-84.

19. [William Vans Murray], *Political Sketches, Inscribed to His Excellency John Adams* (London, 1787), p. 21; Williams, *History of Vermont*, p. 373.

20. Cf. Marshall, *Life of Washington*, II, 91-92; Belknap, *History of New Hampshire*, I, 152-53.

21. Ibid., I, 331; M'Culloch, *Concise History of the United States*, p. 45; Warren, *History of the American Revolution*, I, 147-51.

22. Lipset, *The First New Nation*, pp. 77-78. For a discussion of culture in the new nation see ibid., pp. 6-9, 63-65. "The best Part of a People," wrote Belknap, "is always the lesser; and of that best part, the wisest is always the best-least." *An Election Sermon*.

23. For further discussion of the problem of leadership see Randolph, *History of Virginia*, pp. 176-97.

24 John Jay to Jefferson, Dec. 14, 1786, *Papers of Jefferson*, ed. Boyd, X, 597; Ramsay, *History of the Revolution*, II, 340; Warren, *History of the American Revolution*, III, 346-56. For Shays' Rebellion see J. R. Pole, *Political Representation in England and the Origins of the American Republic* (New York, 1966), pp. 227-44; and Marion Starkey, *A Little Rebellion* (New York, 1955).

25. Quoted in Feer, "George Richards Minot's *History*," p. 207. This is a perceptive analysis of Minot and his work, upon which the discussion here largely relies.

26. For Minot's diary see Massachusetts Historical Society, *Collections*, 1st ser., VIII (1802); and the Sedgwick Papers, Massachusetts Historical Society.

27. Feer, "Minot's *History*," pp. 210-13.

28. Minot, *An Eulogy on George Washington. . . .* (Boston, 1800), pp. 21-22.

29. Mass. Hist. Soc., *Collections*, VIII, 98; Feer, "Minot's *History*," p. 214.

30. Ibid., pp. 214-17.

31. Ibid., p. 217.

32. Ibid., pp. 218, 226; Minot, *History of the Insurrections in the Year 1786* (Boston, 1788), p. 192.

33. Maier, "Popular Uprisings," pp. 3-4. See also Gordon S. Wood, "A Note on Mobs in the American Revolution," ibid., XXIII (1966), 635-42, and *Creation of American Republic*, pp. 319-28.

34. Randolph, *History of Virginia*, pp. 153-56; Burk, *History of Virginia*, II, 233. For the historiography of Bacon's Rebellion see Wilcomb E. Washburn, *The Governor and the Rebel: A History of Bacon's Rebellion in Virginia* (Chapel Hill, 1975), pp. 1-16.

35. Ramsay, *History of the Revolution*, II, 319.

36. Williams, *History of Vermont*, pp. 372-73; Marshall, *Washington*, II, 319. Marshall did not agree that public opinion had determined the outcome of the Revolutionary War. He attributed success to the Continental army and Washington's ability to hold it together. He did concede the importance of public opinion in the years preceding hostilities.

37. Belknap, *History of New Hampshire*, I, 334; Ramsay, *History of the Revolution*, I, 120.

38. Belnap, *History of New Hampshire*, I, 366-67.

39. Brumfitt, *Voltaire*, pp. 104-111.

40. Warren, *History of the American Revolution*, I, 123- 24; Brumfitt, *Voltaire*, p. 108.

41. *Columbian Magazine* (January, 1788), p. 3, cited in Free, *The Columbian Magazine*, p. 103.

42. For an annotated list of biographical dictionaries published from 1794 to 1820 see Danzer, "America's Roots in the Past," pp. 175-77.

43. On Puritan spiritual biography see Murdock, *Literature and Theology*, pp. 67-98; Shea, *Spiritual Biography*; Gay, *A Loss of Mastery*; and Tichi, "Spiritual Biography," pp. 64-85.

44. Ibid., pp. 69-71.

45. Van Tassel, *Recording America's Past*, p. 69.

46. Allen, *Biographical Dictionary*, p. iv; Rogers, *American Biographical Dictionary*, p. iv.

47. Allen, *Biographical Dictionary*, pp. viii, 3-6.

48. James DeWitt Andrews, ed., *The Works of James Wilson* (Chicago, 1896), I, 466; Ramsay, *History of the Revolution*, I, 10; Backus, *History of New England*, I, 246; Morgan Edwards, "Materials for a History of the Baptists of Rhode Island," Rhode Island Historical Society, *Collections*, VI (1838), 302-03.

49. Randolph, *History of Virginia*, pp. 176-93.

50. Ibid., pp. 183-84, 190-91, 208-09.

51. Ibid., pp. 186, 192.

52. Ibid., pp. 167, 168, 179, 181, 178.

53. Ibid., pp. 178-79; Shaffer, intro. ibid., pp. xxi- xxvi.

54. Ibid., p. 5.

55. On Washington's emergence as a national hero see Dixon Wecter, *The Hero in America: A Chronicle of Hero-Worship* (Ann Arbor, 1963), pp. 99-147; Marcus Cunliffe, *George Washington: Man and Monument* (New York, 1960).
56. David Ramsay, *The Life of George Washington* (New York, 1807), pp. 1-3; Marshall, *Life of Washington*, II, 1-3.
57. Ibid., I, xvi.
58. Ibid., V, 379; Ramsay, *Life of Washington*, p. 33.
59. Lipset, *The First New Nation*, pp. 21-26.
60. Barlow, *Advice to the Privileged Orders*, pp. 46-47.
61. Webster, *Revolution in France*, p. iii.
62. Belknap, *History of New Hampshire*, II, 193.

**Chapter VIII**

1. Ramsay, *History of the Revolution*, I, 34; II, 316-17. Although I have a different set of concerns and have drawn different conclusions, I owe a debt to William R. Smith's discussion of the views of Ramsay, Warren, and Marshall on the Constitution and the early national period. *History as Argument*, esp. pp. 57-72, 98-117, 146-71.
2. Ramsay, *History of the Revolution*, I, 356; II, 316, 335-39.
3. Ibid., I, 357; II, 334-35.
4. Ibid., II, 342-43.
5. Ibid., I, 348-54.
6. Ibid., II, 341-42.
7. Belknap, *History of New Hampshire*, I, 378-406; Williams, *History of Vermont*, pp. 234-89; and Morse, *American Geography*, pp. 260-68. Although William Gordon published his *History of the Independence of the United States* before the new Constitution was ratified, he had consistently spoken against any effort to strengthen the national government. "I am not for being betrayed under the plea [weakness of government]," he told John Adams, "into a violation of the Confederation and the great fundamentals upon which it was established, and into a mode of congressional government that, by not suiting the northern climate . . . will after a time bring on fresh wars and fighting among ourselves." Quoted in Page Smith, *John Adams* (New York, 1962), p. 618.
8. M'Culloch, *Concise History of the United States*, p. 163.
9. Catherine Drinker Bowen, *Yankee from Olympus: Justice Holmes and His Family* (New York, 1960), pp. 7-8. 20-21.
10. Ramsay. *History of the United States*, III, 12-14.
11. Ramsay, *Life of Washington*, p. 308.
12. Warren to Henry Knox, March 9, 1789, cited in Donald R. Raichle. "The Image of the Constitution in American History: A Study in Historical Writing from David Ramsay to John Fiske, 1789-1888" (Ph.D. dissertation, Columbia University, 1956), p. 33.
13. Warren, *History of the American Revolution*, III, 293. 295, 303, 304, 338-56, 357.
14. Ibid., p. 369.
15. Ibid., pp. 284, 286, 358-62.

16. Ibid., p. 392.
17. Ibid., p. 367.
18. Philip S. Foner, ed., *The Basic Writings of Thomas Jefferson* (New York, 1944), p. 637.
19. Warren, *History of the American Revolution*, III, 398.
20. Warren only mentioned Jefferson as the author of the Declaration of Independence.
21. Ibid., p. 432.
22. Ibid., p. 400.
23. Ibid., pp. 251-52, 302, 329, 370, 400, 413, 423.
24. Warren's Revolutionary plays were "The Adulateur, a Tragedy," *The Magazine of History*, Extra Number 63 (1918), 225-59: *The Blockheads* (Boston, 1776); *The Defeat* (Boston, 1773); *The Group* (Boston, 1775); and *The Retreat* (n.d.).
25. Quoted in Katherine Anthony, *First Lady of the Revolution: the Life of Mercy Otis Warren* (Garden City, 1958), p. 203.
26. Warren, *History of the American Revolution*, I, iv. I am indebted to Lawrence Friedman's *Inventors of the Promised Land, 1786-1840* (New York, 1975), and a forthcoming article by Friedman and myself in the June issue of the *New England Quarterly* for much of my discussion of Warren's sexual attitudes.
27. Warren to Abigail Adams, Dec. 29, 1774; Warren to Mrs. Robert Temple, June 2, 1775; Warren to Sally Sevier, June 20, 1784; Warren to Mrs. Henry Warren, Nov. 1771; Mercy Warren MS Letterbook, 1770-1800, Mass. Hist. Soc.
28. Ann D. Wood, "The Scribbling Women and Fanny Fern: Why Women Wrote," *American Quarterly*, XXIII (1971), 3-24.
29. Warren, *Poems, Dramatic and Miscellaneous* (Boston, 1790); *History of the American Revolution*, I, iii-iv.
30. For Warren's family background see John J. Waters, Jr., *The Otis Family in Provincial and Revolutionary Massachusetts* (Chapel Hill, 1968), pp. 76-203; also Linda Grant DePauw, "The Forgotten Spirit of 76: Women of the Revolutionary Era," *MS.*, III (July, 1974), 56.
31. For Marshall's political and judicial philosophy see Faulkner, *Jurisprudence of Marshall.*
32. *Marshall's Answers to Freeholders Questions,* reprinted in Albert J. Beveridge, *The Life of John Marshall* (Boston, 1919), II, 577. Cf. also Faulkner, *Jurisprudence of Marshall*, p. 17.
33. Edmund Burke, *Reflections on the Revolution in France* (New York, 1955), p. 69. For Marshall's views of Burke see *Life of Washington*, I. 418; and Smith, *History as Argument*, p. 183n.
34. Cited by Arthur N. Holcombe, "John Marshall as Politician and Political Theorist," in *Chief Justice John Marshall: A Reappraisal*, ed. W. Melville Jones (Ithaca, 1956), p. 29.
35. Even his friend and ally John Adams described Marshall's *Washington* as a "mausoleum, 100 foot square at the base, and 200 feet high." Adams to Thomas Jefferson, July 13, 1813, *The Adams-Jefferson Letters*, ed. Lester J. Cappon (Chapel Hill, 1959), II, 349.

36. Marshall, *Autobiographical Sketch* (1827), cited in Holcombe, "Marshall as Politician and Political Theorist," p. 29.
37. Marshall, *Life of Washington,* IV, 170, 194-95.
38. Ibid., pp. 238-41. Marshall allotted less than two pages to the Philadelphia Convention, and no space to analyzing the document itself.
39. Ibid., III, 358; IV, 143-44.
40. Ramsay, *History of the Revolution,* II, 342; Marshall, *Life of Washington,* IV, 242.
41. Ibid., V, 330-33.
42. P.L. Ford, *The Writings of Thomas Jefferson* (New York, 1892-99), X, 236n.
43. Marshall's preoccupation with practicality and the necessity of experience were not just tactical maneuvers confined to his history: they were also essential ingredients of his judicial philosophy. Cf. Faulkner, *Jurisprudence of Marshall,* pp. 3-44.
44. Marshall, *Life of Washington,* IV, 321, 443. One cannot help but note the close similarity between Marshall's interpretation of the differences between Jefferson and Hamilton and their supporters and the analysis of Stanley Elkins and Eric McKitrick in "The Founding Fathers: Young Men of the Revolution," *Political Science Quarterly,* LXXVI (1961).
45. Marshall, *Life of Washington,* IV, 443-44.
46. Ibid., pp. 444-46.
47. Miller, *Federalist Era,* p. 204.
48. Marshall, *Life of Washington,* V, 378; Faulkner, *Jurisprudence of Marshall,* pp. 116, 129. Cf. pp. 114-92 for a discussion of Marshall's republicanism.
49. Warren, *History of the American Revolution,* III, 304-06. Ramsay offered essentially the same formula in *The History of South Carolina,* II, 140-41.

## Chapter IX

1. For a list of American and European histories published in the United States see Danzer, "America's Roots in the Past," pp. 117-203.
2. Brunhouse, "Ramsay . . . Writings," pp. 225-26.
3. Ibid., pp. 38-48.
4. Danzer, "America's Roots in the Past," pp. 194, 196-97, 106-07.
5. Curti, *Roots of Loyalty,* p. 127.
6. Kaplan, "Belknap as Literary Craftsman," pp. 19-20.
7. Brunhouse, "Ramsay . . . Writings," p. 222.
8. Howe, "Republican Thought and Political Violence," p. 152; Bailyn, *Ideological Origins;* Cecelia Kenyon, "Men of Little Faith: the Anti-Federalists on the Nature of Representative Government," *William and Mary Quarterly,* 3d. ser., XII (1955), 1-43 and "Republicanism and Radicalism in the American Revolution: An Old-Fashioned Interpretation," ibid., XIX (1962), 153-82; Gordon Wood, "Rhetoric and Reality in the American Revolution," ibid., XXIII (1966), 3-32.
9. M'Culloch, *Concise History of the United States,* p. 189; Sullivan, *Thoughts Upon the Political Situation,* p. 27.

10. Howe, "Republican Thought and Political Violence," p. 158.
11. Ramsay to Morse, Aug. 12, 1807, "Ramsay . . . Writings," p. 160.
12. Adams to Plumer, Aug. 16, 1809, quoted in Van Tassel, *Recording America's Past,* p. 83.
13. Bailyn, *Origins of American Politics,* passim.
14. Ramsay, *History of the Revolution,* II, 315; Williamson, *Observations on the Climate in America,* pp. 179-80.
15. Quoted by Kraus, *Writing of American History,* p. 107.
16. Howe, *Political Thought of Adams,* p. 49.
17. Peardon, *Transition in English Historical Writing,* pp. 162-63.
18. Williams, *History of Vermont,* p. 317; Ramsay, *History of the Revolution,* I, 31.
19. Quoted in Bert J. Loewenberg, *American History in American Thought: Christopher Columbus to Henry Adams* (New York, 1972), p. 247.
20. Echevarria, *Mirage in the West,* p. 259.
21. Ibid., pp. 124-25, 215-16.
22. For Burke's influence in the United States see Edward Handler, *America and Europe in the Political Thought of John Adams* (Cambridge, Mass., 1964), pp. 157-59.
23. George H. Callcott, *History in the United States, 1800-1860: Its Practice and Purpose* (Baltimore, 1970), p. 20.
24. Danzer, "America's Roots in the Past," pp. 379-88.
25. Hofstadter, *The Progressive Historians,* pp. 11-12.
26. Ibid., pp. 10-11.
27. For an analysis of American Romantic historians see David Levin, *History as Romantic Art: Bancroft, Prescott, Motley, and Parkman* (New York, 1967), pp. 3-23 and passim.
28. Callcott, *History in the United States,* p. 23.
29. Russel B. Nye, *George Bancroft: Brahmin Rebel* (New York, 1944), pp. 92-96.
30. Levin, *History as Romantic Art,* pp. 49-50; Hofstadter, *Progressive Historians,* p. 13.
27. For an analysis of American Romantic historians see David Levin, *History as Romantic Art: Bancroft, Prescott, Motley, and Parkman* (New York, 1967), pp. 3-23 and passim.
28. Callcott, *History in the United States,* p. 23.
29. Russel B. Nye, *George Bancroft: Brahmin Rebel* (New York, 1944), pp. 92-96.
30. Levin, *History as Romantic Art,* pp. 49-50; Hofstadter, *Progressive Historians,* p. 13.
31. Quoted by Russel B. Nye, *George Bancroft* (New York, 1964), pp. 84-85.
32. For Bancroft as historian see ibid., pp. 136-94; intro. to George Bancroft, *The History of the United States of America,* abridged and ed. by Russel B. Nye (Chicago, 1966), pp. vii- xxvi; Richard C. Vitzthum, "Theme and Method in Bancroft's *History of the United States,*" *New England Quarterly,* XLI (1968), 362-80; Shirley Jane Bill, "The Originality of George Bancroft's Interpretation of the American Revolution" (M.A. thesis, University of Chicago, 1942).
33. Ibid., p. 57.
34. Nye, intro. to Bancroft, *History of the United States,* p. xx.

35. George Bancroft, *The History of the United States of America* (Boston, 1834-74), VII, 301.
36. Nye, *Bancroft,* p. 157.
37. Ibid.
38. For the influence of theology on Bancroft's historical philosophy see Vitzthum, "Theme and Method in Bancroft's *History,*" pp. 364-70.
39. Cf. Callcott, *History in the United States,* pp. 166-73 For eighteenth century views of national distinctions see Jordan, *White over Black,* pp. 223-25, and passim.
40. Brunhouse, "Ramsay . . . Writings," p. 224.
41. Orin G. Libby, "William Gordon's *History of the American Revolution,*" American Historical Association, *Annual Report, 1899* (New York, 1900), pp. 367-88; "Some Pseudo-Historians of the American Revolution," *Proceedings of the Wisconsin Academy of Sciences and Arts,* XIII (1900), 419-25; and "Ramsay as a Plagiarist," *American Historical Review,* VII (1902), 697-703.
42. Gordon, *History of the Independence of the United States,* I, vii.
43. Callcott, *History in the United States,* pp. 136-38.
44. Collingwood, *The Idea of History,* p. 257.
45. Charles Beard, *Economic Origins of Jeffersonian Democracy* (New York, 1915), pp. 1, 109, 159, 237, 242, and *An Economic Interpretation of the Constitution* (New York, 1937), p. 296 and following.
46. Ramsay, *History of the Revolution,* I, 29.

# Bibliography

**I. Primary Sources**

Adams, Amos, *A Concise Historical View of the Planting and Progressive Improvement of New England*. Boston, 1769.

Adams, Hannah, *A History of the Jews*. Boston, 1812.

———, *A Memoir of Miss Hannah Adams Written by Herself with Additional Notices, by a Friend*. Boston, 1832.

———, *A Summary History of New England*. Dedham, Mass., 1799.

Adams, John, *A Dissertation on the Canon and Feudal Law*. Boston, 1765.

———, *Twenty-Six Letters, Upon Interesting Subjects Respecting the Revolution of America*. 2d. ed., New York, 1789.

Allen, Ira, *The Natural and Political History of the State of Vermont, one of the United States of America*. London, 1789.

Allen, Paul, *A History of the American Revolution*. Baltimore, 1822.

Allen, William, *A Biographical Dictionary*. Boston, 1809.

Backus, Isaac, *A History of New England with Particular Reference to the Baptists*. 3 vols., Boston, 1777-97.

Bancroft, Aaron, *An Essay on the Life of George Washington*. Worcester, Mass., 1807.

Bancroft, George, *History of the United States from the Discovery of the American Continent*. 6 vols., Boston, 1834-74.

Barlow, Joel, *Advice to the Privileged Orders in the Several States of Europe Resulting from the Necessity and Propriety of a General Revolution in the Principle of Government*. New York, 1792.

———, *The Columbiad, a Poem*. Philadelphia, 1807.

Barnard, John, *The Throne Established by Righteousness*. Boston, 1734.

Belknap, Jeremy, *American Biography*. 2 vols., Boston, 1794-98.

———, "A Description of the White Mountains" *Transactions of the American Philosophical Society*, II (1786).

———, *A Discourse Intended to Commemorate the Discovery of America by Christopher Columbus*. Boston, 1792.

———, *An Election Sermon, Preached Before the General Court of New Hampshire*. Portsmouth, N.H., 1785.

———, *The Foresters*. Boston, 1792.

———, "Has the Discovery of America Been Helpful or Hurtful to Mankind?" *Boston Magazine*, I (1784).

———, *History of New Hampshire*. 3 vols., Boston and Philadelphia, 1784-92.

Botta, Carlo, *History of the Independence of the United States of America*. 3 vols., Philadelphia, 1820.

Bozman, John Leeds, *The History of Maryland, from its First Settlement in 1633, to the Restoration, in 1660*. 2 vols., Baltimore, 1837.

———, *A Sketch of the History of Maryland*. Baltimore, 1811.

Burk, John Daly, *Bunker Hill; or, The Death of General Warren: An Historic Tragedy, in Five Acts*. New York, 1817.

———, *The History of Virginia, from Its First Settlement to the Commencement of the Revolution*. 3 vols., Petersburg, Va., 1804-05.

———, *An Oration, Delivered on the Fourth of March 1803 to Celebrate the Election of Thomas Jefferson, and the Triumph of Republicanism.* Petersburg, Va., 1803.

Burke, Edmund, *Reflections on the Revolution in France.* New York, 1955.

Callender, James T., *Sketches of the History of America.* Philadelphia, 1798.

Campbell, John W., *A History of Virginia.* Philadelphia, 1813.

Chalmers, George, *Political Annals of the Present United Colonies from their Settlement to the Peace of 1763.* London, 1780.

Champion, Judah, *A Brief View of the Distresses, Hardships, and Dangers our Ancestors Encountered in Settling New England.* Hartford, Conn., 1770.

Chipman, Nathaniel, *Sketches of the Principles of Government.* Rutland, Vt., 1793.

Cooke, Samuel, *A Sermon Preached at Cambridge.* Boston, 1770.

Crevecoeur, J. Hector St. Jean de, *Letters from an American Farmer and Sketches of Eighteenth-Century America.* New York, 1963.

Drayton, William Henry, *Memoirs of the American Revolution, from its Commencement to the Year 1776.* 1779. ed. with additions by John Drayton. Charleston, 1821.

Edwards, Morgan, "Materials for a History of the Baptists of Rhode Island." Rhode Island Historical Society, *Collections,* VI (1838).

Eliot, John, *A Biographical Dictionary.* Boston, 1809.

———, "History of New England." Massachusetts Historical Society, *Collections.*

Filson, John, *The Discovery, Settlement, and Present State of Kentucke.* Wilmington, 1784.

Ferguson, Adam, *An Essay on the History of Civil Society* (1767), ed. with intro. by Duncan Forbes. Edinburgh, 1966.

Gordon, William, *The History of the Rise, Progress and Establishment of the Independence of the United States of America.* 4 vols., London, 1788.

Hale, Nathan, "Review of Benjamin Trumbull, *A Complete History of Connecticut.*" *North American Review,* VIII (Dec., 1818).

———, "Review of Carlo Botta, Storia della Guerra Independenza." *American Review of History and Politics,* I (Jan. 1811).

Hardie, James, *New Universal Biographical Dictionary and American Remembrances of Departed Merit.* 4 vols., New York, 1801.

Hazard, Ebenezer, *Historical Collections.* 2 vols., Philadelphia, 1792-94.

Hewatt, Alexander, *An Historical Account of the Rise and Progress of the Colonies of South Carolina and Georgia.* 2 vols., London, 1779.

"An Historical Journal of the American War." Massachusetts Historical Society, *Collections,* II (1793).

"History of the Late War in America," *Worcester Magazine,* 1786-88.

Holmes, Abiel, *American Annals; or a Chronological History of America.* 2 vols., Cambridge, Mass., 1805.

Howard, Simeon, *A Sermon.* Boston, 1773.

Hubley, Bernard, *The History of the American Revolution.* Northumberland, Pa., 1805.

Hume, David, *An Enquiry Concerning Human Understanding.* London, 1748.

———, *History of England.* 6 vols., London, 1754-61.

Hutchinson, Thomas, *History of Massachusetts Bay.* 3 vols., 1764-1828. ed. Lawrence S. Mayo, Cambridge, Mass., 1936.

Jefferson, Thomas, *Notes on the State of Virginia.* 1784. intro. by Thomas Perkins Abernethy. New York, 1964.

Kingston, John, *New American Biographic Dictionary.* Baltimore, 1810.

Lendrum, John, *A Concise and Impartial History of the American Revolution.* 2 vols., Philadelphia, 1795.

McCall, Hugh, *The History of Georgia, Containing Brief Sketches of the most Remarkable Events up to the Present Day, 1784.* 2 vols., Savannah, Ga., 1811-16.

M'Culloch, John, *A Concise History of the United States.* Philadelphia, 1795.

———, *An Introduction to American History.* Philadelphia, 1787.

Marshall, John, *The Life of George Washington.* 5 vols., Philadelphia, 1804-07.

Miller, Samuel, *A Brief Retrospect of the Eighteenth Century.* 2 vols., New York, 1803.

Minot, George R., *Continuation of the History of the Province of Massachusetts Bay from the Year 1748.* 2 vols., Boston, 1798-1803.

———, *History of the Insurrections in the Year 1786.* Boston, 1788.

Montesquieu, Baron de, *The Spirit of the Laws.* 1748. intro. by Franz Neumann. New York, 1962.

Morris, Gouverneur, *Observations on the American Revolution.* Philadelphia, 1779.

Morse, Jedidiah, *The American Geography; or a View of the Present Situation of the United States of America.* Elizabethtown, N.J., 1789.

———, *The American Universal Geography,* 2 vols., Boston, 1795.

———, *Annals of the American Revolution.* Philadelphia, 1824.

———, and Parish, Elijah, *A Compendious History of New England.* Boston, 1804.

———, *Geography Made Easy.* New Haven, 1784.

———, *The History of America, in Two Books.* Philadelphia, 1790.

Moultrie, William, *Memoirs of the American Revolution,* 2 vols., New York, 1802.

Murray, William Vans, *Political Sketches, Inscribed to His Excellency John Adams.* London, 1787.

Oliver, Peter, *Origins of the American Rebellion: A Tory View,* ed. by Douglass Adair and John Schutz, San Marino, Calif., 1965.

Paine, Thomas, *A Letter to the Abbé Raynal.* London, 1782.

Price, Richard, *Observations on the Importance of the American Revolution.* Boston, 1784.

Priestley, Joseph, *An Essay on the First Principles of the Government and on the Nature Political, Civil and Religious Liberty.* London, 1768.

Prince, Thomas, *A Chronological History of New England in the Form of Annals.* Boston, 1736.

Proud, Robert, *The History of Pennsylvania in North America.* 2 vols., Philadelphia, 1797-98.

Ramsay, David, *An Address to the Freemen of South Carolina on the Federational Constitution by Civis.* Charleston, 1788.

———, A *Chronological Table of the Principal Events which have taken place in the English Colonies, Now United States, from 1607, Till 1810.* Charleston, 1811.

———, *Historical and Biographical Chart of the United States.* N.p., n.d.

———, *History of South Carolina, From Its First Settlement in 1670 to the Year 1808.* 2 vols., Charleston, 1809.

———, *The History of the American Revolution.* 2 vols., Philadelphia, 1789.

———, *The History of the Revolution of South Carolina.* 2 vols., Trenton, N.J., 1785.

———, *History of the United States.* 3 vols., Philadelphia, 1816-17.

———, *The Life of George Washington.* New York, 1807.

———, *An Oration, Delivered on the Anniversary of American Independence, July 4, 1794.* Charleston, 1794.

———, *An Oration on the Advantages of American Independence.* Charleston, 1778.

———, *Universal History Americanized; or, An Historical View of the World, from the earliest Records to the Year 1808.* 12 vols., Philadelphia, 1819.

Randolph, Edmund, *History of Virginia,* ed. with intro. by Arthur H. Shaffer. Charlottesville, Va., 1970.

———, *Letter on the Federal Constitution.* n.p., 1787.

Raynal, Abbé, *Revolution of America.* Boston, 1781.

Rogers, Thomas J., *A New American Biographical Dictionary.* Philadelphia, 1812.

———, "David Ramsay on the Ratification of the Constitution in South Carolina, 1787-88." ed. Robert L. Brunhouse. *Journal of Southern History,* IX (1943).

Root, Erasmus, *An Introduction to Arithmetic for the Use of the Common Schools.* Norwich, Conn., 1796.

Rush, Benjamin, *Essays, Literary, Moral and Philosophical.* Philadelphia, 1798.

Smith, Samuel Stanhope, *Lectures on the Subjects of Moral and Political Philosophy.* Trenton, N.J., 1812.

Smith, Samuel, *The History of the Colony of Nova-Caesaria, or New Jersey.* Burlington, N.J., 1765.

Smith, William, *History of the Province of New York.* London, 1757.

Snowden, Richard, *The American Revolution Written in the Style of Ancient History.* 2 vols., Philadelphia, 1793.

———, *History of America.* Philadelphia, 1805.

Stiles, Ezra, *The United States Elevated to Glory and Honour.* 2d ed., Worcester, Mass., 1783.

Stith, William, *History of the First Discovery and Settlement of Virginia.* Williamsburg, 1747.

Stoughton, William, *New England's True Interest.* Cambridge, Mass., 1670.

Sullivan, James, *Thoughts Upon the Political Situation of the United States.* Worcester, Mass., 1788.

———, *The History of the District of Maine.* Boston, 1795.

Tappan, David, *A Discourse Occasioned by the Ratification of the Treaty of Peace*. Salem, Mass., 1783.

Trumbull, Benjamin, *A Century Sermon*. New Haven, 1801.

——, *A General History of the United States of America*. Boston, 1810.

——, *A Complete History of Connecticut*. 2 vols., New Haven, 1797-1818.

Walsh, Robert, *An Appeal from the Judgements of Great Britain respecting the United States of America*. Philadelphia, 1819.

Warren, Mercy Otis, *The Group*. Boston, 1775.

——, *The History of the Rise, Progress, and Termination of the American Revolution*. 3 vols., Boston, 1805.

——, *Observations on the New Constitution By a Columbian Patriot*. Boston, 1788.

——, *Poems, Dramatic and Miscellaneous*. Boston, 1790.

Webster, Noah, *American Selection of Readings*. 3d ed., Philadelphia, 1787.

——, *Collection of Essays and Fugitiv Writings*. Boston, 1790.

——, *History of the United States*. New Haven, 1832.

——, *The Revolution in France Considered in Respect to its Progress and Effects by an America*. New York, 1794.

——, *Sketches of American Policy*. 1785. ed. Harry R. Warfel. New York, 1937.

Weems, Mason Locke, *The Life of Washington*. 1800. ed. with intro. by Marcus Cunliffe. Cambridge, Mass. 1962.

Williams, Samuel, *A Discourse on the Love of Our Country*. Salem, Mass., 1775.

——, "History of the American Revolution." *Rural Magazine; or, Vermont Repository*. Burlington, Vt., 1795.

——, *The Natural and Civil History of Vermont*. Walpole, N.H., 1794.

Williamson, Hugh, *The History of North Carolina*. 2 vols., Philadelphia, 1812.

——, *Observations on the Climate in Different Parts of America*. New York, 1811.

——, "On the Benefits of Civil History." New York Historical Society, *Collections*, II (1814).

Wood, John, *The History of the Administration of John Adams*, New York, 1802.

## II. Collections

Adams, Charles Francis, ed., *The Works of John Adams*. 10 vols., Freeport, N.Y., 1969.

"Correspondence between John Adams, and Mercy Warren relating to her 'History of the American Revolution,' July-August, 1807." Massachusetts Historical Society, *Collections*, 5th ser., IV. Boston, 1878.

*Belknap Papers*. Massachusetts Historical Society, *Collections*, 5th ser., I, II, 6th ser., IV. Boston, 1877-91.

Brunhouse, Robert L., ed., "David Ramsay, 1749-1815: Selections From His Writings." *Transactions of the American Philosophical Society*, NS, LV, pt. 4, 1965.

Commager, Henry S. and Elmo Girandetti, eds., *Was America a Mistake? An Eighteenth Century Controversy*. New York, 1967.

"The Letters of the Reverend William Gordon, History of the American Revolution." Massachusetts Historical Society, *Proceedings*, LXIII, 1929-30.

Lipscomb, Andrew A. and Albert E. Berg, eds., *The Writings of Thomas Jefferson*. 20 vols., Washington, 1905.

Norton, David F. and Richard H. Popkin, eds., *David Hume: Philosophical History*. Indianapolis, 1965.

Plumstead, A.W., ed., *The Wall and the Garden: Selected Massachusetts Election Sermons, 1670-1775*. Minneapolis, 1968.

Mercy Otis Warren, MS Letterbook, 1770-1800, Massachusetts Historical Society.

## III. Secondary Works Cited

Adair, Douglas G., "The Tenth Federalist Revisited." *William and Mary Quarterly*, ed ser., VIII (1951).

——, "That Politics May be Reduced to a Science: David Hume, James Madison, and the Tenth *Federalist*." *Huntington Library Quarterly*, XX (1957).

Anthony, Katherine, *First Lady of the Revolution: The Life of Mercy Warren*. Garden City, 1958.

Arieli, Yehoshua, *Individualism and Nationalism in American Ideology*. Cambridge, Mass., 1964.

Bailyn, Bernard, *The Ideological Origins of the American Revolution*. Cambridge, Mass., 1967.

——, *The Origins of American Politics*. New York, 1968.

Beard, Charles A., *An Economic Interpretation of the Constitution*. New York, 1937.

——, *Economic Origins of Jeffersonian Democracy*. New York, 1915.

Ben-Israel, Hedva, *English Historians on the French Revolution*. London, 1968.

Beveridge, Albert J., *Life of John Marshall*. 2 vols., Boston, 1919.

Bill, Shirley Jane, "The Originality of George Bancroft's Interpretation of the American Revolution." Master's Thesis, University of Chicago, 1942.

Black, J. B., *The Art of History: A Study of Four Great Historians of the Eighteenth Century*. New York, 1965.

Bonomi, Patricia U., "The Middle Colonies: Embryo of the New Political Order." *Perspectives on Early American History: Essays in Honor of Richard B. Morris*, eds. Alden T. Vaughan and George A. Billias. New York, 1973.

Boorstin, Daniel, *The Lost World of Thomas Jefferson*. New York, 1960.

Bowen, Catherine Drinker, *Yankee From Olympus: Justice Holmes and His Family*. New York, 1960.

Bridenbaugh, Carl, *Mitre and Sceptre: Transatlantic Faiths, Ideas, Personalities, and Politics, 1689-1775*. New York, 1967.

Brumfitt, J. H., *Voltaire, Historian*. London, 1958.

Bryson, Gladys M., *Man and Society: The Scottish Inquiry of the Eighteenth Century*. Princeton, 1945.

Buel, Richard, Jr., *Securing the Revolution: Ideology in American Politics, 1789-1815*. Ithaca, 1972.

Cairns, William B., *British Criticism of American Writings, 1783-1815*. Madison, 1918.

Cappon, Lester J., "American Historical Editors Before Jared Sparks." *William and Mary Quarterly*, 3d ser., XXX (1973).

Callcott, George H., *History in the United States, 1800-1860: Its Practice and Purpose*. Baltimore, 1970.

Chinard, Gilbert, "Eighteenth Century Theories on America as a Human Habitat." *Proceedings of the American Philosophical Society*, XCI (1947).

Colbourn, H. Trevor, *The Lamp of Experience: Whig History and the Intellectual Origins of the American Revolution*. Chapel Hill, 1965.

Cole, Charles W., "Jeremy Belknap: Pioneer Nationalist." *New England Quarterly*, X (1937).

Collingwood, R.G., *The Idea of History*. New York, 1967.

Conkin, Paul and Roland H. Stromberg, *The Heritage and Challenge of History*. New York, 1971.

Connors, Paul W., *Poor Richard's Politicks: Benjamin Franklin and his New American Order*. New York, 1965.

Craven, Wesley Frank, *The Legend of the Founding Fathers*. Ithaca, N.Y., 1965.

Cremin, Lawrence, *American Education: the Colonial Experience, 1607-1783*. New York, 1970.

Cunliffe, Marcus, *Washington: the Man and the Monument*. New York, 1960.

Curti, Merle, *Human Nature in American Historical Thought*. Columbia, Mo., 1968.

——, *Probing our Past*. New York, 1955.

——, *Roots of American Loyalty*. New York, 1946.

Danzer, Gerald A., "America's Roots in the Past: Historical Publication in America to 1860." Ph.D. dissertation, Northwestern University, 1967.

Davis, Herbert, "The Augustan Conception of History." *Reason and the Imagination: Studies in the History of Ideas 1600-1800*, ed. J. A. Mazzeo. New York, 1962.

David, Richard Beale, *Intellectual Life in Jefferson's Virginia, 1790-1830*. Chapel Hill, 1964.

DePauw, Linda Grant, "The Forgotten Spirit of 76: Women of the Revolutionary Era." *MS*, III (1974).

Dos Passos, John, *The Ground We Stand On: Some Examples From the History of a Political Creed*. New York, 1941.

Eliot, Samuel A., "Jeremy Belknap." Massachusetts Historical Society, *Proceedings*, LXVI (1942).

Elkins, Stanley and Eric McKitrick, "The Founding Fathers: Young Men of the Revolution." *Political Science Quarterly*, LXXVI (1961).

Faulkner, Robert K., *Jurisprudence of John Marshall*. Princeton, 1968.

Feer, Robert A., "George Richards Minot's *History of the Insurrections:* History, Propaganda, and Autobiography." *New England Quarterly,* XXXV (1962).

Fisher, Sidney G., "The Legendary and Myth-Making Process in Histories of the American Revolution." *Proceedings of the American Philosophical Society,* LI (1912).

Foran, William A., "John Marshall as a Historian." *American Historical Review,* XLIII (1937).

Frankel, Charles, *The Faith of Reason: The Idea of Progress in the French Enlightenment.* New York, 1969.

Free, William J., *The Columbian Magazine and American Literary History.* The Hague, 1968.

Freehling, William W., "The Founding Fathers and Slavery." *American Historical Review,* LXXVII (1972).

Friedman, Lawrence, *Inventors of the Promised Land, 1786-1840.* New York, 1975.

Gay, Peter, *The Enlightenment: An Interpretation.* 2 vols., New York, 1967-69.

————, *A Loss of Mastery: Puritan Historians in Colonial America.* Berkeley and Los Angeles, 1966.

————, *Style in History.* New York, 1974.

Greene, Jack P., "The Flight From Determinism: A Review of Recent Literature on the Coming of the American Revolution." *South Atlantic Quarterly,* LXI (1962).

Handler, Edward, *America and Europe in the Political Thought of John Adams.* Cambridge, Mass., 1964.

Hartshorne, Thomas L., *The Distorted Image: Changing Conceptions of the American Character Since Turner.* Cleveland, 1968.

Haycox, Stephen W., "Jeremy Belknap and Early American Nationalism: A Study in the Political and Theological Foundations of American Liberty." Ph.D. dissertation, University of Oregon, 1971.

Henretta, James A., "Economic Development and Social Structure in Colonial Boston." *William and Mary Quarterly,* 3d ser., XXII (1965).

Hofstadter, Richard, *The Idea of a Party System: The Rise of Legitimate Opposition in the United States, 1780-1840.* Berkeley and Los Angeles, 1969.

————, *The Progressive Historians: Turner, Beard, Parrington.* New York, 1968.

Holcombe, Arthur N., "John Marshall as Politician and Political Theorist." *Chief Justice John Marshall: A Reappraisal,* ed. W. Melville Jones. Ithaca, 1956.

Howard, Leon, "The Late Eighteenth Century: An Age of Contradictions." *Transitions in American Literary History,* ed. Harry Hayden Clark. Durham, N.C., 1953.

Howe, John R., Jr., *The Changing Political Thought of John Adams.* Princeton, 1966.

————, "Republican Thought and the Political Violence of the 1790s." *American Quarterly,* XIX (1967).

Jensen, Merrill, *The New Nation: A History of the United States During the Confederation, 1781-1789.* New York, 1965.

Johnson, Elmer Douglass, "David Ramsay: Historian or Plagiarist?" *South Carolina Historical Magazine,* LVII (1956).

Jones, Howard Mumford, *O Strange New World; American Culture: The Formative Years.* New York, 1964.

Jones, Maldwyn Allen, *American Immigration.* Chicago, 1960.

Jordan, Winthrop D., *White Over Black: American Attitudes Toward the Negro, 1550-1812.* Chapel Hill, 1968.

Kaplan, Sidney, *"The History of New Hampshire:* Jeremy Belknap as Literary Craftsman." *William and Mary Quarterly,* 3d ser., XII (1964).

Kenyon, Cecelia, "Men of Little Faith: the Anti-Federalists on the Nature of Representative Government." *William and Mary Quarterly,* 3d ser., XII (1955).

——, "Republicanism and Radicalism in the American Revolution: An Old-Fashioned Interpretation." *William and Mary Quarterly,* 3d ser., XXIII (1966).

Kettler, David, *The Social and Political Thought of Adam Ferguson.* Columbus, Ohio, 1965.

Koch, Adrienne, *Power, Morals, and the Founding Fathers: Essays in the Interpretation of the American Enlightenment.* Ithaca, 1961.

Kohn, Hans, *American Nationalism: An Interpretative Essay.* New York, 1961.

Kramnick, Isaac, *Bolingbroke and His Circle: The Politics of Nostalgia in the Age of Walpole.* Cambridge, Mass., 1968.

Kraus, Michael, *The Writing of American History.* Norman, Oklahoma, 1953.

Lemon, James T. and Gary B. Nash, "The Distribution of Wealth in Eighteenth-Century America: A Century of Change in Chester County Pennsylvania, 1693-1802." *Journal of Social History,* II (1968).

Levin, David, *History as Romantic Art: Bancroft, Prescott, Motley, and Parkman.* New York, 1967.

Libby, Orin G., "Ramsay As a Plagiarist." *American Historical Review,* VII (1902).

——, "Some Pseudo-Historians of the American Revolution." *Proceedings of the Wisconsin Academy of Sciences and Arts,* XIII (1900).

——, "William Gordon's *History of the American Revolution."* American Historical Association, *Annual Report, 1899* (1900).

Lipset, Seymour Martin, *The First New Nation: The United States in Historical and Comparative Perspective.* Garden City, 1963.

Lockridge, Kenneth, "Land, Population, and the Evolution of New England Society, 1630-1790." *Past and Present,* no. 39 (1968).

Loewenberg, Bert J., *American History in American Thought: Christopher Columbus to Henry Adams.* New York, 1972.

——, *Historical Writing in American Culture.* Mexico City, 1968.

McWilliams, Wilson Carey, *The Idea of Fraternity in America.* Berkeley and Los Angeles, 1973.

Maier, Pauline, "Popular Uprisings and Civil Authority in Eighteenth-Century America." *William and Mary Quarterly*, 3d ser., XXVII (1970).

Main, Jackson T., *The Social Structure of Revolutionary America*. Princeton, 1965.

Marcou, Jane Belknap, *The Life of Jeremy Belknap*. New York, 1847.

Mayo, Lawrence S., "Jeremy Belknap and Ebenezer Hazard, 1782-84." *New England Quarterly*, II (1929).

Merry, Henry J., *Montesquieu's System of Natural Government*. West Lafayette, Indiana, 1970.

Miller, John C., *The Federalist Era, 1789-1801*. New York, 1960.

Miller, Ralph N., "American Nationalism as a Theory of Nature." *William and Mary Quarterly*, 3d ser., XI (1955).

——, "Samuel Williams' *History of Vermont*." *New England Quarterly*, XXII (1949).

Mitchell, Broadus and Louise Mitchell, *Biography of the Constitution of the United States*. New York, 1964.

Morse, James King, *Jedidiah Morse: A Champion of New England Orthodoxy*. New York, 1957.

Morse, Jarvis M., *American Beginnings*. Washington, 1952.

Murdock, Kenneth B., "Clio in the Wilderness." *Church History*, XXIV (1955).

——, *Literature and Theology in Colonial New England*. New York, 1963.

Nelson, William H., "The Revolutionary Character of the American Revolution." *American Historical Review*, LXX (1965).

Nye, Russel B., *The Cultural Life of the New Nation, 1776-1830*. New York, 1960.

——, *George Bancroft*. New York, 1964.

——, *George Bancroft: Brahmin Rebel*. New York, 1944.

Pearce, Roy Harvey, *Savagism and Civilization: A Study of the Indian and the American Mind*. Baltimore, 1967.

Peardon, Thomas P., *The Transition in English Historical Writing, 1760-1830*. New York, 1933.

Persons, Stow, *American Minds: A History of Ideas*. New York, 1958.

——, "The Cyclical Theory of History in Eighteenth Century America." *American Quarterly*, VI (1954).

Plumb, John H., *The Death of the Past*. Boston, 1971.

Pole, J. R., *Political Representation in England and the Origins of the American Republic*. New York, 1966.

Raichle, Donald R., "The Image of the Constitution in American History: A Study in Historical Writing from David Ramsay to John Fiske, 1789-1888." Ph.D. dissertation, Columbia University, 1956.

Risjord, Norman K., *Forging the American Republic, 1760-1815*. Reading, Mass., 1973.

Sabine, Lorenzo, *Biographical Sketches of Loyalists of the American Revolution*. Boston, 1847.

Schargo, N. N., *History in the Encyclopedia*. New York, 1947.

Sellers, Charles G., Jr., "The American Revolution: Southern Founders of a National Tradition." *Writing Southern History: Essays in Historiography in Honor of Fletcher M. Green,* ed. Arthur S. Link and Rembert W. Patrick. Baton Rouge, 1965.

Shaffer, Arthur H., "John Daly Burk's *History of Virginia* and the Development of American National History." *Virginia Magazine of History and Biography,* LXXVII (1969).

Shea, Daniel B., *Spiritual Biography in Early America.* Princeton, 1968.

Shelley, Fred, "Ebenezer Hazard: America's First Historical Editor." *William and Mary Quarterly,* 3d ser., XXII (1955).

Shulim, Joseph I., "John Daly Burk: Irish Revolutionist and American Patriot." *Transactions of the American Philosophical Society,* new ser., LIV, pt. 6 (1964).

Simpson, Lewis P., "Literary Ecumenicalism of the American Enlightenment." *The Ibero-American Enlightenment,* ed. A. Owen Aldridge, Urbana, 1971.

Sirmans, M. Eugene, *Colonial South Carolina: A Political History 1663-1763.* Chapel Hill, 1966.

Sloan, Douglas, *The Scottish Enlightenment and the American College Ideal.* New York, 1971.

Smith, Page, "David Ramsay and the Causes of the American Revolution." *William and Mary Quarterly,* 3d ser., XVII (1960).

——, *The Historian and History.* New York, 1964.

——, *John Adams.* 2 vols., New York, 1962.

Smith, William R., *History As Argument: Three Patriot Historians of the American Revolution.* The Hague, 1966.

——, "The Necessity of the Circumstances: John Marshall's Historical Method." *The Historian,* XXVI (1963).

Spencer, Benjamin T., *The Quest for Nationality: An American Literary Campaign.* Syracuse, 1957.

Starkey, Marion, *A Little Rebellion.* New York, 1955.

Stromberg, Roland N., "History in the Eighteenth Century." *Journal of the History of Ideas,* XII (1951).

Teggert, Frederick J., *Theory and Process of History.* Berkeley and Los Angeles, 1962.

Tholfsen, Trygve R., *Historical Thinking: An Introduction.* New York, 1967.

Thomas, Keith, *Religion and the Decline of Magic: Studies in Popular Beliefs in Sixteenth and Seventeenth Century England.* London, 1971.

Tichi, Cecelia, "Spiritual Biography and the Lord Remembrancers." *William and Mary Quarterly,* 3d ser., XXVII (1971).

Trefz, Edward K., "The Puritan View of History." *Boston Public Library Quarterly,* IX (1957).

Trevor-Roper, Hugh, "The Historical Philosophy of the Enlightenment." *Studies on Voltaire and the Eighteenth Century.* ed. Theodore Besterman, XXVII (1963).

Tuveson, Ernest Lee, *Millenium and Utopia: A Study in the Background of the Idea of Progress.* New York, 1964.

―――, *Redeemer Nation: The Idea of America's Millenial Role.* Chicago, 1968.

Van Schaack, Henry C., *The Life of Peter Van Schaack.* New York, 1842.

Van Tassel, David D., *Recording America's Past: An Interpretation of the Development of Historical Studies in America, 1607-1884.* Chicago, 1960.

Varg, Paul, *The Foreign Policy of the Founding Fathers.* Baltimore, 1972.

Vaughan, Alden T., "The Evolution of Virginia History: Early Historians of the First Colony." *Perspectives on Early American History: Essays in Honor of Richard B. Morris,* ed. Alden T. Vaughan and George A. Billias. New York, 1973.

Vitzthum, Richard C., "Theme and Method in Bancroft's *History of the United States." New England Quarterly,* XLI (1968).

Washburn, Wilcomb E., *The Governor and the Rebel: A History of Bacon's Rebellion in Virginia.* Chapel Hill, 1957.

Waters, John J., Jr., *The Otis Family in Provincial and Revolutionary Massachusetts.* Chapel Hill, 1968.

Wechter, Dixon, *The Hero in America: A Chronicle of Hero-Worship.* Ann Arbor, Michigan, 1963.

Whitehall, Walter Muir, *Independent Historical Societies.* Boston, 1962.

Wood, Ann D., "The Scribblings of Women and Fanny Fern: Why Women Wrote." *American Quarterly,* XXIII (1971).

Wood, Gordon S., *The Creation of the American Republic, 1776-1787.* Chapel Hill, 1969.

―――, "A Note on Mobs in the American Revolution." *William and Mary Quarterly,* 3d ser., XXIII (1966).

―――, "Republicanism as a Revolutionary Ideology." *The Role of Ideology in the American Revolution,* ed. John R. Howe, Jr., New York, 1970.

―――, "Rhetoric and Reality in the American Revolution," *William and Mary Quarterly,* 3d ser., XXIII (1966).

Zilversmit, Arthur W., *The First Emancipation: The Abolition of Slavery in the North.* Chicago, 1967.

# Index